HIKES
of Newfoundland

KATIE BROADHURST
ANNE ALEXANDRIA FORTIN
MARY SMYTH
FRED HOLLINGSHURST

BOULDER
BOOKS

Library and Archives Canada Cataloguing in Publication

Title: Hikes of Newfoundland / Katie Broadhurst, Anne Alexandra Fortin,
   Fred Hollingshurst, Mary Smyth.
Names: Broadhurst, Katie, author. | Fortin, Anne Alexandra, author. |
   Hollingshurst, Fred, 1942- author. | Smyth, Mary, 1953- author.
Description: Includes bibliographical references and index.
Identifiers: Canadiana 20200197010 | ISBN 9781989417096 (softcover)
Subjects: LCSH: Hiking—Newfoundland and Labrador—Guidebooks. |
   LCSH: Trails—Newfoundland and Labrador—Guidebooks. |
   LCSH: Newfoundland and Labrador—Guidebooks. | LCGFT: Guidebooks.
Classification: LCC GV199.44.C22 N48 2020 | DDC 917.1804/5—dc23

Published by Boulder Books
Portugal Cove-St. Philip's, Newfoundland and Labrador
www.boulderbooks.ca

Printed in China

© 2020 Katie Broadhurst, Anne Alexandra Fortin, Fred Hollingshurst, Mary Smyth

Editor: Stephanie Porter
Copy editor: Iona Bulgin
Design and layout: Todd Manning and John Andrews
Cover photos (clockwise from left): Paul Wylezol, Henrik Thorbun, Mary Smyth,
Katie Broadhurst, Mary Smyth.

We acknowledge the financial support of the Government
of Newfoundland and Labrador through the Department of
Tourism, Culture, Industry and Innovation.

Newfoundland
Labrador

Funded by the   Financé par le
   Government   gouvernement
   of Canada   du Canada

Table of Contents

Acknowledgements

This book would not have been possible without the help and support from the Boulder team, our families, friends, and the always helpful people of this great island. We send a big thank you to: IATNL chair Paul Wylezol; our parents, Brenda and Lindsay Broadhurst and Lisette Fortin and Daniel Trudel; our partners, Will Bennett and Cory Bertrand; the instructors of the Adventure Tourism programs in Gaspé, Québec, and Pembroke, Ontario; our friends Caroline Swan and Jamie Harnum. We also have to give a big shoutout to the many Newfoundlanders that helped us along the way by directing us to trailheads, teaching us more about their area, and showing us profound hospitality and kindness. All of this assistance provided us with incredible experiences in unique places that we are proud to share with you.

—*Alex and Katie,*
authors of the western trails, hikes #1–#71

This book includes some of the best hikes you will encounter in the world. It is a collection of trails from all parts of the island of Newfoundland, and we are proud to be a part of it. We wish to express our appreciation to all those individuals and groups who have built and maintained hiking trails across this province. They have created a wonderful asset for us all to enjoy now and for years to come. For helping us in our discovery of new trails for this book and our previous *Hikes of Eastern Newfoundland*, we thank: Neil Hardy, Sharon Collett, Charlie Elton, Fraser Carpenter, Fred Bridger, Joe and Val Earles, Ed Delaney, Randy Murphy, and David Smyth. Also thanks to David Peddle and Freeman Rumbolt, who were enthusiastic guides on the spectacular new Coastal Ridge Trail. Thanks to Rebecca Smyth and Piers Evans for braving the elements for a photo of the new Silver Mine Head bridge. A special thank you to all those who have joined us in the many hikes over the years and shared a Thermos of tea and a sandwich along these wonderful trails. As always, to our editor, Stephanie Porter, and publisher, Gavin Will, thank you for all the support.

—*Fred and Mary,*
authors of the eastern trails, hikes #72–#157

Newfoundland and Labrador, at the eastern edge of Canada, borders the Atlantic Ocean.

Introduction

Is there anything that is better
than to be out, walking, in the clean air?
—*Thomas A. Clarke, Glennock, Scotland*

Convincing seasoned hikers of the benefits of a walk on a breathtaking coastal trail is preaching to the converted. But for those just discovering hiking, we hope the joy of the activity and appreciation of the natural environment of the island of Newfoundland will make converts of you, too.

With its rugged beauty and dramatic landscapes, Newfoundland has captured our hearts. Hiking has always offered the best way to access many of the more remote and untouched parts of the island, including cliffs, beaches, wetlands, woodlands, and wildlife.

We could not include every hike or community trail on the island—otherwise, we would have written something the size of an encyclopedia. Many more trails can be found in almost every region, and we encourage hikers to refer to other tourism resources to find out more (to start, see "Further information" on page 372). Visitors will no doubt find additional trails worth exploring, and new ones are being developed all the time.

This book is organized by region, loosely from west to east, following the island's vehicle transportation routes. The first trails are in the southernmost region of Newfoundland, nearest to the ferry docks at Port aux Basques. Many visitors to the island begin there, and the southwest coast is a spectacular place to start a hiking adventure. The last section explores the spectacular East Coast Trail on the eastern coast of the Avalon Peninsula.

We hope that our fellow hikers find this a useful resource. There is no better way to enjoy the beauty of the natural world than on foot. We look forward to seeing you on the trails.

How to use this book

Our intent is to give you the information and tools you need to success-fully get to the start and end of each hike. The hike descriptions have been organized to be user-friendly, instructive, and, we hope, inspiring. Each hike is described over 1–4 pages.

Nearest community/ town name (or park or route number)

Trail number and name

Bar colour indicates region*

Rating: Easy (1) Moderate (2) Difficult (3) Strenuous (4) Wilderness (W)

Tent icon indicates an overnight hike; compass icon indicates an unmarked trail (map and compass skills required)

Footnotes: information to help you plan your hike

Trail description

Trail map: not to be used for navigation

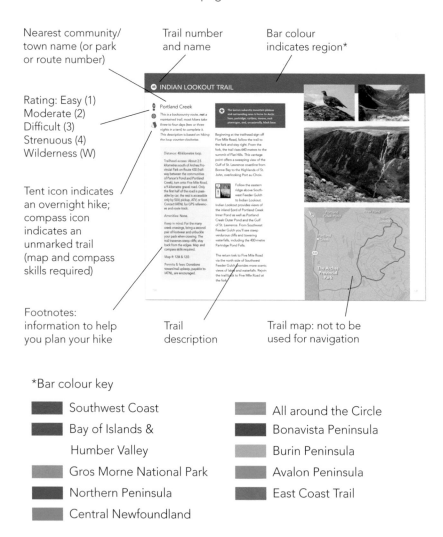

*Bar colour key

Southwest Coast

Bay of Islands & Humber Valley

Gros Morne National Park

Northern Peninsula

Central Newfoundland

All around the Circle

Bonavista Peninsula

Burin Peninsula

Avalon Peninsula

East Coast Trail

Page Layout

Trail ratings

The trails in this book have been rated as Easy, Moderate, Difficult, Strenuous, or Wilderness. The first four categories are based loosely on the ratings used by the East Coast Trail Association (www.eastcoast-trail.ca), with some changes to account for the terrain of Newfoundland's west coast and the specific hikes described in this book.

Please read the ratings descriptions below carefully; when we rated hikes, we considered ease of access, duration, distance, elevation changes, trail conditions, and signage.

1 **Easy:** Beginner-friendly trails accessible for most fitness and experience levels. Trails are easy to access and, in general, well signed, range from less than 1 kilometre to 7 kilometres return, and have elevation changes up to 50 metres. Trail surfaces are generally gravel walkways, boardwalks, or footpaths, and trails are in good condition.

2 **Moderate:** Easy-to-access trails ranging from 4 to 11 kilometres return. Trails generally have elevation changes up to approximately 150 metres; these changes will occur more frequently than on "easy" hikes. Trail surfaces are typically gravel walkways or footpaths over uneven terrain, and trails are in good condition.

3 **Difficult:** Easy-to-access trails ranging from 9 to 17 kilometres in length. Expect elevation changes, often greater than 250 metres; trails are good to very rugged footpaths and may include steep climbs or scrambles. Boardwalks, bridges, or logs may cover some wet spots.

4 **Strenuous:** Trails are easy to access and up to 17 kilometres or more in length; major elevation changes will occur, and for prolonged durations. Footpaths, ranging from good to very rugged, may include steep climbs or scrambles, sometimes with logs, boardwalks, or bridges in wet areas.

W **Wilderness:** Backcountry routes and trails for fit and experienced hikers. Remote trailheads may require a four-wheel drive or boat to access. Map and compass skills are essential; the route is usually unmarked. Expect major elevation changes. These routes may call for overnighting in tents, often without designated campsites.

 A second "boot" icon indicates a second trail or optional add-on hike, or that the difficulty level falls between two levels. Please read the trail description for details.

Other icons

 These routes require overnighting in tents for one or more nights. If the tent icon is greyed-out, camping is optional—read the trail description for details. Tent sites indicated on the map are approximate locations and subject to change. Amenities vary with the site.

The trail or route is unmarked and map and compass skills are mandatory. Do not rely only on a Global Positioning Device (GPD), such as a cell phone, or Global Positioning System (GPS). A greyed-out compass indicates an optional backcountry hike add-on.

Trail description
An overview of the hike, describing major junctions, lookout locations, landmarks along the intended route, and other noteworthy information.

Trail map
The maps accompanying each trail description contain information gathered from the Toporama website of Natural Resources Canada and are subject to a degree of error. They are intended to give a general idea of the terrain, the location of main junctions and trailheads, and a bird's-eye view of the hike. Depending on the scale of the map, topographic lines are shown in either feet or metres; topography lines may not be shown on all maps. Not all roads or landmarks are shown. **The maps provided in this guide should not be used for navigation purposes.** Please purchase a reliable government topographic map for any backcountry hiking or other trail requiring navigation. The East Coast Trail Association has produced a detailed set of maps of their trails.

Map legend

———	Road	●	Trailhead	🗼	Lighthouse
∿	Hiking trail	▲	Campsite		

Footnotes

Distance: The hike length in kilometres and trail type (loop, linear, or network). Estimated hiking times are not included. Most people of average fitness can walk 4 to 5 kilometres per hour on a smooth road; that pace will slow considerably on a trail, especially one with uphill climbs.

Trailhead: Location of trailhead. Often the driving route to the trailhead is outlined; this will include boat access information, if relevant. It also identifies parking areas and provides the decimal degrees of the main trailhead commonly used by GPS. Be sure to correct for declination. GPS information is from Natural Resources Canada via Toporama and is subject to a degree of error.

Amenities: Facilities or services available on the trail or at the trailhead.

Highlights: What to watch for along the trail (east coast hikes).

Keep in mind: Cautions specific to the trail. Please take all warnings seriously.

Permits & fees: Brief information about day passes, permits, or donations, if relevant.

Map #: Refers to the Natural Resources Canada topographic maps of the terrain in which the trail is located. Map numbers are included only for wilderness trails. Topographic maps may be obtained from a map dealer, GeoGratis website (www.geogratis.ca), a regional distribution centre, or a certified map printer. The Gros Morne visitor centre has topo maps for the Long Range and North Rim traverses.

 Interesting information: Historical notes, natural feature highlights, geologic information, personal observations, and recommendations.

Good to know before you go ...

Newfoundland weather

The island of Newfoundland is surrounded by the Atlantic Ocean, which creates a temperate climate; however, the weather is change-able and difficult to predict. It is always best to be prepared for a range of conditions and temperatures. We have found that Environment Canada (weather.gc.ca) provides the most accurate and up-to-date forecasts.

Tides, wind, and fog

Each day two low and two high tides occur at approximately six-hour intervals. Tides could leave you stranded on a beach or island if you are not keeping track of them. Keep in mind that tides do not always reach the same height; fluctuations depend on the pull of the moon and sun; as well, neap and spring tides are higher or lower than usual. For a schedule of the tides for specific locations, visit Fisheries and Oceans Canada: www.waterlevels.gc.ca/eng/station/list.

The ocean occasionally brings fog, which can roll in quickly and severe-ly reduce visibility, onto the shoreline. Fog is particularly dangerous if you are venturing near cliffs or travelling at higher elevations and it can cause you to lose the trail and become disoriented. Waiting for the fog to clear is safer than heading out in the wrong direction.

Beware of high winds by cliffs and mountaintops: they can be extremely powerful all around Newfoundland, reaching speeds of 100+ kilometres per hour.

Animals

Wild animals are unpredictable, even if they appear tame. Do not get too close and do not feed them. Do keep binoculars and cameras with you at all times. Remember that anything odorous in your tent—food, and even toothpaste and deodorant—attracts wildlife.

Moose
Moose, which are native to Labrador, were introduced to the island of Newfoundland at Gander Bay in 1878 and in 1904 four moose were introduced at Howley. The moose population has flourished to over 150,000 due to the abundance of food and virtually no natural predators. Its main threat is humans. Moose is an important game animal, with approximately

22,000 animals harvested yearly. The fact that Newfoundland has the highest density of moose in the world poses problems of moose-vehicle collisions and deforestation as well as the introduction of other non-native species (possibly wolves) to help control the moose population.

Be cautious around moose, especially in the spring when the cow (female) has calves, as they are extremely protective of their new offspring. Females have been known to charge and will trample anything in their path. In the fall, be wary of rutting bulls (males).

Learn to recognize a moose's warnings: raising the long hair on its shoulder hump, laying back its ears (like a dog or cat does), or licking its lips, huffing, or grunting. When you encounter a moose, whether or not it sees you, avert your eyes (but watch it from the corner of your eye), and back away slowly; find another route or return to the trailhead. If the moose approaches or charges, look for the nearest tree, fence, car, or other obstruction to duck behind. When a moose charges, it often kicks forward with its front hooves, so get behind something solid. It is usually a good idea to run from a moose (unlike bears) because they won't chase you far and you can run around a tree faster than a moose can. Moose are not agile—weaving and circling or getting into thick brush usually deters them.

If a moose knocks you down, it may continue running or stomp and kick with all four hooves. Either way, curl up in a ball, protect your head with your hands, and hold still. Don't move or try to get up until the moose moves a safe distance away.

Black bears and polar bears
Black bears are native to the island and sometimes polar bears cross on the ice pack in the winter from Labrador onto the Northern Peninsula. Both are curious and intelligent and tend to avoid or ignore people, but both can be dangerous. Bears do not like surprises, so when you're hiking, announce your presence by making a noise, singing, talking loudly, or by tying a bell to your pack. Never approach or provoke a bear—it could be just passing through, but it could become aggressive if it has young cubs nearby or is protecting a kill, or if you've strayed too close.

When you are backcountry camping, cook away from your tent. Store all food away from your campsite and, ideally, hung out of reach of bears. If the area is treeless, store all food in airtight or specially designed bear-proof containers. Dogs and their food may also attract bears. Always keep a clean camp by washing dishes thoroughly, burning garbage completely in a  hot fire (or packing it out), and eliminating food smells from clothing. As food and garbage attract bears, treat them both with equal care.

If you see a bear, try to avoid it, and give it every opportunity to avoid you. If you do encounter one at close range, remain calm. Attacks are rare. Most bears are interested only in protecting food, cubs, or their "personal space." Once the threat has been removed, they will move on. If you encounter a bear, remember:

■ Identify yourself: Let the bear know you are human. Talk to the bear in a normal voice. Wave your arms. Help the bear recognize you. If a bear cannot tell what you are, it may come closer or stand on its hind legs to get a better look or smell. A standing bear is usually curious, not threatening. Try to back away slowly, diagonally, but if the bear follows, stop and hold your ground.

■ Don't run: You can't outrun a bear. They have been clocked at speeds up to 56 kilometres per hour and, like dogs, they will chase fleeing animals. Bears often make bluff charges, sometimes to within 3 metres of their adversary, without making contact. Continue waving your arms and talking to the bear. If it comes too close, raise your voice and be more aggressive. Bang pots and pans. Use noisemakers. Never imitate bear sounds or make a high-pitched squeal.

■ If attacked: If a black bear makes contact, fight back regardless of circumstances. If a polar bear attacks, fight back unless the attack is by a mother protecting her cubs, in which case you should remove yourself as a threat by curling up in a ball and remaining passive.

The above information is reprinted with permission from the Alaska Department of Fish and Game. Visit their website for more details, www.adfg.alaska.gov/ (Living with Wildlife).

Coyotes
Coyotes are considered a native species to Newfoundland and Labrador; they arrived in the province and extended their range naturally, through their own efforts. However, they have only been on the island since the mid-1980s. Coyotes tend to have a natural fear of humans and are usually easily scared off. Be alert in the woods and watch for signs such as scat or tracks. Attacks are extremely rare and are usually related to a coyote's habituation to people and their food. If you are approached, it is probably because the coyote has become used to being fed by people. Stop, remain calm, and assess your situation.

If you encounter a coyote, remember:

■ Never approach or crowd the coyote—give it an escape route.
■ If the coyote seems unaware of you, move away quietly when it is not looking in your direction.

- If the coyote is aware of you, respond aggressively: wave your arms, shout, and maintain eye contact. Carry a whistle and blow it to startle the animal.
- Throw rocks or sticks at the coyote.
- If the coyote continues to approach, back away slowly and move toward buildings or human activity. Do not turn away or run. If the coyote attacks you, fight back.

The above information is reprinted with permission from the Newfoundland & Labrador Department of Wildlife and Conservation website: www.env.gov.nl.ca/env/wildlife/all_species/living.html.

Hunting seasons

Hunting, trapping, and angling are not only a way of life in Newfoundland and Labrador but also a valuable part of the province's economy. Open hunting and fishing season dates are species dependent and can vary year to year. Check the provincial Department of Environment and Conservation website for the most up-to-date information: www.env.gov.nl.ca/env/wildlife/season_dates/.

Generally, big game (moose, caribou, bear) seasons open between the end of August and early October and close by the end of January. Small game snaring and shooting seasons are generally from mid-September to the end of February. Trapping is typically open by the end of October and ends around mid-March. Open season on coyotes usually runs from mid-September through to early July.

Be safe and be seen. Wear blaze orange during hunting season; this also applies to pets.

Ferries and boat transportation

For provincial ferry services and schedules, contact the Marine Services Division of the provincial Department of Transportation and Works (www.tw.gov.nl/ferryservices or [888] 638-5454).

Reservations for the Western Brook Pond boat tour (the boat transports hikers to the trailhead of the Long Range Traverse and the North Rim Traverse) can be made with Bon Tours at www.bontours.ca or (888) 458-2016 or (709) 458-2016.

Other trailheads may require a boat to access. Contact IATNL for information: www.iatnl.com.

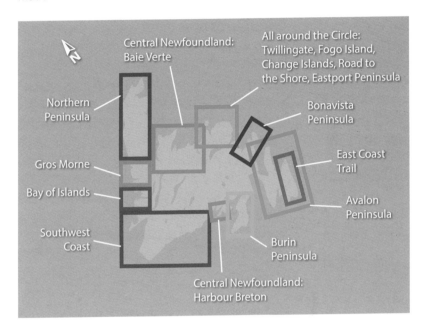

Planning your hike

Venturing out into the wilderness requires preparation and planning. Some things to consider:

■ Which trail will you hike? Using the ratings given for each trail, determine which hikes are suitable by considering how long you can comfortably hike, the terrain you prefer, what you want to see, and how you will get to the trailhead.
■ When will you hike? It is always best to start hiking as early in the day as possible so you can be off the trail well before darkness sets in. Consider the weather—does the forecast call for rain or other unpleasant weather? Will it be windy? When is high/low tide?

■ Who are your hiking partners? Answering this will also determine which hike you do and when you can go. Be aware of the abilities and limitations of all group members, and remember you're only as fast as your slowest person.

■ Do you have a route plan? It is good practice to prepare a brief route plan, particularly before backcountry hikes, and leave it with a reliable person. Include the trail name, intended route with GPS reference points, start time, expected hike duration, the hikers' names, and a brief description of clothing and tent. At the very least, you should always tell someone where you are going and when you expect to be back, and then stick to the plan. For overnight or multi-day treks, a route plan is an excellent way to plan your trek and can be a valuable asset should you require assistance.

■ What will you bring? For sample basic equipment checklists for day hikes and multi-day hikes, see pages 370 and 371.

Clothing

Clothes don't make the hiker, but the right clothing can make the experience a more comfortable one. Experienced hikers will know what works best for them. Dressing in layers so you can dress up or down as conditions change is a good idea. Wet-weather gear is a must any time of year. A hat provides protection from sun and rain, and gloves are good to have at the bottom of the backpack for those days when it is cool or fog rolls in.

Footwear

Feet are a hiker's best friends, so it is important to be kind to them. Waterproof hiking boots makes for a happy hiker. If you are going to venture out on easy trails only occasionally and in good conditions, you can probably get by with running or trail shoes.

Gaiters are useful in wet and muddy conditions and can also protect your legs in places where brush and branches have grown over the path.

Communication devices

Many cell phones will work in Newfoundland, some even in remote areas; however, gullies and mountains can block reception. Check with your cell phone provider to see their coverage area maps and never rely solely on cell phones when hiking in the backcountry. More remote communities do not have any cell phone coverage at all. When hiking in remote areas, marine radios, satellite phones, or SPOT GPS Messengers can be handy in case of an emergency. Marine radios offer the widest range of reception all around the coast and a coast-guard-specific channel. They are also the most reliable and cost-effective communication devices.

Always tell someone where you are going, when you will return, and what to do if you don't show up within a specified time range (whom to contact in case of emergency and for what/whom they are looking).

Hiking with pets

Pets are allowed within most national and provincial park boundaries; however, some trails (for example, Gros Morne Mountain) do not permit dogs due to the delicate nature of the mountaintop. Check with specific parks about their current policies.

Pets should always be leashed when hiking on busy trails out of respect for other users and especially when you're near a community. Clean up after your pet—no one likes dog poop on the trails. Some backcountry trails are ideal for letting your dog run free: keep in mind that your pet may disturb the wildlife and Conservation Officers can fine you for this. Wild animals are unpredictable; a moose or bear may charge your dog if the dog has disturbed it. A blaze orange vest for your dog is an excellent idea, especially during open hunting season for coyotes.

Practice the Leave No Trace Principles

Whether you are hiking in Newfoundland or any other place around the world, you should apply the Leave No Trace Principles. They are meant to protect and preserve the environment. Always carry in everything you need for your trip and carry out all of your garbage and belongings. Take pictures of what you see and/or find instead of bringing it back with you. These principles include:

- Plan ahead and prepare
- Travel and camp on durable surfaces
- Dispose of waste properly
- Leave what you find
- Minimize campfire impacts
- Respect wildlife
- Be considerate of other visitors

For details of these seven principles and how to apply them, visit www.leavenotrace.ca.

Assumption of risk

Walking and hiking in Newfoundland is inherently risky due to many factors, including, but not limited to, unpredictable weather, falling rocks, falling trees, and animal encounters. Most of the hikes in this book have marked and maintained trails and we strongly advise that you remain on these trails.

This guide is designed to provide general guidelines about each hike. Trail descriptions have been carefully researched by local professionals; however, conditions not mentioned in the hike descriptions may be encountered. Trailheads, signage, parking, and trail status are also subject to change. It is the ultimate and sole responsibility of the user to determine which hikes are appropriate to their skill and fitness level, for being aware of changes, and alert to hazards that may have arisen since the writing of this book.

Newfoundland T'Railway Provincial Park:
A section of the Trans Canada Trail

Once completed, the Trans Canada Trail will connect St. John's, Newfoundland, to Victoria, British Columbia, and eventually lead up to Tuktoyaktuk, Northwest Territories, and, at 22,000 kilometres, will be the world's longest trail network.

The railway in Newfoundland was decommissioned in 1988 and the railbed was repurposed as a multi-use trail. Frequented by hikers, snowshoers, cross-country skiers, ATVs, and snowmobiles, the trail provides access to almost all parts of Newfoundland. Like many other sections of decommissioned railway in Canada, this section—the 833 kilometres of railbed linking St. John's to Channel-Port aux Basques—became part of the Trans Canada Trail. We did not include the T'Railway in the hikes in this book due to its size and many uses. More information and interactive maps can be found on the Trans Canada Trail and Newfoundland T'Railway websites (www.tctrail.ca, www.trailway.ca).

The Newfoundland section of the Trans Canada Trail is maintained by the Newfoundland T'Railway Council and the provincial government. Maintenance is also supported by donations and volunteer work.

International Appalachian Trail (IAT)

 IAT is the extension of the Appalachian Trail (AT) located in the United States; it stretches along the east coast from Georgia to Maine. These trails were designed to showcase the Appalachian Mountains.

IAT links the AT to the rest of the Appalachian Mountain range. Beginning in Maine, IAT enters eastern Canada in New Brunswick, crosses into the Gaspé Peninsula in Quebec, heads back into New Brunswick, across Prince Edward Island, then traverses Cape Breton in Nova Scotia, and finishes its Canadian section in western Newfoundland. IAT also has trails in Greenland, Iceland, the Faroe Islands, Norway, Sweden, Denmark, the Netherlands, England, Scotland, Ireland, Wales, Spain, France, Portugal, and Morocco.

The building of these trails would not be possible without volunteers and donations. Kilometres of trail are added every year. Please help IAT continue to flourish by visiting their website www.iat-sia.org or our local chapter, the International Appalachian Trail of Newfoundland and Labrador, at www.iatnl.com. Annual memberships start at $15.

SOUTHWEST COAST

The southwest coast of Newfoundland spans from Port aux Basques to the Lewis Hills and includes François, Grey River, Ramea, Burgeo, and the Port au Port Peninsula. The landscape offers a shifting palette: ancient orange mountains, dense green forests, and shades of blue and grey in the ever-changing ocean and sky. The vibrant scenery is the perfect backdrop for leisurely beach walks or adventurous multi-day treks.

Sheltered by the Long Range Mountains, this region has milder weather than the rest of the island. The Codroy Valley holds traditional farmlands and a large estuary to which thousands of birds migrate every year. You'll also find some of the province's most dramatic cliffside lighthouses, such as the Rose Blanche lighthouse, made of granite, or the Cape Anguille lighthouse, perched at the westernmost point of Newfoundland.

The southwest coast is home to the first section of the International Appalachian Trail of Newfoundland and Labrador (IATNL). The International Appalachian Trail (IAT) spans from Mount Katahdin in Maine through eastern Canada and western Newfoundland, to Greenland and Iceland, and, finally, into Europe. Some of the hikes in this region, such as the Grand Codroy Way and the Lewis Hills Trail, are part of the IATNL, and may require camping. The IATNL routes bring hikers to remote areas and incredible views that only the most adventurous experience.

A few of our favourite community trails are also noted on the map (location shown in red). These are generally shorter, well-maintained trails in some of the towns and communities in the area, and well worth checking out.

A. Rose Blanche Trail / Rose Blanche / 1.75-kilometre trail
B. Barachois Falls Hiking Trail / Rose Blanche / 1.6-kilometre trail
C. Harbour le Cou trail / Habour le Cou–Rose Blanche / 1.2-kilometre trail
D. Sgt. Craig Gillam Memorial Trail / South Branch / 5-kilometre trail
E. Walk-a-Ways Park and Trails / Stephenville / 16.5-kilometre trail network
F. Fossil Footpath / Stephenville / 0.7-kilometre trail

Trails of the Southwest Coast

1. Harvey Trail / Isle aux Morts
2. Grand Bay West Trailway / Channel-Port aux Basques
3. Table Mountain Trail / Cape Ray
4. Grand Codroy Way / Cape Ray–Tompkins
5. Wetlands Trail / Upper Ferry
6. Starlite Trail / Tompkins
7. Cow Hill & Beach Trail / Burgeo (Sandbanks Provincial Park)
8. Aaron's Arm Trail / Burgeo
9. Man O'War Hill & Ramea Walking Trails / Ramea
10. Grey River Trails / Grey River
11. Francois Trail Network / Francois
12. Boutte du Cap & Breadcrumb Trails / Cape St. George
13. Gravels Walking Trails / Port au Port West
14. Indian Head Range Trail / Stephenville Crossing–Noels Pond
15. Lewis Hills Trail / Cold Brook–Serpentine Lake
16. Erin Mountain Trail / Barachois Provincial Park

Isle aux Morts

The Harvey Trail starts from the Isle aux Morts craft store, a small red building at the end of Cemetery Road. Well-maintained and fairly easy to walk on, the trail follows the gently rolling shoreline. Hikers will experience little elevation gain.

Several small trail offshoots lead from the main trail down to the water's edge, often to secluded coves and beaches which are

 Panels along the trail tell the story of the Harvey family and their Newfoundland dog, Hairyman, who saved almost 200 lives in two daring rescues in the early 1800s.

Trail maps are **not to be used for navigation.**

worth exploring if you have time. At the highest point, a gazebo gives hikers a 360-degree view of the Gulf of the St. Lawrence and Cabot Strait, and the picturesque community of Isle aux Morts. No large trees grow on this barren coastal lowland, and visibility is excellent (weather permitting); this is an ideal location to photograph seaside panoramas.

At the trail's farthest point is its highlight: a mural of local heroes, the Harvey family. From the mural, the trail loops back toward town and returns to the parking area and craft store.

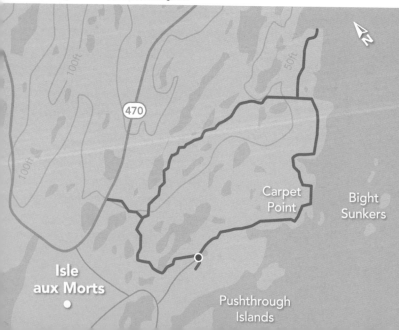

Distance: 4-kilometre loop.

Terrain/elevation: 10-metre elevation gain.

Trailhead: Follow Route 470 east to Isle aux Morts. Turn right on LeGallais Street, left on Water Street East, then left at Cemetery Road. Drive until the road changes to gravel and turn right before the gate, and park. The red building is the craft store and the trailhead: 47.5846, -58.9682.

Amenities: Craft shop, visitor centre, picnic tables, gazebos, café, and outhouses. Guided tours available.

Keep in mind: Be aware of slippery rocks, tides, and ocean waves.

Permits & fees: Donations toward trail upkeep are payable to the Town of Isle aux Morts.

Channel-Port aux Basques

From the Kyle Lane trailhead, the Grand Bay West Trailway begins as a boardwalk along white sand beaches and delicate sand dunes and transitions into a gravel walkway at the barrens. Along the gravel section are platforms with playground equipment and viewpoints overlooking the Gulf of St. Lawrence—this is a beautiful spot to watch the sun set.

> ★ The endangered piping plover lives in this area. Respect its habitat and stay on the trail. Many ships have been wrecked off this coast; look for the interpretation panels that tell their stories.

The trail meanders along the shoreline and arrives at an old barn and some family gardens, which are still maintained. After rounding the barn, you may either follow the four-wheeler trail straight back to the Kyle Lane parking area to complete the small loop or stay to the left and continue down the trail along the beach.

If you opt for the beach route, you'll be rewarded with views of the coast and the Long Range Mountains. This trail will bring you to the Grand Bay Road West parking area. Return to Kyle Lane via Grand Bay Road West to complete a loop or walk back along the trail.

Distance: 6-kilometre trail network.

Trailhead access:

There are two trailheads:

■ Exit TCH at Grand Bay Road West. Drive through the community of Grand Bay West, and turn right onto Kyle Lane. Drive to the end, and park: 47.5831596, -59.1844214.

■ Grand Bay Road West, about 1 kilometre from TCH: 47.5960168, -59.184591.

Amenities: Interpretation panels, play equipment.

Keep in mind: This hike is in the Channel-Port aux Basques Municipal Wetland Stewardship Zone; stay on established trails.

Permits & fees: Donations toward trail upkeep are payable to the Town of Channel-Port aux Basques.

Grand Bay Road W.

100ft

50ft

100ft

50ft

N

1

To Port aux
Basques

**Grand
Bay East**

**Grand
Bay West**

Pole
Rock

Salt Water
Pond

Second
Pond

First
Pond

50ft

Rocky
Barachois
Bight

50ft

100ft

Little
Point

Granby
Point

Trail maps are **not to be used for navigation.**

Cape Ray

The Table Mountain Trail follows a winding gravel road up a steep, narrow valley. A smooth climb, it leads to a set of communication towers, at an elevation of approximately 425 metres, overlooking Newfoundland's southwest coast and the Gulf of St. Lawrence.

 Local resident Lauchie MacDougall ("the human wind gauge") was reputed to have accurately predicted weather changes. He was even hired to inform the railway company if trains could safely pass, a service he performed from 1935 until his death in 1965.

 As you cross the plateau, the trail changes from a gravel road to a quad track. At the fork, you may go either way to reach the lookouts, but most hikers go to the right. On a clear day you'll see the Codroy Valley to the north, Port aux Basques to the south, Cape Ray, and the lowlands, known as the Wreckhouse, due west. The Wreckhouse is infamous for hurricane-force winds that historically blew trains off the tracks, and still periodically blow transport trucks off the road.

Long Range Mountains

Wreckhouse

Big Pond

Cook Stone

650ft

1400ft

1250ft

750ft

1000ft

250ft

1

Billys Pond

Sugar Loaf

500ft

650ft

350ft

Red Rock Point

To Cape Ray

150ft

Trail maps are not to be used for navigation.

As you climb out of the valley, you'll probably feel the winds. Imagine the full force of Wreckhouse winds and the importance of MacDougall's role in transporting supplies across the island.

Return via the same road and enjoy the view of Sugar Loaf Mountain and the surrounding lowlands and ponds as you descend.

Distance: 5-kilometre linear trail (10-kilometre return).

Trailhead access: The gravel road intersects with TCH 0.3 kilometres north of the Cape Ray exit. Park either on the east side of TCH or drive in the road, over a small bridge, and park across from the cabin: 47.6641897, -59.2766323.

Amenities: None.

Keep in mind: In an area notorious for high winds, be cautious of changing weather when up on the mountain.

Permits & fees: Donations toward trail upkeep are payable to IATNL. See page 15.

Note: This trail can be combined with Grand Codroy Way (hike #4) for an overnight hike.

Cape Ray–Tompkins

*This is a backcountry route, **not** a maintained trail; most hikers take two or three days (one or two nights in a tent) to complete it.*

The Grand Codroy Way follows the barren, high country between the Table Mountain Trail (hike #3) in the south and Starlite Trail (hike #6) in the north.

This scenic route follows the cliff edge, allowing for panoramic views of the vibrant Codroy estuary before heading inland to the high, rolling grasslands above the Grand Codroy River Valley. The Codroy estuary hosts over 150 identified bird species, including 19 species of waterfowl, which you can learn more about at the Codroy Valley International Wetlands Interpretation Centre.

Starting from the Table Mountain Trail, this route will take you across the barren plateau of the Long Range Mountains—the perfect habitat for caribou, Arctic hare, and black bears—and beside vistas of green gulches and numerous waterfalls. It finishes at Campbells Lake, where you descend via the Starlite Trail into the Little Codroy River Valley, near Tompkins.

Farley Mowat speculated in his book *The Farfarers: Before the Norse* (2000) that these high, fertile grasslands were once used by the Alban people to graze cattle and winter inland, away from shores that became increasingly hostile as the Vikings pushed south.

Distance: 32-kilometre linear trail.

Trailhead access:
There are two trailheads:

■ The southern trailhead is on the east side of TCH, 0.3 kilometres north of exit to Cape Ray (Table Mountain Trail, hike #3): 47.6641897, -59.2766323.

■ The northern trailhead is off TCH, just south of Tompkins (Starlite Trail, hike #6): 47.7829781, -59.2330455.

Amenities: Codroy Valley International Wetlands Interpretation Centre is located on Route 406 in Upper Ferry; no amenities on trail.

Keep in mind: This area is notorious for high winds and thick, low-lying fog; be alert to changeable weather in the mountains. This is not a marked route: map and compass skills are required, as is a government-issued topographic map. Contact IATNL for a GPS track of the route, but do not rely solely on GPS.

Permits & fees: Donations toward trail upkeep are payable to IATNL.

Map #: 11014 & 11011.

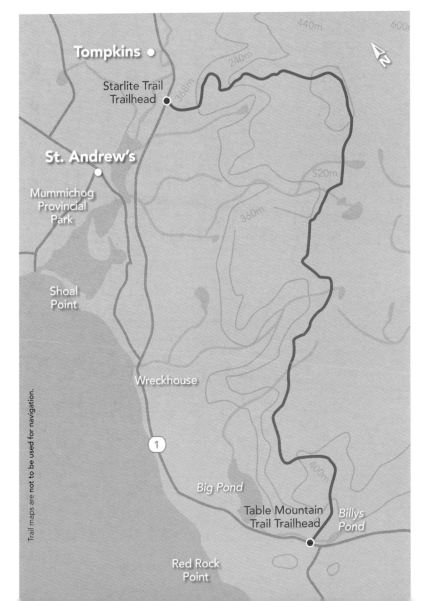

Tompkins ●

Starlite Trail
Trailhead ●

St. Andrew's ●

Mummichog
Provincial
Park

Shoal
Point

Wreckhouse

① 1

Big Pond

Table Mountain
Trail Trailhead ○

Billys
Pond

Red Rock
Point

440m

240m

368m

600

520m

360m

400m

N

Trail maps are not to be used for navigation.

27

Upper Ferry

This gentle walking trail follows the Grand Codroy Estuary and offers many vantage points to observe birds and wildlife. The well-defined path meanders through forests to reach bird viewing areas overlooking the estuary and ponds. Many interpretation panels along the trail will help you learn more information about the Grand Codroy Estuary.

Distance: 1.9-kilometre (3.8-kilometre return) linear trail.

Trailhead access: The trailhead is across from the Codroy Valley International Wetlands Interpretation Centre in Upper Ferry (Codroy Valley) off Route 406: 47.843641, -59.248645.

Amenities: Restrooms at the Wetlands Centre, and benches and picnic tables along the trail.

Keep in mind: This is a birding hotspot; be considerate to others on the trail. It is also home to the endangered Piping Plover and some rare plants.

Permits & fees: Donations toward trail upkeep are payable to the Wetlands Centre.

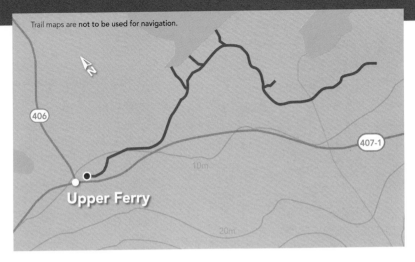

Trail maps are **not to be used for navigation.**

406

407-1

10m

20m

Upper Ferry

The Grand Codroy Estuary was designated as a "wetland of significance" in 1987 by the Ramsar International Convention. Over 540 acres of protected land provides shelter to a great array of birds. More than half the birds found in Newfoundland have been sighted here. Spring and fall offer great sighting opportunities for migrating birds.

Pick up a pamphlet at the Wetlands Centre about the different birds which inhabit the area. Don't forget your binoculars!

29

Tompkins

The Starlite Trail starts gently, taking you over boardwalks through forest. After 1 kilometre or so, you'll begin to climb up along the side of the mountain. The ascent is gorgeous, offering multiple views of the ocean and Little Codroy River Valley from a height of about 360 metres. Be sure to take a break and absorb the view!

> ⭐ Table Mountain is part of the Anguille Mountains, which belong to the Long Range Mountains that span the entire west coast of Newfoundland. The Long Range Mountains belong to the greater Appalachian Mountain Range, which formed during the middle Ordovician Period, about 485–444 million years ago.

 The trail eventually forks, and signs indicate "Mountain Trail" to the left and "Campbells Lake" to the right. If you stay left, the trail will continue to climb through meadows and barrens, finally leading to a flat summit area from which you'll see a breathtaking gorge, lush with vegetation, surrounding Campbells Lake. This is an ideal place for a snack or picnic and pictures and is where most hikers turn around.

Experienced hikers may decide to explore northward: approximately 3.5 kilometres farther is a gorge with a waterfall and sheer cliffs. A topographic map and compass are recommended if you wish to extend your hike to the gorge; there is no marked trail.

Return via the same route to the parking area.

Distance: 3-kilometre linear trail (6-kilometre return) to summit.

Terrain/elevation: Moderate terrain/360-metre elevation gain.

Trailhead access: On the east side of TCH, just south of Tompkins, is a large parking area with a trail map for IATNL and Starlite Trail: 47.78262, -59.23341.

Amenities: A small shelter in the parking area.

Keep in mind: If you explore the mountaintop, be advised that there are no trails. You must have good orientation skills, a map, and a compass. Weather may change rapidly, and thick fog can disorient hikers.

Permits & fees: Donations toward trail upkeep are payable to IATNL.

Map #: 11014.

Note: This trail can be combined with Grand Codroy Way (hike #4) for an overnight hike.

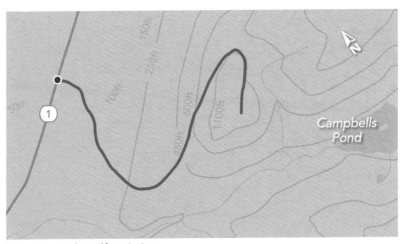

Trail maps are not to be used for navigation.

Burgeo (Sandbanks Provincial Park)

Distance:
8-kilometre trail network.

Terrain/elevation:
Single track, gravel paths, boardwalks, beaches/ 10 metre elevation gain.

Trailhead access: In Burgeo, turn right onto Main Street, right onto Messieurs Road, and right again on Park Road and drive to the park. Park in the day-use area: 47.6073806, -57.6454407.

Amenities: Washrooms, tent areas, picnic tables, beach volleyball court, and play-ground equipment; benches and garbage bins along trails.

Keep in mind: No smoking. All pets must be kept on leash. Sand dunes are a delicate environment; stay on trails.

Head to Sandbanks Provincial Park and wander the 7 kilometres of white sand beaches. The soft sand will make you feel like you're in the tropics … until you step into the very refreshing water! Climb the stairs to the summit of Cow Hill and enjoy the 360-degree view of Burgeo and surrounding islands while you pick raspberries. If you visit near the end of summer, you may be lucky and find bakeapples.

The trail network starts between camp-sites D13 and A15, and between A17 and C19. You can also sea kayak along the whole park and rest at one of its many quiet beaches.

Don't forget your binoculars—watch for sandpipers, plovers, and, especially in the fall, migrating ducks and geese.

The park showcases outstanding eco-logical diversity. You'll see peat bogs,

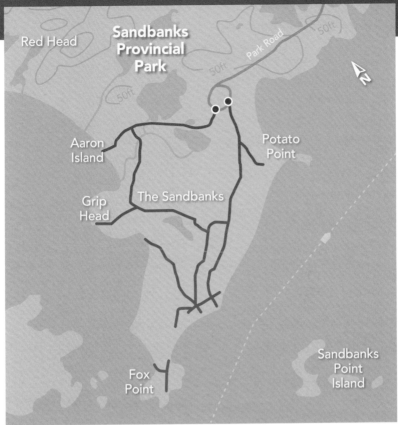

Red Head

Sandbanks Provincial Park

Park Road

50ft

50ft

50ft

Aaron Island

Potato Point

Grip Head

The Sandbanks

Fox Point

Sandbanks Point Island

Trail maps are **not to be used for navigation.**

boreal forest, delicate sand dunes, ponds, and rocky tidal pools—something to satisfy hikers of all ages, abilities, and interests. This trail connects to Aaron's Arm Trail, detailed on the next page.

An abandoned cemetery on Fox Point at the tip of the peninsula is all that remains on the grounds of an old church that was built in the 1880s by Reverend Blackmore. It was blown down by a gale only one year after being built.

Burgeo

The first part of the trail follows a little stream through the forest before reaching a cove. A short distance past the cove, a staircase will lead you up to breathtaking views of many islands and pristine white sandy beaches. Enjoy the scenery from a picnic table or as you pick juicy berries—through the summer and early fall you'll find blueberries, blackberries, partridgeberries, bakeapples, and raspberries along this trail.

From the viewpoint, boardwalks carry you across barrens where pitcher plants grow. Aaron's Arm

 The sand beaches and dunes were created by the glaciers of the last ice age as they melted and left deposits of sand. Some of the wooden boards on the trail have been engraved with names of pets, grandchildren, and names in memory as a fundraiser for trail maintenance.

Trail meets up with Western Beach, which can also be accessed from Sandbanks Provincial Park (hike #7). To keep hiking, walk to the western end of the beaches where you can pick up the trail. It will take you back through the forest and to different beaches. Worth the extra distance.

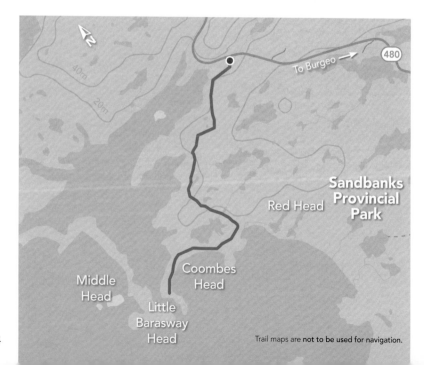

Trail maps are **not to be used for navigation.**

Distance:
3.6-kilometre (7.2-kilometre return) linear trail.

Terrain/elevation:
Boardwalk, single track trail/10-metre elevation change.

Trailhead access: The trailhead is located on the right side of route 480 before the town of Burgeo (about 2.5 kilometres before Foodland). Next to a big trail sign is a small parking lot: 47.627157, -57.652263.

Amenities: Picnic tables.

Keep in mind: The dunes and beaches are very fragile environments, stay on trails.

Permits & fees: Donations toward trail upkeep are payable to the Town of Burgeo.

Ramea

This scenic trail takes hikers around the island and community of Ramea and through the community; it is a must-do on your visit.

You can enter and exit the trail at a number of points for a shorter stroll. Hike to the top of Man O'War Hill for a breathtaking view of Ramea and surrounding islands. Hike and visit the light station at Northwest Point. A shorter hike to the observation deck on Goodknock gives another panoramic view of the community and area.

> ⭐ Geocache hunting (using GPS) is a fun way to explore the island of Ramea:
> Rock Island Cache: 44.30747, -57.24558
> Scotch Cove Cache: 47.31562, -57.22918

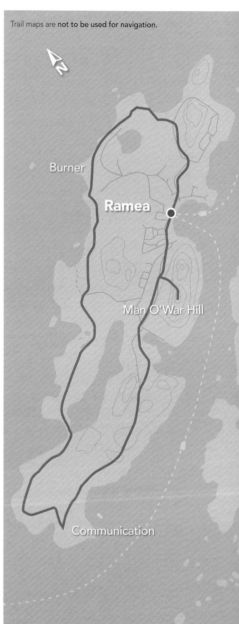

Trail maps are **not to be used for navigation**.

Burner

Ramea

Man O'War Hill

Communication

Distance: 6.5-kilometre loop.

Terrain/elevation: Easy natural surface, <10-metre elevation change.

Trailhead access: From the ferry dock, you can hike clockwise or counter clockwise. There are three trailheads:

- Muddyhole Road:
  47.51641, -57.39671
- Man of War Road:
  47.52253, -57.39661
- Scotts Cove Road:
  47.52676, -57.38285

Amenities: None on the trail.

Map #: 11P11.

2 Grey River

Follow these local trails, footpaths, and snowmobile trails to the top of the hills that surround the community. The trails will take you to a lower and an upper lookout, before eventually disappearing. You can wander where you like—just keep track of the way back to the trail. Enjoy the views of tundra and heath landscapes and the towering cliffs of the fjord.

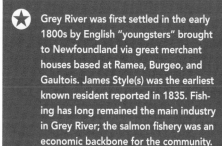

Grey River was first settled in the early 1800s by English "youngsters" brought to Newfoundland via great merchant houses based at Ramea, Burgeo, and Gaultois. James Style(s) was the earliest known resident reported in 1835. Fishing has long remained the main industry in Grey River; the salmon fishery was an economic backbone for the community.

Trail maps are **not to be used for navigation.**

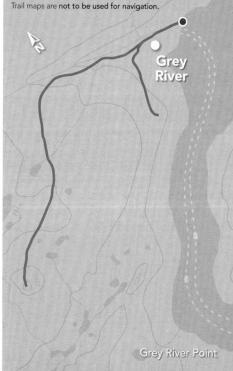

Grey River

Grey River Point

Distance: ~5-kilometre trail.

Terrain/elevation: Natural surfaces/250-metre elevation change.

Trailhead access: From the ferry dock, follow the river uphill. For the lower lookout, turn off and head towards the cemetery. For the upper lookout, continue uphill and veer southwest.

Amenities: None on the trail.

Keep in mind: The area has ferry access only, so plan accordingly. There is no cell phone service.

Map #: 11P11.

François

François boasts some of the most spectacular views of the entire south coast. Three trails will get you out enjoying the area.

 Access to this outport community is by ferry only, and Francois maintains its rural heritage and lifestyle. Connect with local residents to learn the stories and history of the area.

■ **Charlie's Head Lookout Trail:** Just past the town's cemetery, begin climbing the steep stairway. This brings you up to tundra-like scenery and a lookout platform poised 107 metres above the fjord. Francois is dwarfed by towering cliffs.

■ **Pond Trail:** This trail is a mix of boardwalk and natural surface that encircles the pond. Enjoy colourful wildflowers, including pink lady slippers and white bunchberries in early summer, or the reds of shrubbery in the fall.

■ **The Friar:** From Pond Trail, follow the yellow markers that lead northward up the valley to the communication tower. Enjoy the views, then continue to the Friar, minding the cliff edge. Carry on southeast and follow the trail down the valley to the ocean. Follow the shoreline back to Francois.

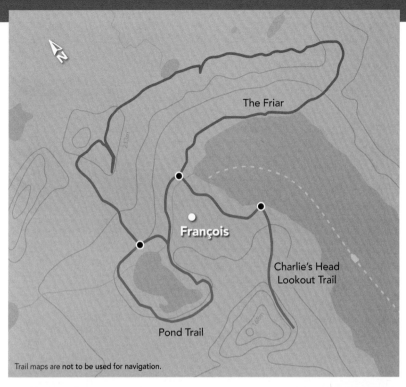

The Friar

François

Charlie's Head
Lookout Trail

Pond Trail

Trail maps are not to be used for navigation.

■ **Charlie's Head Lookout Trail**
Distance: <2 kilometres.

Terrain/elevation: Boardwalk, stairs, and natural surfaces/ 25-metre elevation change.

Trailhead access: From the ferry dock, head southwest towards the staircase.

■ **Pond Trail**
Distance: 3 kilometres.

Terrain/elevation: Boardwalk and natural surface/25-metre elevation change.

Trailhead access: From the ferry dock, walk into town and head north, past the school. Veer left and go up the hill to the pond.

■ **The Friar**
Distance: 3.5 kilometres.

Terrain/elevation: Steep, rocky natural surface paths/350-metre elevation change.

Trailhead access: From the pond, turn right/north and look for the yellow markers.

Amenities: None along the trails.

Keep in mind: Visiting the area requires a commitment as the weather can keep you in or out for days. Plan a few extra days in case. Do not count on cell phone service in the area.

Map #: 11 P 10.

Permits & Fees: None.

Cape St. George

The Port au Port Peninsula is the cradle of Newfoundland and Labrador's francophone culture. The first French fishers settled there centuries ago; many of the peninsula's communities have French names, and many local residents speak French.

The Breadcrumb Trail is an easy, flat trail of less than 1 kilometre that leads hikers along the cliff edge from which whales and a rich diversity of seabirds can be observed. Seascape views await; try this trail during sunset.

Hikers may follow the cliff edge (not too closely!) to the north-northeast and pick up the Boutte du Cap Trail, which heads uphill toward two kittiwake colonies, including the largest kittiwake colony on the west coast of Newfoundland. Wooden posts with red painted tops indicate the way through stunted tuckamore forests and exposed barrens and along the 213-metre-high cliffs.

You'll know you've arrived at the first colony by the noise (and perhaps the smell, if you are

This trail offers a glimpse into the life of the Acadians who lived in this area in the 19th century. Boutte du Cap Park holds the only Acadian monument in Newfoundland. The traditional bread oven is for public use, and bread is baked in it during the summer.

downwind). Farther along the trail is a second kittiwake colony (at approximately 48.48444, -59.25257); the trail is not well-marked after this second colony, and GPS, map, and compass are recommended if venturing farther. Return by the same route.

Distance: 3-kilometre (6-kilometre return) linear trail.

Trailhead access: Take Route 460 to the Port au Port Peninsula. Stay left and drive to the community of Cape St. George, and turn into Boutte du Cap Park. Park by the bread oven or the interpretation panels at the end of the road: 48.4644273, -59.2628114.

Amenities: Benches, interpretation panels.

Keep in mind: Be extremely cautious during windy or foggy days; stay back from the cliff edge as cliffs may be undercut and unstable.

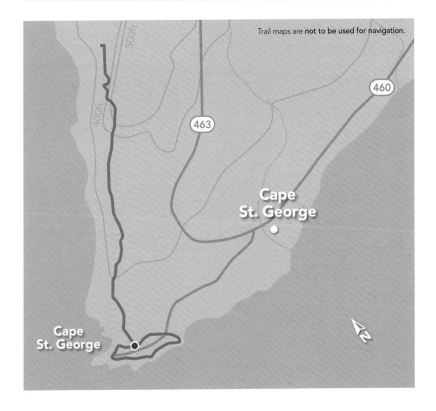

Trail maps are **not to be used for navigation.**

460

463

500ft

400ft

Cape St. George

Cape St. George

1 Port au Port West

Beginning from the west end of the parking area, follow the trail along the coast as it winds between the stunted boreal forest and the limestone shoreline.

 The limestone coast hosts many fossils from the Ordovician Period (485–444 million years ago), including trilobites, ammonites, and fossilized plants.

Hikers will be treated to a view of the Lewis Hills in the background and unique eroded limestone designs in the foreground. The ocean in this area is remarkably clear: from most points on the trail you can see its bottom.

The Gravels Walking Trail is well-maintained, with stairs, wooden bridges, and small offshoot trails that lead to the sea or back toward the main road. Take the side trail to Aguathuna to visit Our Lady of Mercy church, one of Newfoundland's oldest and largest wooden buildings. The site also hosts a separate museum and tearoom. Guided tours are available.

Return to the Gravels Trail parking area by following the main road or returning along the trail.

Distance: 3.5-kilometre trail network.

Trailhead: From Stephenville take Route 460 to Port au Port West. Along the isthmus, Gravels Pond is on your left and the parking area on your right. The trail begins at the west end of the parking area: 48.559, -58.7287.

Amenities: Picnic tables, garbage cans, and benches along the trail; interpretation signs and picnic tables at trailhead.

Keep in mind: Be wary about getting too close to the ocean; waves are powerful and the water cold.

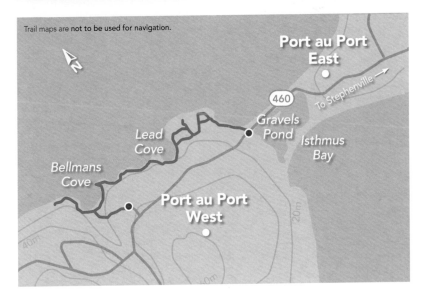

Trail maps are **not to be used for navigation.**

Port au Port East

460

To Stephenville →

Gravels Pond

Lead Cove

Isthmus Bay

Bellmans Cove

Port au Port West

20m

40m

Stephenville Crossing–Noels Pond

The Indian Head Range Trail begins about 50 metres from the Noels Pond parking area. From the lot, walk left along a quad track until you see a sign for the trail on the right—once you're on it, it's easy to follow and well-marked.

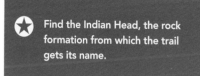

⭐ Find the Indian Head, the rock formation from which the trail gets its name.

This trail is rough and wet in places, with a few easy creek crossings. The trail passes main-ly through forests, and terrain changes are fairly gradual with only a few short, steep rises to access the barrens. From the 160-metre-high lookout, you can

see Stephenville, Bay St. George, Port au Port, and the Lewis Hills.

Trail maps are **not to be used** for navigation.

The trail then leads you down toward Stephenville Crossing, ending at Seal Cove Road. Return by the same trail or arrange a shuttle back to the Noels Pond trailhead.

Distance: 6.2-kilometre (12.4-kilometre return) linear trail.

Terrain/elevation: Rugged single track/350-metre elevation change.

Trailhead access: There are two trailheads:

■ From TCH, take Route 460. On your left, 1.3 kilometres before Noels Pond, is the parking lot: 48.56346, -58.458977.

■ From TCH, take Route 490. About 4 kilometres before Stephenville Crossing, turn onto Seal Cove Road. Stay left until 48.540059, -58.458977, park by the side of the road.

Amenities: None.

Keep in mind: Logs placed to assist crossings may be slippery or unstable.

Permits & fees: Donations are payable to the Town of Stephenville.

Cold Brook–Serpentine Lake

*This is a backcountry route, **not** a maintained trail; most hikers take two to three days (one or two nights in a tent) to complete it. This description is from south to north.*

> All three of Newfoundland's carnivorous plants are found in the Lewis Hills: butterwarts, pitcher plants, and sundews.

 Starting at the southern trailhead off Cold Brook Road, the Lewis Hills Trail crosses 2 kilometres of wetland, revealing spectacular views of a rust-coloured peridotite mountain range before descending to cross Fox Island River. After the river crossing, the trail rises again, through a peridotite valley with many waterfalls. This section brings hikers to a height of about 640 metres, before the final 4-kilometre ascent (174-metre elevation gain) to the Cabox, Newfoundland's highest point, at 814 metres.

From the Cabox, the route continues west across the hills to the rugged Molly Ann Gulch, a steep fjord-like valley with views of the Gulf of St. Lawrence. This excellent camping spot provides sheltered areas as well as prime sunset viewing.

From Molly Ann Gulch, continue north to Rope Cove Canyon and then cross the barrens, heading northeast toward Buds Lake overlooking the awe-inspiring Serpentine Valley. Be alert for caribou herds and moose.

Serpentine Lake
Blue Hill Brook
Logger School Road

Rope Cove Canyon

640m

720m

640m

Cold Brook Road

Shag Island

Cabox 814 m

600m

480m

400m

360m

Lewis Hills

*Trail maps are **not to be used for navigation.***

Descend Red Rocky Gulch, named for the peridotite rocks and boulders strewn along the valley floor. Along the descent, the route provides views of Serpentine Lake and the Blow Me Down Mountains before crossing Blue Hill Brook and connecting to Logger School Road at the northern trailhead.

51

Distance: 32-plus-kilometre linear route.

Terrain/elevation: Rugged, uneven/640-metre elevation change.

Trailhead access: A four-wheel drive with good clearance is needed to access trailheads; roads may be washed out.

■ Southern trailhead: Turn off Route 460 2.5 kilometres past Noels Pond into Cold Brook. Before the community, on the right is a logging road and parking area. Drive in approximately 28 kilometres following the few IATNL blazes. Park at 48.76629, -58.41228.

■ Northern trailhead: Exit the Trans Canada Highway about 10 kilometres west of Corner Brook onto Logger School road. Follow Logger School road for about 30 kilometres, turn left at 48.84569, -58.17162 and drive another 16 kilometres; just before Serpentine Lake the trailhead is on the left at 48.87822, -58.32012.

Amenities: None.

Keep in mind: Navigation is essential throughout this trek. Take extra precautions during low cloud or fog situations. The weather, particularly the wind, along the coast can be extreme. This is not a marked route. A map, compass skills, and a government-issued topographic map are necessary. Do not rely solely on GPS.

Permits & fees: Donations are payable to IATNL.

Map #: 12B16 & 12B15.

Note: This multi-day hike can be combined with Blow Me Down Mountain Traverse (hike #21).

Barachois Provincial Park

The first section of the Erin Mountain Trail travels over well-maintained boardwalks through boreal forest to a lower lookout. The trail from the lower lookout to the top of Erin Mountain climbs steadily through forest and, in some places, crosses over exposed rock, making the route to the summit more challenging.

The waters and forests of Barachois Pond have long been important to residents of St. George's Bay. Moose, caribou, and rabbit hunting provided fresh meat; white pine, fir, and spruce were used for house and boat construction and fuel. By 1958, commercial lumbering combined with blister rust disease had exhausted most of the white pine stands. Barachois Pond and surrounding area became a park in 1962.

Look for plagioclase and blue-green pyroxene crystals in the bedrock.

At the 340-metre summit, you'll be rewarded with a panoramic view of Bay St. George and the blue waters of the Gulf of St. Lawrence. Look behind you to see the top of the Long Range Mountains. The summit is a scenic picnic area; you may even be lucky enough to see moose near the ponds to the east.

Follow the same route back to the campground, but pause to enjoy the views. A beach and swimming area at Barachois Park is ideal for a refreshing post-hike dip.

Trail maps are **not to be used for navigation.**

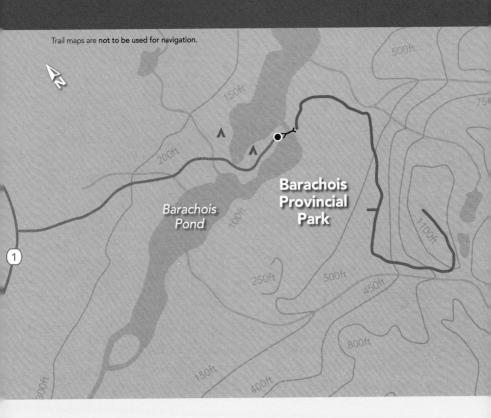

500ft

150ft

75

200ft

Barachois
Pond

100ft

1100ft

**Barachois
Provincial
Park**

250ft

500ft

450ft

1

800ft

300ft

150ft

400ft

Distance: 4-kilometre linear trail (8-kilometre return).

Trailhead access: Barachois Park entrance is on the TCH between the two exits for Stephenville. Pay at the check-in and drive to the end of the peninsula, where a small parking area marks the trailhead: 48.48115, -58.26100.

Amenities: Campsites and a day-use area with picnic tables, playground, drinking water, and toilets.

Keep in mind: Pace yourself—some sections of this trail rise steeply. Always look out for moose, caribou, and other large wildlife.

Permits & fees: Required for access to all provincial parks.

BAY OF ISLANDS & HUMBER VALLEY

The trails in the Bay of Islands and Humber Valley rival those in Gros Morne National Park for their diversity of distances, terrain, and scenery. All of the Bay of Islands and Humber Valley trails listed below are used year-round by hikers, snowshoers, and cross-country skiers.

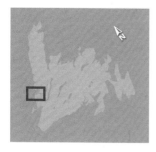

The Bay of Islands is steeped in history. The area was first charted by Captain James Cook. In his 1767 survey, Cook mapped the Port au Port Peninsula, the Port au Choix Peninsula, and also measured the depths of both St. George's Bay and the Bay of Islands. He also travelled 24 kilometres up the Humber River to map the nearby mountains and the river's depth. Cook's name appears twice on maps of the Bay of Islands, at Cooks Cove and Cooks Brook; he named places after his survey ships (the *Lark* in Lark Harbour, for example) and used English river names (Humber River). Visit Cook's Lookout in Corner Brook to learn more about this world traveller and his importance to Newfoundland.

Bay of Islands and the Humber Valley have been recognized as one of the best places in the province for adventure tourism, not only for hikers but also for sea kayakers, salmon fishers, hunters, downhill and cross-country skiers, and snowmobilers. Access to the trailheads is easy and the variety of landscapes, routes, and urban and remote areas will suit everyone's needs and interests.

Community trails to check out (shown on the map in red):

A. Humber Valley Nature Trail / Deer Lake / 5.6-kilometre trail / Easy
B. Murray Mountain Trail / Lark Harbour / 4-kilometre trail / Strenuous

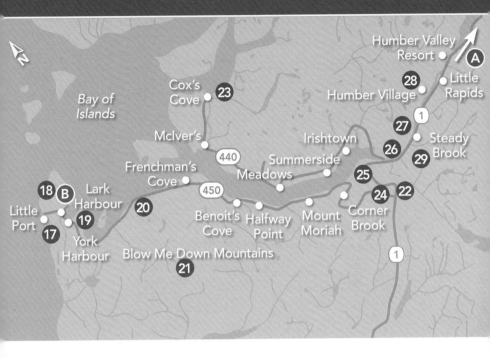

Trails of Bay of Islands & Humber Valley

17. Cedar Cove & Little Port Head Lighthouse Trails / Little Port
18. Bottle Cove & Southhead Lighthouse Trails / Lark Harbour
19. James Cook Heritage Trail / Lark Harbour (Blow Me Down Provincial Park)
20. Cape Blow Me Down Trail / York Harbour
21. Blow Me Down Mountain Traverse / York Harbour
22. Tipping's Pond Trail / Massey Drive
23. North Arm Traverse / Cox's Cove–Trout River
24. Ginger Route / Corner Brook
25. Corner Brook Stream Walking Trails / Corner Brook
26. Old Man in the Mountain to Wild Cove / Corner Brook
27. Wild Cove to Humber Village / Wild Cove–Humber Village
28. Humber Village to Humber Valley Resort / Humber Village–Humber Valley Resort
29. Marble Mountain & Steady Brook Falls Trails / Steady Brook

1 Cedar Cove Trail

Turning left onto the Cedar Cove Trail takes you along the base of Little Port Head and directly out to Cedar Cove Beach. The trail is

Outer Bay of Islands
Enhancement Committee

well-maintained and -marked, with little elevation change. The beach is scattered with driftwood, and it's a favourite place for kite flying. Follow the trail back out to the parking area.

3 Little Port Head Lighthouse Trail

Little Port Head Lighthouse Trail heads toward the harbour. You'll begin to ascend immediately; the narrow trail has a steep drop-off on your right. At the modern light station, you'll have a view of the mouth of the Bay of Islands. Guernsey Island, the tallest island in the bay, is to the north-northwest. Continue to the 250-metre summit and traverse across the head to see the Lewis Hills to the south and Lark Harbour and Blow Me Down Mountains to the east. The descent is very steep and may be slippery, but ropes are available to assist you. At the trail junction, turn right to go to Cedar Cove Beach or left to return to the parking area.

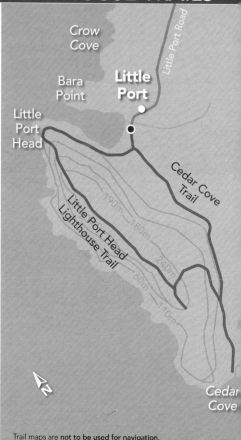

Trail maps are **not to be used for navigation.**

 The Bay of Islands was originally mapped by Captain James Cook, between 1764 and 1767. York Harbour and Lark Harbour, two of the four communities that make up the Outer Bay of Islands (with Bottle Cove and Little Port), were named after Cook's ships HMS *York* and HMS *Lark*, which belonged to the Royal Navy's Newfoundland squadron. The first permanent settlers in the Outer Bay of Islands arrived early in the 19th century as the area developed its fishery and lumber industries.

Distances: 1.8-kilometre linear and 3-kilometre loop trail options.

Trailhead access: Take Route 450 toward Lark Harbour. Turn left after the gas station toward Little Port (on Little Port Road). Drive to the end of the road and park on the far left near the stairs. Ensure your vehicle is not obstructing traffic: 49.1058, -58.4702.

Amenities: None.

Keep in mind: The ascent and descent of Little Port Head are steep and can be slippery year-round. Use extreme caution along the trail, especially near cliff edges, as they may be undercut. Extremely high winds can make hiking challenging and potentially dangerous.

Permits & fees: Donations are payable to Outer Bay of Islands Enhancement Committee (OBIEC) via the towns of Lark Harbour or York Harbour or at www.obiec.ca.

Bottle Cove Trail

Bottle Cove Trail is a 1-kilometre network between Bottle Cove Beach and Miranda Cove that showcases

Outer Bay of Islands
Enhancement Committee

steep cliffs, sea caves, and white sand beaches. Seals and whales often swim here—and so can you, during the warmer months. A sea cave at the south end of Bottle Cove Beach is accessible at low tide. From the Bottle Cove parking lot, start hiking at the large trailhead sign. Built into the boardwalk at Bottle Cove is a replica of the *Grenville*, the ship James Cook used to survey Newfoundland.

Southhead Lighthouse Trail

Follow the signs from the Bottle Cove parking lot for the 3.3-kilometre Southhead Lighthouse Trail. The trail passes a communication station and heads toward the Murray Mountains, meandering through forest and bog and into a valley. The next section is a steady climb up the valley. The 350-metre elevation gain is gratifying, as it brings you to a breathtaking view of Guernsey Island, the Bay of Islands, and the North Arm Hills (across the bay). The trail loops at the end, and hikers return via the same route.

Distances: 1-kilometre trail network and 3.3-kilometre linear trail (6.6-kilometre return) options.

Trailhead access: Follow Route 450 to Lark Harbour. Turn left after the gas station onto Little Port Road; when the road branches, stay right. Follow the gravel road and take the first left into the Bottle Cove parking area: 49.1170, -58.4060.

Amenities: Porta-loo.

Keep in mind: As these trails follow high cliffs, stay back from the edges. Be aware of the tides when venturing to the sea cave.

Permits & fees: Donations toward trail upkeep are payable to OBIEC via the towns of Lark Harbour or York Harbour or at www.obiec.ca.

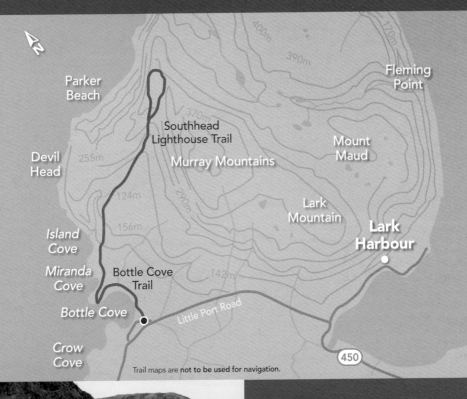

Parker
Beach

Fleming
Point

Southhead
Lighthouse Trail

Mount
Maud

Devil
Head

255m

Murray Mountains

124m

Lark
Mountain

**Lark
Harbour**

Island
Cove

156m

Miranda
Cove

Bottle Cove
Trail

142m

Bottle Cove

Little Port Road

Crow
Cove

450

Trail maps are **not** to be used for navigation.

400m

390m

370m

290m

170m

 Southhead Lighthouse was established on a stone cliff at Southhead in 1925 to help ships reach the Corner Brook pulp and paper mill. It was built as a square wooden structure topped by an open wooden framework that supported an acetylene gas lantern. The dwelling at South-head was intentionally burned in 1989, leaving just the octagonal concrete tower; this was demol-ished in 2010 and replaced with a cylindrical, red-and-white-striped fibreglass tower that supports a solar-powered light. The lantern room from the original octag-onal tower is on display at the trailhead.

3 Lark Harbour (Blow Me Down Provincial Park)

From the day-use parking lot at Blow Me Down Provincial Park, walk to the rocky beach and observe starfish, crabs, seabirds, and perhaps seals. The trail starts on the north end of the beach at the Governor's Staircase, which is built into the rocks and cliffside. Another trail access off the parking lot eliminates Governor's Staircase and the beach (take this trail if the staircase is inaccessible due to tides). The two trails meet before heading uphill.

> ★ **The Governor's Staircase** showcases the geology of 450-million-year-old rock. Look for quartz veins and interesting sedimentary rock formations.

A 250-metre steep climb brings hikers to a viewing platform overlooking the Blow Me Down Mountain Range and the Bay of Islands. From the platform, hikers can turn around or head to the tip

Trail maps are **not to be used for navigation.**

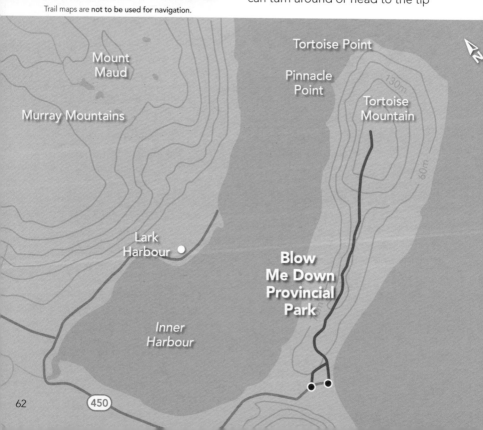

450

of the peninsula and the top of Tortoise Mountain, following the ridge through forest and across barrens.

On a clear day, the top of Tortoise Mountain offers a 360-degree view of the communities of Lark Harbour and York Harbour, as well as the Murray Mountains, Blow Me Down Mountains, and the Bay of Islands. Return by the same route.

Distance: 4.5-kilometre linear trail (9-kilometre return).

Trailhead access: Take Route 450 toward Lark Harbour and watch for signs for Blow Me Down Provincial Park on your right, just before you enter the community: 49.090799, -58.3655517. The trail starts from either the day-use parking lot or its camping loop and the beach.

Amenities: Picnic tables and washrooms at campsite; picnic table at lookout platform.

Keep in mind: Governor's Staircase is inaccessible at high tides. The stairs on the trail's first section may be wet and slippery during heavy rains. No smoking is allowed on trails; all pets must be leashed.

Permits & fees: Required to access all provincial parks.

York Harbour

Park across from the old copper mine, founded in 1893, and enjoy the view before starting your climb.

 The view from the Blow Me Down peak may include caribou, moose, and other wildlife. In late summer, the blueberries found along the trail will be ripe for picking.

Outer Bay of Islands Enhancement Committee

Ascend a set of stairs, then follow trail markers—it's a steady climb to the Blow Me Down peak, but several lookouts and rest places are scattered along the way. Each lookout rewards hikers with a view of the Bay of Islands. The trail's first section climbs and meanders through dense forest. When it reaches the open barrens, there is an intersection for the backcountry trail (hike #21)—take the left trail toward the summit. Bogs and barrens change into subalpine landscape as you approach the 650-metre summit.

The view of Bay of Islands, Corner Brook, Lark Harbour, and other communities is stunning, especially when the landscape is inflamed at sunrise or sunset.

Return to the parking area by the same route. From the parking area, another short trail leads to a waterfall, and is worth the detour. This trail is just off to the side, past the stairs to the main trail, at the end of the parking lot.

Trail maps are not to be used for navigation.

Distance: 3.8-kilometre linear trail (7.6-kilometre return).

Trailhead access: Follow Route 450 from Corner Brook. About 10 kilometres past Frenchman's Cove, look for the trail sign on the left with an uphill gravel road leading to the parking area: 49.0618, -58.3046.

Amenities: Benches at parking area and along the trail.

Keep in mind: The trail's first section is steep, and muddy and slippery when it rains.

Permits & fees: Donations toward trail upkeep are payable to OBIEC at www.obiec.ca.

York Harbour

*This is a backcountry route, **not** a maintained trail; most hikers take two to three days (one or two nights in a tent) to complete it.*

Starting from the northern trailhead, the first part of the trail is the same as that for the Cape Blow Me Down Trail (hike #20) and is well-marked.

Take the trail to the right at the fork in the open barrens, and trek 16 kilometres south across the mountaintop to arrive at Red Gulch. IATNL suggests a route

The peridotite mantle rock of Red Gulch was heaved up through plate tectonics and is the same as that of the Tablelands in Gros Morne National Park. It is part of the Bay of Islands ophiolite complex. This orange-brown rock has toxic amounts of heavy metals, making it difficult for most plants to survive—hence the Mars-like landscape.

The plateau meadows and bogs contain a rich diversity of wildflowers and plants. In late summer, blueberries are abundant and may attract black bears. This plateau is home to moose and herds of caribou.

(shown on the map), but hikers can explore the mountain plateau. Must-sees are Red Gulch, with its orange-brown peridotite rocks; Simms Gulch, which is half peridotite and half slate grey; and Blow Me Down Gulch and its waterfall.

On the south side of the Blow Me Down plateau, Serpentine Lake and valley with the Lewis Hills as its backdrop are a remarkable sight. The trail wanders through marsh, bogs, forests, and rocky terrains. Be ready to bushwhack if exploring around the plateau.

Heading west from Red Gulch, the trail descends into the steep and meandering Simms Gulch until it reaches Serpentine Lake, where hikers must cross Serpentine River, to reach the Logger School Road trailhead access. This route requires a shuttle or arranged pickup and drop-off.

Lark
Harbour

**Blow
Me Down
Provincial
Park**

York
Harbour

Bear
Head

Blow Me Down
Peak

Copper Mine
to Cape Trail

450

*Mad Dog
Lake*

Blow
Me Down
Gulch

Blow Me Down
Mountain Trail

Simms
Gulch

Red
Gulch

*Serpentine
Lake*

Benoit's
Cove

320m
600m
480m
540m
520m
600m
540m

Trail maps are **not to be used for navigation.**

Distance: 35+ kilometres.

Note: This hike can be combined with the Lewis Hills Trail (hike #15).

Trailhead access: A four-wheel drive with good clearance is strongly recommended; roads may be washed out and rough. The multiple logging roads can be confusing: accurate backcountry maps and a compass will be required for navigation. Contact IATNL for GPS reference points and route track.

■ Northern trailhead: Follow Route 450 from Corner Brook; about 10 kilometres past Frenchman's Cove is an IATNL trail sign on the left (49.0618, -58.3046). An alternate trail access: Blow Me Down Nature Trail, 4 kilome-

tres from Frenchman's Cove (this is a rougher, wetter access point, but the peridotite and gabbro valley is stunning): 49.06108, -58.23123.

■ Southern trailhead: Exit Route 1 onto Logger School Road, approximately 10 kilometres west of Corner Brook. Drive approximately 30 kilometres, turn left at 48.84569, -58.17162. Drive another 17.5 kilometres until you get to the lake. Park here and head toward Serpentine Lake. Park at the end of the road.

Keep in mind: This is a wilderness route. Do not rely solely on GPS, as the signal can be greatly reduced during cloudy days.

Map: 12B16, 12G1 & 12G2.

Massey Drive

This is a very gentle, well-maintained trail with only minor elevation changes. A few wooden platforms and benches offer nice views and a place to rest.

The trail meanders between deciduous trees and the more common spruce trees, taking you all the way around the pond.

Also know as Tippin's Pond, this is a very popular swimming spot in the summer months. Massey Drive used to be under Corner Brook's jurisdiction before becoming its own community.

Trail maps are **not to be used for navigation.**

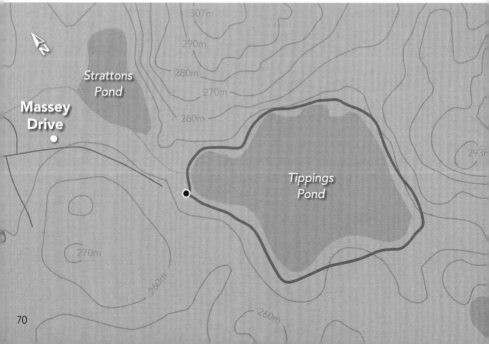

Distance: 2.2-kilometre loop.

Trailhead access: The trailhead is located at the top of the hill in the town of Massey Drive. The parking is on the left: 48.932114, -57.884901.

Amenities: Picnic tables; dock (in summer) for swimming.

Keep in mind: Dogs should be kept on leash.

Permits & fees: Donations towards trail upkeep are payable to the Town of Massey Drive.

Cox's Cove–Trout River

This remote and wild area is perfect for the experienced off-trail hiker. Plateaus at 600 metres elevation are accessible from the north, east, and south, with unparalleled views of the Bay of Islands, Trout River Pond, and the Tablelands.

As part of the Cabox Aspiring Global Geopark and the Ultramatrex, the North Arm Mountain massif is special. It contains the most complete ophiolite sequences in western Newfoundland. It is composed of ultramafic rocks, layered with gabbro that show sheeted diabase dyke complexes and pillow basalts erupted on the ancient sea floor.

431

**Trout
River**

Trout River Pond
Boat Accesss

Overfalls
Trailhead

Hughes Brook
Road

North Arm
Road Access

Stowbridge
Cabin

N

Trail maps are **not to be used for navigation.**

Distance: 35–50-plus-kilometre backcountry route taking 2–3-plus days.

Trailhead access:

■ Northern access: either via boat via the Overfalls Trail or hike in via the Elephant Trail.

■ Overfalls Trail: Park at the boat dock located at the western end of Trout River Pond, near the community of Trout River. It's a 45-minute boat ride across Trout River Pond to the trailhead at 49.36713, –57.96755.

■ Elephant Trail: Park at 49.43864, -58.13158, about 3.5 kilometres past the Trout River Campground. Hike southeast on the ATV trail toward the mountains for 3.3 kilometres. The trailhead is at 49.41920, -58.10680.

■ Eastern access: Drive down Hughes Brook logging road. At kilometre 35, turn left onto North Arm Road and drive 4.25 kilometres, staying right. After 500 metres, turn right on an old road. Go another 750 metres and look for an ATV

trail on the right. This is the trailhead, 49.22936, -57.91066.

■ Southern access is via boat from the community of Cox's Cove with drop-off at Stowbridge Cove.

Amenities: At Stowbridge Cove a cabin is available for rent (49.21677, -58.09666). Contact IATNL for details.

Keep in mind: This trail includes several brook crossings; carry a second pair of footwear and be sure to unbuckle your pack when crossing. The trail traverses steep cliffs; be sure to stay back from the edges. The only access to this remote country is by boat or by skidoo in the winter. Hikers must be proficient navigators and be prepared for survival situations.

We recommend that all hikers request the GPS track for this route from the IATNL, www.iatnl.ca.

Map #: 12G08, 12G01, 12H05, 12H04.

Corner Brook

The Ginger Route is just one of many new local multi-use trails being added to the Corner Brook area, all built by volunteers.

Ginger Route is primarily a mountain biking trail, but it has been designated as a multi-use trail; meaning hikers can enjoy it too.

The Ginger Route trail has several narrow sections and steep switchbacks near the end that can make a gradual climb for hikers. Ginger Route connects to hike #25.

Distance: 2.3-kilometre linear trail (4.6-kilometre return).

Trailhead access: Access the bottom (west end) of the trail via the upper parking lot at Margaret Bowater Park or from the top (east end) at Crocker's Road.

Amenities: Margaret Bowater has ample parking. Toilets/ change rooms and swimming facilites are available in the summer.

Keep in mind: Mountain bikers are the primary users of the trail. Hikers should yield to riders, and downhill riders should yield to uphill riders.

Permits & fees: Donations toward trail upkeep are payable to Cycle Solutions: www.cyclesolutions.ca/tour/trails.

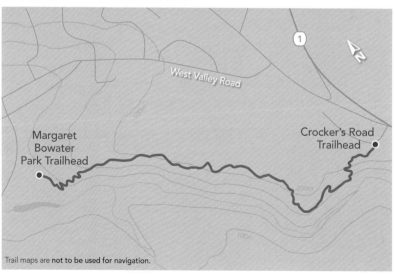

Margaret Bowater Park Trailhead

Crocker's Road Trailhead

West Valley Road

1

Trail maps are **not to be used for navigation.**

Corner Brook

The Corner Brook Stream Walking Trail network is made up of three main trails: Glynmill Inn Pond trail, Three Bear Mountain trail, and Corner Brook Gorge trail. Glynmill Inn Pond trail, the easiest and most accessible, consists of 2 kilometres of gravel walkways. During the summer, many events are held around the Glynmill Pond and in Margaret Bowater Park.

Three Bear Mountain trail has more elevation gain than the Glynmill Inn Pond trail but is only about 1 kilometre long. Side trails lead to views of the city; interpretation panels of Corner Brook's history and development are displayed along the trail.

Corner Brook Gorge trail is approximately 4 kilometres long and rated a moderate trail. It leads up to Corner Brook Gorge, where hikers can view the waterfalls and return via the same route or hike down to Crocker's Road. This trail meanders through the forest and along the wooden pipeline and crosses the Corner Brook stream.

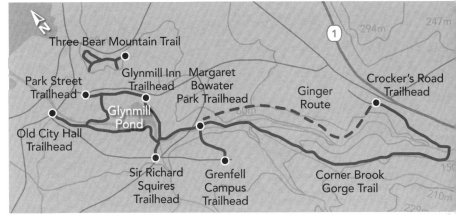

Trail maps are **not to be used for navigation.**

Distance: 7-kilometre trail network.

Trailhead access: The main entry area is at Margaret Bowater Park on O'Connell Drive: 48.9445528, -57.9351942. Other access points: Glynmill Inn, Park Street, Cobb Lane, Old City Hall (corner of Main St. and Mt. Bernard), Crocker's Road, and Sir Richard Squires Building; most have parking areas.

Amenities: Trails have rest spots, picnic areas, and lookouts. Margaret Bowater Park has multiple playgrounds, an unsupervised swimming area, canteen, and bathrooms.

Keep in mind: The swans in Glynmill Inn Pond, although used to visitors, can be dangerous if aggravated. Keep dogs leashed and clean up after your pet.

Permits & fees: Donations toward trail upkeep are payable to the Corner Brook Stream Development Corporation (CBSDC). Participation in the memorial program is appreciated.

Corner Brook

Humber Valley Trail Section 1

This section of the Humber Valley Trail follows the hilltops along the north side of the lower Humber River, from the southern trailhead near Ballam Bridge to the Old Man in the Mountain Lookout. You may hike this trail as a half-day out-and-back hike, or a full-day linear hike.

For the half-day hike, you'll begin with a 300-metre ascent up an old wood-cutting trail and creek bed. At the first pond, stay right to access the first viewpoint. Follow the ridge east toward the next hill, where you will climb a steep switchback leading to the second viewpoint and a view of the entire Bay of Islands. Head downhill, still on an easterly bearing, and follow a path through the forest. You'll come by a third pond (where the trail gets boggy), continue on down the hill. Just before the fourth pond, the trail takes a sharp right, following the pond to the other side.

As you start to climb again, the

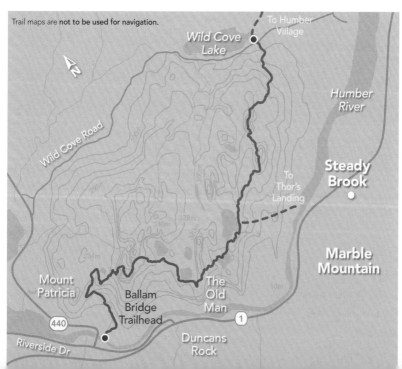

Trail maps are **not to be used for navigation**.

trail forks. Stay right to reach the top of the Old Man in the Mountain. This viewpoint offers a breathtaking view of the Humber River and Shellbird Island. Return by the same route.

To extend you hike, when you reach the fork in the trail (48.95121, -57.86647), head northeast along the ridge through birch stands down to Wild Cove Road.

A branch off the main trail will take you down to Thor's Landing, where an old cabin beside the Humber River is available for hikers to use as a warm-up shelter or overnight hut. Boat transfers can be arranged via IATNL.

Distance: Half-day hike: 2.5-kilometre (5-kilometre return) linear trail. Full day hike: 9.3 kilometres one way.

Trailhead access: The southern trailhead is located just off Route 440. Immediately after Ballams Bridge, turn right on a gravel road. Follow this road about 40 metres and park in the parking area on the left: 48.9532917, -57.8860611.

The northern trailhead is off Wild Cove Road at 48.97013, -57.82567.

An additional access point is at Thor's Landing: 48.95902, -57.82666.

Amenities: None.

Keep in mind: This area is used for hunting moose (September to February) and small game (all year). Wear blaze orange in the fall and be cautious with dogs off leash. This trail is not well-maintained; be prepared with a GPS-enabled device or map and compass.

Permits & fees: Donations toward trail upkeep are payable to the IATNL.

Map #: 12A13 & 12H4.

Wild Cove–Humber Village
Humber Valley Trail Section 2

This is the second section of the Humber Valley Trail that follows the hilltops along the north side of the lower Humber River. This section is a local favourite in the fall.

From Wild Cove road, head northeast and climb through large stands of birch forest. At Barry's Lookout (310 metres) stop to enjoy panoramic views of the Humber Valley from the Blow Me Down Mountains in the west to the North Arm Hills in the north and Marble Mountain ski hill in the south.

Keep hiking until you intersect with the access trail at 48.98793, -57.78325 and take a right (east) to head downhill toward Humber Village.

 The Humber River is one of the world's best Atlantic salmon fishing rivers, attracting people from all over the world.

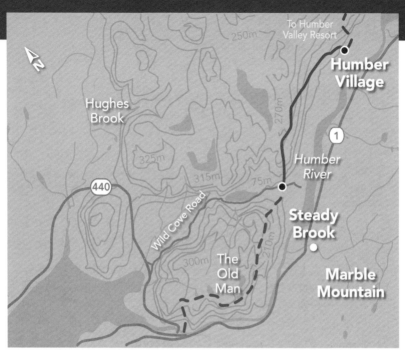

Trail maps are not to be used for navigation.

Distance: 5-kilometre linear trail.

Trailhead access:

■ Southern trailhead: On Wild Cove Road, 6 kilometres past Ballam Bridge on Route 440. Drive in about 10 kilometres to the east end of the pond, turn left, and park on the right. The trail is 480 metres down the road at 48.97013, -57.82567.

■ Northern trailhead: In Humber Village, take the first left and follow the main road, turn left onto Pine Street, and stay right (it changes to Marble View Drive). Park about 50 metres past the tower at 48.98496, -57.77422. Do not block the road. The trailhead will be on the uphill side, with signs.

Keep in mind: This area is used for hunting moose (September to February) and small game (all year). Wear blaze orange in the fall and be cautious with dogs off leash. This trail is not well-maintained; be prepared with a GPS-enabled device or map and compass.

Permits & fees: Donations toward trail upkeep are payable to IATNL.

Map #: 112A13 & 12H4.

Humber Village–Humber Valley Resort
Humber Valley Trail Section 3

Starting in Humber Village, the access trail to this section of the Humber Valley Trail is an old snowmobile trail and quite wide. It climbs gradually for 250 metres through boreal forest and intersects with the Humber Valley Trail at 48.98793, -57.78325.

The ridgetop trail then heads steadily northeast toward Little North Pond, crossing old sections of forestry cutovers and logging roads. There are few signs or trail markers until you will reach the plateau and viewpoint above Little North Pond at 49.03773, -57.71014.

At the northern end of the plateau, the trail is routed atop a gorge carved into the landscape before intersecting with a Humber Valley Resort service road. The trailhead is located next to the water reservoir (Little North Pond's south shore).

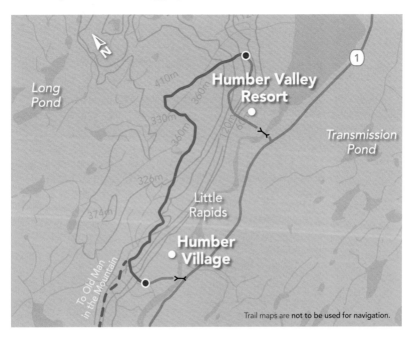

Trail maps are **not to be used for navigation.**

Distance: 13-kilometre linear trail.

Trailhead access:

■ Southern trailhead: In Humber Village, take the first left and follow the main road, turn left onto Pine Street, and stay right (it changes to Marble View Drive). Park about 50 metres after the tower at 48.98496, -57.77422. Do not block the road. The trailhead will be on the uphill side, with signs.

■ Northern trailhead: In Humber Valley Resort, drive past the Golf Club and take the second left. Park at the pumphouse building on the right and walk or, if vehicle clearance allows, drive up the road about 2.5 kilometres until the little round-about at 49.03706, -57.69353. Park here. Walk down the road 20 metres, take the right road (IAT is written in white on the rock) and walk to the pond. The trail starts on the left. Watch for white paint or pink flagging tape.

Keep in mind: This area is used for hunting moose (September to February) and small game (all year). Wear blaze orange in the fall and be cautious with dogs off leash. Be prepared with a GPS-enabled device or map and compass.

Permits & fees: Donations toward trail upkeep are payable to IATNL.

Map #: 12A13 & 12H4.

Marble Mountain Trail

Follow the gravel access road and either take the Steady Brook trail or stay on this road and climb gradually. Both trails merge at the chlorine treatment hut. Continue straight on the gravel road until the road forks. Take the right road, go around the gate, and keep climbing the road past the two ski lifts and up to the Doppler weather station—a white tower with a big ball on top—at about 550 metres.

At the top of Marble Mountain is a panoramic view of the Bay of Islands, Corner Brook, Blow Me Down Mountains, North Arm Hills, Humber Valley, and Steady Brook. If you can, hike to the summit just before sunset and watch as the sun sets over the horizon of the Gulf of St. Lawrence. Start your return just after sunset to make it back before dark. Bring a flashlight! Descend along the same route.

★ The climb up Marble Mountain actually brings you to the summit of Musgrave Mountain. The nearby town of Steady Brook has a network of walking trails across the highway from the ski hill.

Distance: 5-kilometre linear trail (10-kilometre return).

Trailhead access: Exit Route 1 into Steady Brook and follow the road behind Tim Horton's. Before the bridge, turn right into a gravel parking area: 48.94978, -57.8235719. The road up the hill is the trail.

Steady Brook Falls Trail

From the parking area, start up the gravel access road, turn left and cross the little bridge and follow the signs for Steady Brook Falls. The first section leads up to stairs and a wooden lookout platform. Continuing up the stairs will take you up the trail along the edge of Steady Brook Gorge to the top of the waterfall. Return by the same route.

Keep in mind: This trail is located on a ski hill. Be courteous to users. The section from the chlorine water treatment hut to the Doppler is closed December 15 to April 15. Dogs can be off leash.

Trail maps are available inside Marble Mountain ski lodge.

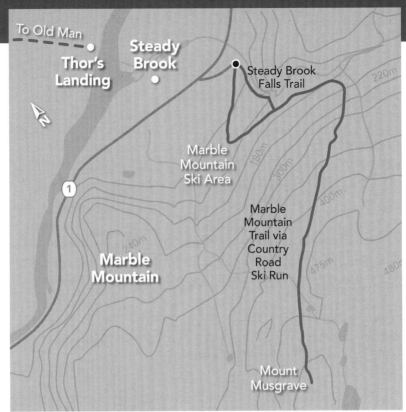

To Old Man

Thor's Landing

Steady Brook

Steady Brook Falls Trail

220m

Marble Mountain Ski Area

180m

300m

400m

1

Marble Mountain Trail via Country Road Ski Run

240m

Marble Mountain

475m

480m

Mount Musgrave

Trail maps are **not to be used for navigation.**

GROS MORNE NATIONAL PARK

It's no surprise that Gros Morne National Park, designated a UNESCO World Heritage Site in 1987 for its geological history and natural beauty, contains some of the most majestic scenery in Canada.

See for yourself, as you hike the wide variety of trails throughout the park. Explore the glacially carved valleys, ancient mountaintops, coastal flatlands, and unearthly Tablelands (used as a Mars analogue by NASA researchers). Each trail offers something special, from geological wonders to wildlife sightings and towering waterfalls, and always a story to tell. Come here for a fully illustrated guide to plate tectonics or to see the earth's mantle—exposed. Welcome to some of the best hiking in western Newfoundland!

Trails of Gros Morne National Park

30. Overfalls Trail / Trout River
31. Trout River Trails / Trout River
32. Trout River Pond Trail / Trout River
33. Green Gardens Trail / Route 431
34. Tablelands Trail / Route 431
35. Lookout Trail / Woody Point
36. Stanleyville Trail / Lomond
37. Lomond River Trail / Lomond
38. Stuckless Pond Trail / Lomond
39. Burnt Hill Trail / Norris Point
40. James Callaghan Trail (Gros Morne Mountain) / Route 430
41. Baker's Brook Falls Trail / Route 430
42. Coastal Trail / Route 430
43. Snug Harbour Trail / Route 430
44. North Rim Traverse / Route 430
45. Long Range Traverse / Route 430
46. Cow Head Lighthouse Trail / Cow Head

Permits & fees

■ All trails require a park pass. Daily and annual passes can be purchased at the Discovery Centre in Woody Point, the information kiosk off Route 430 before Wiltondale, or at the visitor centre at the Norris Point turnoff.

■ Extra fees apply for the use of backcountry trails and campsites.

■ Some trails require boat access; extra fees apply.

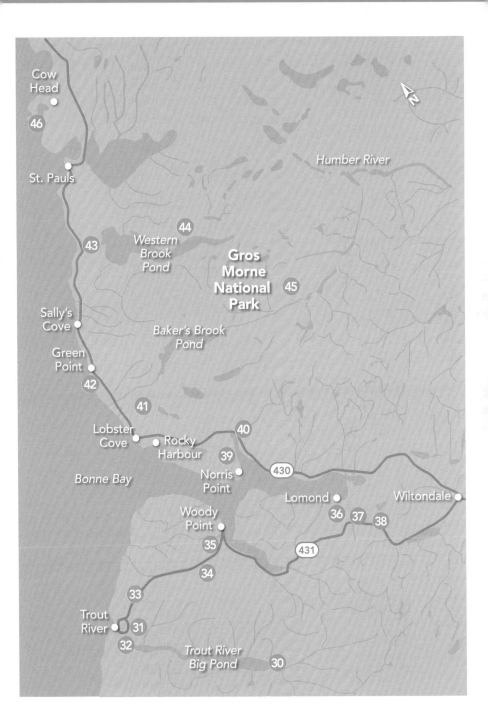

Trout River

To reach the Overfalls Trail, you must take a boat shuttle from Trout River to the eastern end of Trout River Pond. The boat trip is about one hour and travels along the south edge of the Tablelands, providing an excellent opportunity to view this favourite destination of geologists.

Walk southwest on the beach, away from the Tablelands, until you see a trail, signs, or flagging tape leading into the forest. Follow the dry, even trail along the west branch of Trout River. The trail climbs from sea level to about 200 metres by the Overfalls. About midway, there is a side loop that you can climb to a lookout that provides views of Trout River Pond valley, the Tablelands, and the Overfalls.

The main trail does not lead to the base of the Overfalls but instead traverses the rim of the small valley created by the Overfalls waterfall, and is still quite rough. As of writing, the trail to the top of the falls is incomplete, but it is worth the trek to where the trail ends to have a better view of the falls. Return the way you came, meeting your return shuttle at the beach. Watch for caribou and moose—both are commonly encountered along this trail.

 The Overfalls Trail is the first IATNL-Gros Morne National Park partnership trail, established in 2011. It will eventually provide access to the North Arm hills and more IATNL trails.

Distance: 5-kilometre (10-kilometre return) linear trail.

Trailhead access: Take Route 431 to Trout River. At the stop sign, turn left onto Main Street. Follow Main Street (stay left) until the parking area: 49.1061, -58.1267. You must boat across Trout River Pond (contact IATNL) to get to the trailhead: 49.36713, -57.96755.

Amenities: None.

Keep in mind: This trail may be quite rough in sections. Arrange a boat shuttle for a round-trip. Some stream crossings are challenging early in the season or after heavy rains.

Map #: 12 H 05.

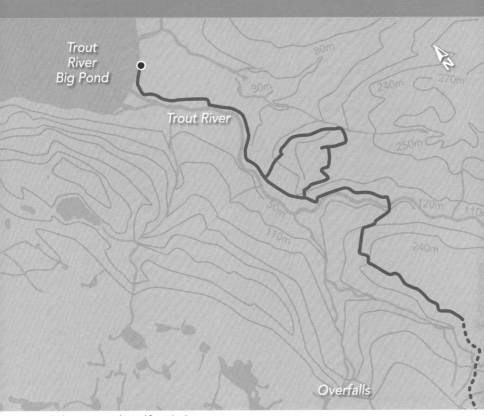

Trout
River
Big Pond

80m

30m

240m

270m

Trout River

250m

50m

120m

110m

110m

240m

Overfalls

Trail maps are **not to be used for navigation.**

Trout River

There are two lovely trails on the outskirts of town where you can enjoy gentle hikes along the coast. Locals attest this is the best place in Gros Morne National Park to watch the sunset!

Eastern Point Trail

Distance: 1-kilometre linear trail.

Terrain and elevation: Boardwalk and natural surface, 50-metre elevation gain.

Trailhead access: Parking and entrance is at the northern end of Main Street at 49.48338, -58.12192.

Old Man/Lighthouse Trail

Distance: 2-kilometre linear trail.

Terrain and elevation: Natural surface, 80-metre elevation gain.

Trailhead access: Parking and entrance is off Riverside Drive at 49.47809, -58.13131.

Amenities: None on the trails.

Keep in mind: These are community trails (not Parks Canada trails); we encourage users to contribute toward keep them clean and consider donating to the Trout River Trail Committee.

Eastern Point Trail: A short flight of stairs leads to the top of the cliff that extends out toward the ocean. This is a ruggedly scenic trail that provides fabulous views of the water, beach, town, and cliffs. Some friendly sheep may make an appearance.

Old Man/Lighthouse Trail: This winding trail leads directly to interesting rock formations while offering the opportunity to take marvelous photographs of the Town of Trout River, the river itself, fishing boats, and mountains. Walk up to the large rock structure the locals call The Old Man. You can carry on past the natural statue along soft fields to view the ocean and cliffs.

 The Old Man formation was once accompanied by an Old Woman, who has since crumbled. The sheep in the area roam free, grazing all summer long. This practice goes back generation in this area.

Trail maps are **not to be used for navigation.**

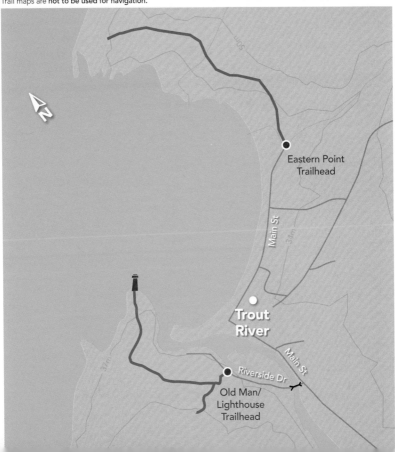

Eastern Point
Trailhead

Main St

Trout
River

Riverside Dr

Main St

Old Man/
Lighthouse
Trailhead

Trout River

Trout River Pond Trail is well signed, with a kilometre marker about every 500 metres or so. The first 3.5 kilometres has little elevation change as it travels through the forest, with occasional scattered views of Trout River Pond. The scenery gradually transitions to smaller trees and tuckamore.

Eventually the trail brings you to exposed barrens covered by orange peridotite and serpentine rocks. You'll have to make a few small stream crossings, but these are easily done by hopping from rock to rock. The trail provides access to rocky beaches along the way.

Within the final 3 kilometres of trail, you'll climb to an elevation of about 110 metres. Enjoy the lookout where Trout River Pond narrows before it opens up again. Continue hiking to the second lookout—red Adirondack chairs await you. Sit and appreciate the scenery of the Tablelands and the cliffs surrounding the pond.

Return to the parking area the way you came.

 This trail takes you along the edge of the Tablelands and up the glacial valley of Trout River Pond.

Trail maps are **not to be used for navigation.**

Distance: 7-kilometre linear trail (14-kilometre return).

Trailhead access: Take Route 431 to Trout River. Turn left onto Main Street and follow the signs for the trail (not the campground). The trail starts at the parking lot: 49.4607471, -58.1164384.

Amenities: Picnic tables, wash-rooms, a shelter, a playground, and a dock at the parking area; halfway along the trail is an outhouse.

Keep in mind: Some parts of the trail may be muddy and slippery. Stream crossings may be challenging after the snow melts; during summer, crossings are easier.

Route 431

The trail down to Green Gardens leads directly to the coast and, because of this, is a popular trail in the park. The trail is 9 kilometres return, and it takes between four and six hours to do the round trip.

The trail begins at the Long Pond parking area and heads off across a barren landscape of frost-cracked, orange-brown peridotite boulders. The trail rises to a viewpoint where the rock type changes and forest begins. Turn left at the junction, where the trail then descends through forest to the coast. This shorter route ends in a staircase leading down to a beach beside a cliff of pillow lava. Return by the same route. It is uphill most of the way and steep in places.

Green Gardens

280m

380m

Trout River Gulch

260m

240m

130m

160m

265m

431

260m

290

Long Pond

Tablelands

220m

● Long Pond Trailhead

Trail maps are not to be used for navigation.

Distances: 4.5-kilometre linear trail (9-kilometre return).

Trailhead access: Frollow Route 430 in Gros Morne National Park and make a left turn in Wilton-dale onto Route 431. In Woody Point turn left to stay on Route 431, following the signs for Trout River. The Long Pond trailhead is 13 kilometres from Woody Point (3 kilometres from Trout River).

Amenities: Outhouses in parking areas and at the coast; tent platforms provided.

Keep in mind: Stay back from cliff edges as some places may be undercut; stay on the trails.

 The rugged coastline is a geologist's paradise of volcanic formations. These eruptions occurred over 600 million years ago when the continents were splitting and oceans forming.

Watch for a sea cave, accessible during low tide, along the Long Pond to Green Gardens short route.

Route 431

As you drive to the Tablelands trailhead, notice how the road separates the orange, barren terrain of the Tablelands to the south from the lush green hills to the north. The valley floor is an ancient fault line; to the north are metamorphosed gabbro and other types of oceanic crust, while to the south is the ophiolite complex known as the Tablelands.

Tablelands Walk: The trail leads to a viewing platform beside Winterhouse Brook in the centre of the

majestic Winter House Gorge. This is an easy trail along a well-maintained gravel walkway with little elevation gain. Return along the same route.

Tablelands Climb: Past the viewing platform, the trail is immediately uneven as you walk from boulder to boulder. As you make your way

Tablelands Walk

Distance: 2-kilometre linear trail (4-kilometre return).

Trailhead access: Follow Route 431 toward Trout River. The parking area and trailhead are on the left, about 4.5 kilometres past the Discovery Centre: 49.4782798, -57.9738196.

Tablelands Climb

Distance: 8.5-kilometre loop.

Trailhead access: From the platform at the end of the Tablelands Walk, continue south up Winterhouse Brook Gorge.

Amenities: Outhouse and garbage bins in parking lot.

Keep in mind: The snow melts slowly on the north face of the Tablelands and may cover parts of the trail early in the season.

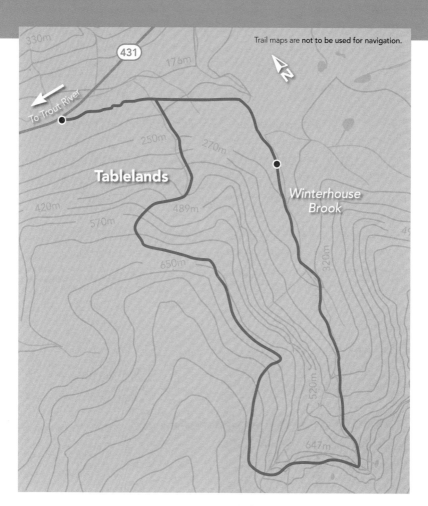

up the valley, be prepared to cross the brook a few times. After about 1.5 kilometres, the route begins to climb steeply. At 49.44210, -57.96685, you are at the top. Head northwest along the rim of the valley to the lookout at 49.45393, -57.96907. To descend, make your way north to Trout River Bowl at 49.46880, -57.97534. Make your way down into the bowl and stay to one side of the brook.

Woody Point

This often-overlooked trail grants hikers access to one of the greatest views of Gros Morne National Park. From the Discovery Centre trailhead, you'll quickly climb 350 metres through boreal forest to reach the barren, boggy summit and the lookout. The first section is linear, but the trail then splits into a loop that goes around the top of Partridge Berry Hill. Stay to the right to reach the viewing platform more quickly.

From the platform, the stunning landscape of Bonne Bay, the Tablelands, and Gros Morne Mountain can be appreciated. Whales and icebergs may be sighted during appropriate times of the year. Continue on to complete the loop of Partridge Berry Hill, or return the way you came.

Distance: 5-kilometre loop.

Trailhead access: Follow Route 431 toward Woody Point, turn left toward Trout River. Turn right at the Discovery Centre and park: 49.4944532, -57.9241429. The trailhead is well signed.

Amenities: Washrooms, phones, and park information at the Discovery Centre; benches and chairs at the lookout.

Keep in mind: Parts of the trail may be muddy during periods of heavy rain in early spring and late fall. Extreme winds may be experienced on the exposed summit.

The landscape of this trail is a complete contrast to the landscape of the Tablelands. Well vegetated, the trail travels over metamorphosed gabbro and other types of oceanic crust, which contains the required elements for plant life. The summit provides a perfect habitat for pitcher plants, Newfoundland and Labrador's provincial flower and one of three carnivorous plants found in the province.

An exceptional hike to start a journey through Gros Morne National Park, it offers a bird's-eye view of all the major park features and helps you get your bearings. However, if you are hiking on a foggy or cloudy day, remember that visibility may be reduced.

Trail maps are **not to be used for navigation.**

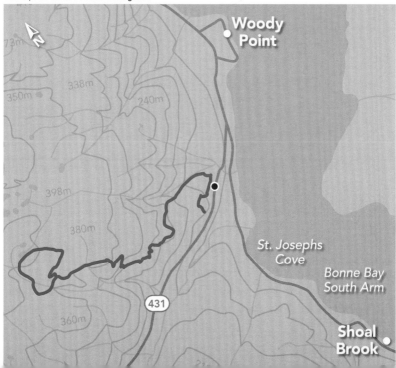

2 Lomond

Stanleyville Trail starts with a gradual ascent and a few bridges over small streams. Next, a steeper section with stairs leads to the highest point, about 110 metres. From this summit, look back toward Lomond and the east arm of Bonne Bay—a gorgeous landscape of hills and cliffs—before descending to the beach of Paynes Cove and Stanleyville.

From the beach you may see whales, seals, and seabirds. Stanleyville has been deserted for over 80 years and it's a lovely place to explore—garden plants and logging machinery are visible reminders of settlement. When you're ready, turn around and return the way you came. Watch for moose along the trail.

★ In the early 1900s, logging was a major industry and white pine the main source of lumber. In 1899, the McKie brothers built a sawmill in Stanleyville and from this started commercial lumbering. The site was abandoned in the 1920s when the St. Lawrence Timber, Pulp, and Steamship Company set up a larger operation in Lomond Cove, where this trail begins. Look for remnants of this abandoned community along the shoreline.

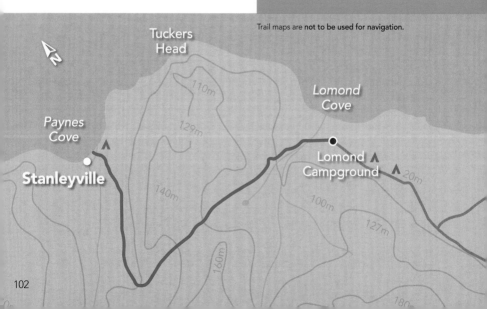

Trail maps are **not to be used for navigation.**

Tuckers Head · 110m · 129m · Lomond Cove · Paynes Cove · Lomond Campground · 20m · Stanleyville · 140m · 100m · 127m · 160m · 180m

Distance: 2-kilometre linear trail (4-kilometre return).

Trailhead access: On Route 431, 16 kilometres from Wiltondale, turn right and follow signs for Lomond Campground: 49.4591664, -57.7599048. The trailhead is at the end of the campground parking lot behind two brown buildings.

Amenities: Washrooms, showers, picnic tables, and a shelter at the trailhead; at Stanleyville beach, an outhouse, picnic table, chairs, and a primitive campsite.

Keep in mind: Many moose live in this area. Use extreme caution if encountering a cow with calf in the spring or a male in the fall mating season. Be careful in steep sections as the trail may be muddy and slippery during rainy periods.

Lomond

Distance: 6-kilometre linear trail (12-kilometre return).

Trailhead access: There are two trailheads:

◼ From Wiltondale, follow Route 431 for about 16 kilometres until you see the trailhead sign and parking area on your right: 49.4268104, -57.7390852.

◼ The second trailhead is on the access road for Lomond Campground and is marked with a trail map: 49.4506875, -57.7548265.

Amenities: Outhouse and garbage bins in the Lomond / Stuckless Pond parking lot.

Keep in mind: Some sections of the trail become muddy and slippery. Be aware of tidal changes.

Lomond River Trail meanders along the Lomond River, with about 60 metres of elevation change, out to the estuary of the east arm of Bonne Bay.

From the parking lot, follow the signs and boardwalk down to the trail and turn left. The trail wanders through a mature forest and leads down to the Lomond River, crossing a few bridges and offering access to rock and sand beaches along the way. The tides from Bonne Bay affect the river's water level; if you explore the beaches, be vigilant about the tides or you may become trapped.

The meeting of Lomond River and the east arm of Bonne Bay creates an estuary full of diverse aquatic life. This region is home to many species of birds and in the fall ducks rest here during their migration south. The Lomond River is also an Atlantic salmon and sea-run trout route during the summer.

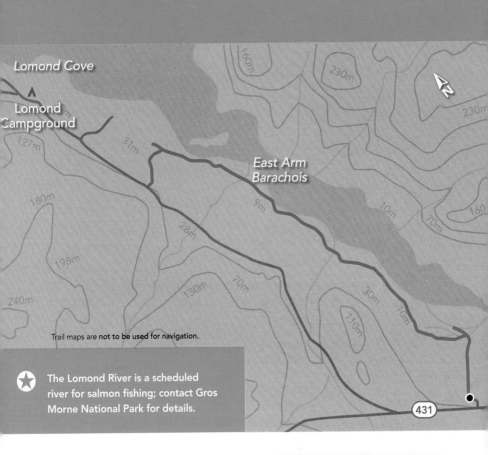

Lomond Cove

Lomond
Campground

East Arm
Barachois

127m

31m

160m

230m

230m

180m

198m

240m

28th

130m

70m

9m

10m

70m

30m

110m

10m

160

10m

Trail maps are not to be used for navigation.

431

★ The Lomond River is a scheduled river for salmon fishing; contact Gros Morne National Park for details.

Hike to the Lomond Campground access road trailhead. Return by the same trail or follow the access road to Route 431, turn left and walk along Route 431 to the parking area. This trail also connects with the Stuckless Pond Trail (hike #38).

Lomond

Leave the trailhead parking area and take the boardwalk down to the trail. Follow the signs for Stuckless Pond and veer to the right.

Descend a short downhill section and cross the Lomond River on a suspension bridge. This trail is a loop around Stuckless Pond; when the trail forks, go either right or left. The trail rolls up and down, with the highest point at an elevation of about 125 metres.

The pond can be accessed for a swim at a few locations. Birch stands, meadows, beaver dams, and the serenity of the area make this an enjoyable and relaxing hike. When

Distance: 10-kilometre loop.

Trailhead access: From Wiltondale, follow Route 431 for about 16 kilometres. The well-signed parking area is on the right: 49.4268104, -57.7390852.

Amenities: Outhouse and garbage bins at the main trailhead.

Keep in mind: This is a shared-use trail for bikers and hikers.

you return to the fork, head back toward the Lomond River Bridge and the parking lot.

Most of this trail is located within the forest, making for good opportunities to see moose or other animals—you may encounter a moose grazing in a meadow or see a beaver at work.

Trail maps are **not to be used for navigation.**

2

Norris Point

A forest fire threw a scare into the people of Norris Point in 1898. A Mr. Tucker was boiling pitch to seal his boat when the contents of the tin caught on fire. The boat was soon ablaze, which ignited the nearby trees and in a short time the whole hill was on fire. The fire burned itself out before it reached the property of any of its residents.

Since that time, much of the hill has regained its growth of trees and bears the name Burnt Hill. The hill also is locally known as Neddy Hill or Big Hill. It is surrounded by water on three sides and the town of Norris Point on the other.

Distance: 2.5-kilometre loop.

Terraine/Elevation: Engineered trail with single-track natural surface, 90-metre elevation gain.

Trailhead access: Park in the large parking area beside the Marine Station and Cat Stop restaurant. Walk to the trailhead at 49.51804, -57.87560.

Amenities: None on the trail.

Keep in mind: This is a community trail (not a Parks Canada trail); consider donating to help with maintenance.

A single-track trail carries you slowly upward. Stop at the many lookouts to enjoy the views and catch your breath. The spectacular view of Bonne Bay, the Tablelands, and town of Norris Point are worth the climb.

Trail maps are **not to be used for navigation.**

Route 430

Gros Morne means "Big Lone" in French. The mountain was given its name because it stands higher than the surrounding hills and is often hidden in the clouds. The trail is named after former United Kingdom prime minister James Callaghan (1976–79) for his conservation efforts.

From the parking lot, the trail climbs steadily to the base of Gros Morne Mountain. At about 300 metres elevation is a platform, an outhouse, and information signs; it makes a suitable rest spot.

The next section brings you to the gully, the steepest and hardest part of this trail; many of the rocks are loose. At the trail intersection, keep going straight up the gully. It is safer for all hikers to hike the mountain loop clockwise.

At the top of the gully, the trail crosses the summit of 806 metres and then follows the edge of Ten Mile Gulch. As the trail descends, it wraps around the mountain to Ferry Gulch. The trail passes a small pond, where there are outhouses, picnic tables, and a backcountry campsite; if flies are abundant, keep moving! Follow the trail until it merges with the gully access trail. Return to the platform and continue to the parking lot.

Trail maps are not to be used for navigation.

Gros Morne's summit is 806 metres, making it the second-highest mountain on the island of Newfoundland. The Cabox, in the Lewis Hills, is the tallest, at 814 metres. The mountain is home to caribou, moose, Arctic hare, and rock ptarmigan.

Distance: 16-kilometre loop.

Trailhead access: Trailhead is off Route 430, about 3 kilometres south of the Gros Morne visitor centre: 49.5653697, -57.8325148.

Amenities: Outhouses in the parking area, at the platform, and at the backcountry campsite; tent platforms and picnic tables at the backcountry campsite.

Keep in mind: It is easy to become disoriented when the fog rolls in, and this summit is exposed to high winds, lightning, and other extreme conditions. Heed all weather warnings.

Gros Morne Mountain is not open to hikers until July 1 in order to protect wildlife during critical weeks of reproduction and growth. No dogs allowed on this trail.

Pack out your garbage; do not remove anything (rocks, fossils, plants), and stay on the trail.

Route 430

From the parking lot of Berry Hill Campground, follow the trail along boardwalks and footpaths through a mix of forest, meadow, and boggy wetlands. This easy stroll takes you to Baker's Brook and the waterfall, Baker's Brook Overfalls.

Moose, squirrels, and grey jays are the most common wildlife along the trail but, if you're interested in local botany, the bogs and meadows boast a wide array of wildflowers.

Most of the trail has little elevation change, but at the end, you descend 30 to 40 metres with the help of stairs to see the falls up close. The falls are stunning and worth the hike—the brook runs over a series of ledges, creating a cascade effect.

Trail maps are **not to be used for navigation.**

Distance: 5-kilometre linear trail (10-kilometre return).

Trailhead access: Turn off Route 430 at Berry Hill Campground: 49.6250013, -57.927896. Pay fees at the gate and then drive straight, following the signs to the trailhead; the parking area is on the left.

Amenities: Washrooms, showers, picnic tables, a shelter, and campsites at Berry Hill Campground.

Keep in mind: Baker's Brook has a strong current and the water is cold; keep a close eye on small children near the water.

During the winter, this is an excellent snowshoeing and cross-country ski trail.

Route 430

This trail is part of the old Winter Mail Road that continues up to the Northern Peninsula. Before the road was cleared, dog teams hauled mail along this route, stopping at every community along the way.

Beginning at Green Point Campground, the trail follows the coastline south, with little elevation change, crossing rocky shoreline, tuckamore forests, marshy ponds, and a traditional lobster cage. It offers fantastic views of the coastline; Green Gardens with its interesting rock formations can also be seen. Watch brilliant sunsets from the trail, and use your binoculars

★ Green Point displays a 30-million-year record of deep ocean sediments in the exposed layers of shale. Gros Morne National Park offers a guided walk called "Stroll through Strata," in which park interpreters share the details of this exceptional geological site.

Trail maps are **not to be used for navigation.**

for sightings of migrating whales, ducks, and seabirds.

In 2000, Green Point was designated a Global Stratotype Section and Point (GSSP) and represents the division between Cambrian and the Ordovician periods (542–443 million years ago). In these limestone layers geologists found the first *Iapetognathus fluctivagus*, a conodont fossil that lies 4.8 metres below the earliest known planktic graptolite fossil.

Walk as far as you like and return along the coastline.

Distance: 3-kilometre linear trail (6-kilometre return).

Trailhead access: There are two trailheads on Route 430:

■ Green Point Campground: 49.6793501, -57.9574785.

■ The parking area at Baker's Brook Bridge: 49.8292314, -57.8560289. Signs indicate the trail.

Amenities: Picnic tables, outhouses, a shelter, and campsites at the campground.

Keep in mind: Most of the trail is exposed to the ocean and wind. Be aware of tidal changes.

Route 430

The Snug Harbour trail takes hikers to a backcountry campsite at the foot of the Long Range Mountains.

Follow the gravel road toward Western Brook Pond. At the split, stay left until you reach the river crossing of Western Brook. Walk upstream, just above the outflow from the pond, to cross. This is where the water is shallowest and the current weakest.

Distance: Snug Harbour: 8-kilometre linear trail (16-kilometre return).

Note: This trail connects to the North Rim Traverse (hike #44).

Trailhead access: Follow Route 430 approximately 28 kilometres past the visitor centre to the large parking area for Western Brook Pond: 49.7882564, -57.870836.

Keep in mind: If you're doing the Snug Harbour Trail, be prepared to ford Western Brook; the water may be deep in the spring or after a heavy rainfall. Bring extra footwear (sandals or water shoes) for crossings.

The trail is in poor condition and is very muddy. Moose are plentiful in this area: keep your distance, especially in spring and fall.

A backcountry permit is required for camping in Snug Harbour and to continue on the North Rim Traverse.

 Western Brook Pond, a freshwater pond, was once connected to the ocean, making it a true fjord. When the glaciers receded, the boggy lowlands rebounded, breaking off the fjord from the ocean. The cliffs and waterfalls along the pond are spectacular and the boat tour is well worth the ticket price.

In places the trail follows the shoreline—keep an eye out for markers indicating where the trail re-enters the forest. The beach at Snug Harbour is a great place to rest or camp. From Snug Harbour, a rough trail provides access to the mountain plateau and the North Rim Traverse. Unless you are carrying on to the traverse, return by the same route.

Trail maps are **not to be used for navigation.**

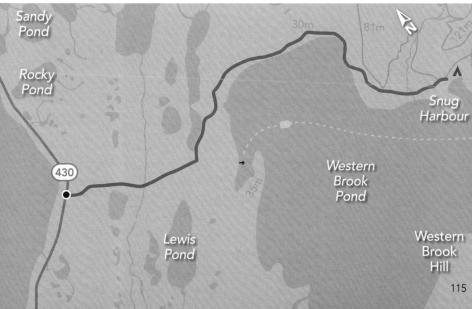

Route 430

*This description is based on hiking in at Snug Harbour (hike #43) and boating out at Western Brook Pond. This is a backcountry route, **not** a maintained trail; most hikers take three to five days (two to four nights in a tent) to complete it.*

Start your hike with the Snug Harbour Trail (hike #43). Snug Harbour campsite has a meadow for tents, a food hang, and an outdoor toilet.

From Snug Harbour, walk to the end of the beach to a trail sign, and make your way uphill. There are two routes up to the North Rim: the right branch is steep and leads to a barren scrubby area; the left, more gradual, leads to a boggy meadow. Both branches rejoin the main trail and continue up

onto the North Rim. An optional side trail leads to a lookout—the view is worth it!

Campsites are available at Long Pond and beside a small pond (about six hours from Western Brook Pond, see GPS coordinates on Gros Morne website). There are no facilities at this site.

Continue toward the back of Western Brook fjord. Follow the brook that feeds into Western Brook fjord, keeping to the south side. Coming down into the fjord is very steep: stay left of the water-fall. After the waterfall, follow the brook to the campsite at the dock. Be ready at the appropriate time for boat pickup. Hike out to the parking area from the dock.

Trail maps are **not to be used for navigation.**

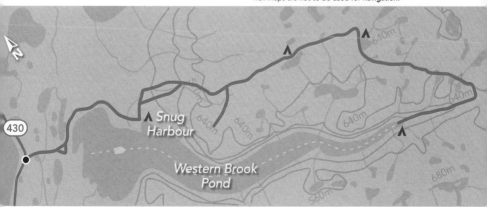

Distance: 27-kilometre linear trail.

Note: North Rim Traverse can be combined with Long Range Traverse (hike #45). North Rim is less travelled and said to be more challenging than Long Range due to the bushwhacking required.

Trailhead access: On Route 430, approximately 28 kilometres past the visitor centre, park in the large parking area for Western Brook Pond: 49.7882564, -57.870836. Do the loop in either direction (hike in via Snug Harbour, boat out via Western Brook Pond, or vice versa).

Amenities: Outhouse and picnic tables at parking area; washrooms and concession at dock. Some backcountry campsites have wooden platforms, pit toilets, and food lockers or bear poles.

Keep in mind:

■ See hike #45 Long Range Traverse

Permits & fees

■ Book hiking dates in advance to avoid disappointment; there is a small window of good hiking weather.

■ Arrive at least one day before your departure to attend a mandatory pre-trip planning session, which includes a map and compass skills assessment.

■ Reservation and backcountry camping fees apply.

■ When booking hiking dates, book boat tickets as well (see information at the back of this book).

Map #: 12H12 & 12H13.

Route 430

This description is based on boating in via Western Brook Pond and hiking out at Gros Morne Mountain (southern trailhead, see hike #40). This is a backcountry route, **not** a maintained trail; most hikers take three to five days (two to four nights in a tent) to complete it.

A gravel access road will lead you to the docks, from which you'll take the tour boat across Western Brook Pond. Bring your backcountry permit and transceiver. You'll be dropped off at the far end of the pond on a small dock in the shadow of steep cliffs.

The next section is challenging: you'll hike up and out of the fjord through meadows and forest, gaining approximately 500 metres.

Western Brook Pond Trail

Western Brook Pond

Baker's Brook Middle Pond

Sally's Cove

Baker's Brook Pond

650m

640m

430

Gros Morne Mountain

Two Mile Pond

James Callaghan Trail

Lobster Cove

Rocky Harbour

Trail maps are not to be used for navigation.

Follow the stream and stay to the right of the waterfall. Don't forget to stop and look behind you. The view of the fjord is impressive.

From the top of the fjord, head south toward Little Island Pond campsite (coordinates on Gros Morne website). Be prepared to bushwhack, cross streams and bogs, and deal with bugs. You'll encounter ponds of all sizes during your hike, so follow your map. As you continue south, use Marks Pond campsite, Harding's Pond campsite, Green Island Pond campsite, and Ferry Gulch as waypoints. Watch for caribou herds, moose, and ptarmigan and a diversity of flora, from bogs to barrens.

Eventually you'll see the rounded shape of Gros Morne Mountain, 806 metres high, as you pass Baker's Brook Gulch, and traverse the edge of Ten Mile Gulch. An array of great views of Bonne Bay, Rocky Harbour, the Tablelands, Ten Mile Pond, and many other communities reward you. Head down Ferry Gulch to the Gros Morne backcountry campsite—this section is very steep!

From the campsite, you'll be on a marked trail. Either hike to the summit of Gros Morne Mountain or walk out Ferry Gulch toward the parking area. Take your transceiver back to the visitor centre.

Distance: 35-kilometre linear route.

Note: Long Range Traverse can be combined with North Rim Traverse (hike #44).

Trailhead access: Two trailheads, both on Route 430.

■ Northern trailhead: parking lot for Western Brook Pond, approximately 28 kilometres past the visitor centre: 49.78916, -57.87238.

■ Southern trailhead: Gros Morne Mountain trailhead: 49.5653697, -57.8325148.

Amenities: Outhouses and picnic tables at the parking area; washrooms and concessions at the Western Brook Pond dock. Some backcountry campsites have wooden platforms, pit toilets, and food lockers or bear poles.

Keep in mind:

■ This is not a marked trail. Do not rely solely on GPS. You must have map and compass skills and a topographic map.

■ Visibility may be greatly reduced when the fog rolls in, forcing you to stop hiking to wait it out.

■ You'll receive a transceiver from the park, which must be returned at the end of your hike. Bring an emergency communication device: a marine radio, satellite phone, or SPOT. Cell phones do not work.

■ Cook and store food away from camp to discourage black bears.

■ Campfires are not permitted.

■ Don't be fooled: Herds of caribou and moose make paths all over the mountains. Stick to your map route.

■ Hiking dates must be booked in advance. This is a popular route, and only nine people per campsite per night are allowed.

■ Arrive at least one day before your departure to attend a mandatory pre-trip planning session, which includes a map and compass skills assessment.

■ Reservation and backcountry camping fees apply.

■ When booking your hiking dates, book boat tickets as well, www.bontours.ca.

Map #: 12H12.

Cow Head

Cow Head Lighthouse Trail leads to a small lighthouse that was built in 1909. In 1960, it became automated; it is no longer in use. From the lighthouse, you may continue along the trail onto the coast at Sandy Point. Walk among the 500-million-year-old breccias that make up the beach.

The next trail leads out to Cow Head. You can access the beach from the head when the tide is right. All trails are well-marked and -maintained. The trails wind through tuckamore, meadows, and coastline. There is no major elevation gain, only one small 60-metre hill.

The tip of the trail offers incredible views of the coastline and ocean, along with interesting rock formations. Look for whales and berries.

★ The coastline, formed of 500-million-year-old rocks, is a geologist's paradise.

You may notice archaeological dig sites along the trails. These 4,000-year-old sites are from three different groups: Maritime Archaic, Dorset Eskimo, and Groswater Paleoeskimo.

Distance: 4-kilometre loop.

Trailhead access: Exit Route 430 into Cow Head. From Main Street turn onto Pond Road, which takes you onto the peninsula (the head). Stay left and park by the community outdoor theatre near the communication tower: 49.9196649, -57.8141024.

Amenities: Outhouses in parking area; viewing platforms along the trails.

Keep in mind: Watch the tide if exploring the beaches or rocky outcrops—don't get stranded! The coastline's exposure to wind and waves can create a dangerous environment.

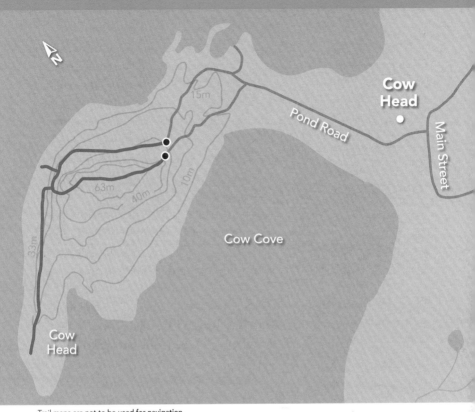

Cow
Head

Pond Road

Main Street

Cow Cove

Cow
Head

15m

63m

40m

10m

33m

Trail maps are **not to be used for navigation.**

NORTHERN PENINSULA

Commonly referred to as "The Great Northern Peninsula," this region boasts some of the most rugged and dramatic landscapes on the island. The coastline is home to many of Newfoundland's wonders: towering cliffs, Viking ruins, and whale and iceberg sightings. In fact, where the tip

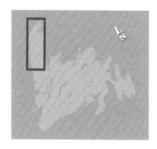

of the Northern Peninsula reaches out into the Labrador Current is known worldwide as Iceberg Alley, spectacular for its annual parade of glassy blue ice giants. Hiking along the shore in late spring and even throughout the summer will bring you to small coves and bays where icebergs may be grounded or bergy bits scattered on the beaches.

This region is also steeped in history. Visit L'Anse aux Meadows National Historic Site to see where the Vikings landed, Conche to admire the French Shore Tapestry, and St. Anthony to explore the Grenfell Historic Properties.

The Northern Peninsula is rugged and remote, with many unique features. Enjoy the beauty of the small communities, the landscape, the marine environment, and the warmth of the people you meet while you explore this region by foot.

Community trails to check out (shown on the map in red):

A. Underground Salmon Pool Trail System / Main Brook / 2.5-kilometre trail
B. Fishing Point Park Trails / St. Anthony / 3.7-kilometre loop
C. St. Anthony Area Community Short Trails / trail network, most <2 kilometres

Trails of the Northern Peninsula

47. Devil's Bite Trail / Parson's Pond
48. Indian Lookout Trail / Portland Creek
49. Point Riche Lighthouse Trail / Port au Choix

50. Englee Trail Network / Englee
51. French Shore Trail / Conche
52. Conche Trail Network / Conche
53. Treena's Trail / Ship Cove
54. Whale Point Trail / Wild Bight

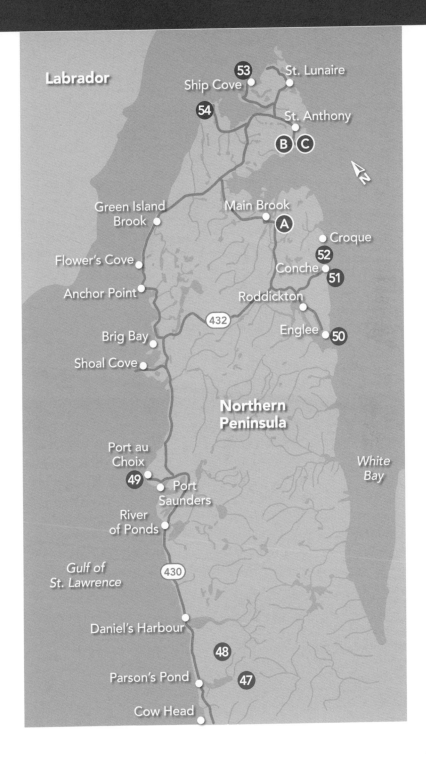

Labrador

St. Lunaire

53 Ship Cove

54

St. Anthony

Ⓑ Ⓒ

Green Island Brook

Main Brook

Ⓐ

Croque

52

Flower's Cove

Conche

51

Anchor Point

Roddickton

432

Englee

Brig Bay

50

Shoal Cove

Northern Peninsula

White Bay

Port au Choix

49

Port Saunders

River of Ponds

Gulf of St. Lawrence

430

Daniel's Harbour

48

Parson's Pond

47

Cow Head

Parson's Pond

*This is a backcountry route, **not** a maintained trail; most hikers take three to four days (two or three nights in a tent) to complete it. This description is based on hiking the loop counter-clockwise.*

Devil's Bite Trail brings adventurous hikers to the remote landlocked fjord of Inner Parson's Pond and passes some of the area's largest waterfalls. You must be shuttled by fishing boat to the trailhead—sit back and absorb the view during the ride.

From the trailhead, hike up and into Western Brook Gulch. As you ascend, you'll pass the 300-metre waterfall of Western Brook (of Parson's Pond) Gulch. When crossing from Western Brook Gulch to Parson's Pond Inner Pond Gulch, take an 8-kilometre round-trip side trek

> ★ Local residents refer to the jagged ridge visible throughout most of the hike as Devil's Bite, said to be created when the devil bit into the mountain precipice.

to the Devil's Bite landmark and lookout. Head next into Parson's Pond Inner Pond Valley and to beautiful Freake's Falls. Cross the stream above the falls, then hike to the top of Parson's Pinnacle to view the surrounding mountains and valleys.

After Parson's Pinnacle, descend into and cross Corner Pond Valley. The trail then rises along the eastern rim of Parson's Pond Inner Pond Gulch, affording unsurpassed views from the sheer 600-metre cliffs of Inner and Outer Parson's Ponds, the Devil's Bite, and the distant Gulf of St. Lawrence. The trail then encircles Main Gulch and Little Gulch before winding around and down the northern corner of East Brook Gulch and back toward Parson's Pond and the north Middle Brook trailhead.

The Arches Provincial Park

430

Parson's
Pond

*Outer
Parson's Pond*

*Inner
Parson's Pond*

640m

480m

280m

600m

640m

120m

640m

120m

560m

560m

Trail maps are **not** to be used for navigation.

Distance: 45-kilometre loop.

Trailhead access: From the community of Parson's Pond, take a 14-kilometre boat shuttle to the trailhead. The trailheads are both at Middle Brook (one to the south, one to the north). Middle Brook connects Parson's Pond Inner and Outer Ponds (labelled Parson's Pond River on some maps). You'll need to arrange a return shuttle. Contact IATNL for shuttle arrangements and GPS references and route track.

Amenities: Cabins for rent at the trailhead; no facilities on the trails.

Keep in mind: This trek involves many creek crossings; bring a second pair of footwear and unbuckle your pack when crossing. The trail traverses steep cliffs; stay back from the edges. The only access to this remote high country is this trail or by skidoo in winter.

Map #: 12H13 & 12H14.

Permits & fees: Donations toward trail upkeep, payable to IATNL, are encouraged.

Portland Creek

*This is a backcountry route, **not** a maintained trail; most hikers take three to four days (two or three nights in a tent) to complete it. This description is based on hiking the loop counter-clockwise.*

 The barren subarctic mountain plateau and surrounding area is home to Arctic hare, partridge, caribou, moose, rock ptarmigan, and, occasionally, black bear.

Distance: 40-kilometre loop.

Trailhead access: About 2.5 kilometres south of Arches Provincial Park on Route 430 (halfway between the communities of Parson's Pond and Portland Creek), turn onto Five Mile Road, a 9-kilometre gravel road. Only the first half of the road is passable by car; the rest is accessible only by SUV, pickup, ATV, or foot. Contact IATNL for GPS references and route track.

Amenities: None.

Keep in mind: For the many creek crossings, bring a second pair of footwear and unbuckle your pack when crossing. The trail traverses steep cliffs; stay back from the edges. Map and compass skills required.

Map #: 12I4 & 12I3.

Permits & fees: Donations toward trail upkeep, payable to IATNL, are encouraged.

Beginning at the trailhead sign off Five Mile Road, follow the trail to the fork and stay right. From the fork, the trail rises 640 metres to the summit of Flat Hills. This vantage point offers a sweeping view of the Gulf of St. Lawrence coastline from Bonne Bay to the Highlands of St. John, overlooking Port au Choix.

 Follow the eastern ridge above Southwest Feeder Gulch to Indian Lookout. Indian Lookout provides views of the inland fjord of Portland Creek Inner Pond as well as Portland Creek Outer Pond and the Gulf of St. Lawrence. From Southwest Feeder Gulch you'll see steep verdurous cliffs and towering waterfalls, including the 400-metre Partridge Pond Falls.

The return trek to Five Mile Road via the north side of Southwest Feeder Gulch provides more scenic views of lakes and waterfalls. Rejoin the trail back to Five Mile Road at the fork.

Trail maps are **not to be used for navigation.**

Port au Choix

The Point Riche Lighthouse Trail network is made up of several interconnecting trails. Leaving the lighthouse parking area, the Coastal Trail follows the limestone coast, where hikers can look for fossils of ancient sea life found nowhere else in Canada. This trail passes Philip's Garden, a Paleo-eskimo archaeological site. Along this section are statues depicting Aboriginal ways of life.

 Maritime Archaic Indians, the Groswater and Dorset Paleoeskimo, and the Recent Indians (ancestors of the Beothuks) once lived in this area. These archaeological sites are 5,000 years old.

From Philip's Garden, continue on the Coastal Trail toward Old Port au Choix and the Philip Drive trailhead or walk through the archaeological site and connect with the Dorset Trail, which will take you inland through stunted spruce forest and past small ponds and back to the visitor information centre.

The trails are well-maintained with gentle elevation changes. A few caribou live on this peninsula; if you are lucky enough to see these majestic animals, please keep a safe distance from them.

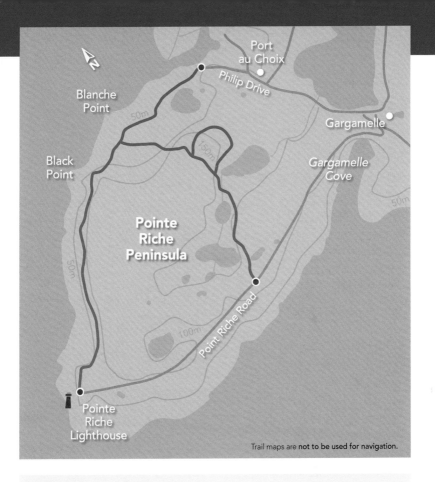

Trail maps are **not to be used for navigation.**

Distance:
10-kilometre trail network.

Terrain/elevation:
Gentle trails with some obstacles; <10-metre elevation change.

Trailhead access: Parking and trailheads are at the Parks Canada visitor information centre, the Point Riche Lighthouse (50.6989439, -57.40905), and in Old Port au Choix on Philip Drive (50.7168682, -57.369876).

Amenities: Visitor information centre, outhouses, picnic tables, and interpretation panels.

Keep in mind: This trail is along exposed coastline; winds and waves can be extreme. Fossils are not to be removed or collected from this or any site.

Permits & fees: Pay a day fee to enter this National Historic Site or purchase a Viking Trail pass, which provides entry to Gros Morne National Park, L'Anse aux Meadows, Red Bay, Port au Choix National Historic Site, and the Grenfell Historic Properties provincial site, valid for seven consecutive days.

Englee

The Englee Trail Network has four trails, totalling 4.7 kilometres, which can be hiked separately or, if you connect them by walking through the community, all together.

■ **White Point Trail** is a linear, 1.5-kilometre (3-kilometre return) trail with lookout points spanning the west side of Englee Island.

■ A 0.7-kilometre loop encircling Barr'd Island, **Barr'd Island Trail** has many stairs and views of Englee Harbour and Canada Bay. In season, you may even see icebergs or whales.

■ **Locker's Point Trail** is a 1.5-kilometre (3-kilometre return) linear traverse of the mountains behind the community. This trail has strenuous uphill sections. Three lookouts are on the trail, including the 120-metre George's Lookout, accessed by a side trail. At Locker's Point, check out the ridges and beds of sandstone, marble, schist, and limestone.

■ The 1-kilometre (2-kilometre return) linear **Shoe Pond Trail** starts as an easy walk but quickly rises before you reach the gazebo at the top of Eastern Hill and views of Englee, Canada Bay, and Bide Arm.

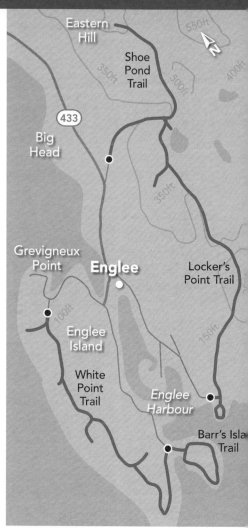

Trail maps are **not to be used for navigation.**

Distance:
See trail description above.

Trailhead access:

White Point Trail: This trail has two access points:

■ From Main Street, turn right and cross the bridge, then turn right onto Heights Cove Road and drive past the fish plant. Take the next left and park at the top of the road: 50.731190, -56.112956.

■ Barr'd Island Trail trailhead.

Barr'd Island Trail:

■ From Main Street, turn right, cross the bridge, then turn left onto Marine Side Drive and drive to the end. Park at the trail signs: 50.723323, -56.109747.

Locker's Point: This trail has two access points:

■ From Main Street turn left at the stop sign onto Dorset Drive. Follow to the end: 50.737560, -56.096992. Park at the trail sign, then walk along the gravel road past the last house and around the point. The trail heads into the forest and into the hills.

■ Shoe Pond trailhead.

Shoe Pond Trail:

■ Turn off Main Street onto Macdonald Drive. If you are driving a small car, park by the basketball court. Otherwise, drive straight but stay left at any intersections until you see the trailhead sign: 50.737789, -56.096321.

Amenities: Gazebos or platforms at lookouts.

Keep in mind: Be mindful of high winds, cliff edges, and tides.

Conche

*This is a backcountry route, **not** a maintained trail; most hikers take two days (one night in a tent) to complete it. This description is based on hiking in from Southwest Crouse.*

The French Shore Trail is a 13-kilometre linear trail along the eastern coastline of the Northern Peninsula between Conche and Croque, two communities on the historic French Shore. Watch for cairns, of unknown origin, which dot the trail.

The trail begins at the communication tower off Route 434 overlooking the communities of Conche and Southwest Crouse, follows the rolling seaside hills north, and takes hikers out onto the Cape Rouge Peninsula. Along the way are views of the surrounding headlands, coves, islands, and ocean, as well as the abandoned fishing communities which dot Crouse Harbour.

From a sheltered campsite on the northern shore of Crouse Harbour, the trail climbs about 170 metres to a scenic lookout at Pyramid Point on the northern end of Cape Rouge Peninsula. The trail then winds across barren hilltops north until it reaches a stream-fed cove halfway between Conche and Croque. Hikers can choose to return via the same route or arrange a boat shuttle to return to Southwest Crouse.

In the early 1500s French fishers crossed the Atlantic in pursuit of the large cod stocks around Newfoundland, particularly in the waters off its northern coast—thus the area became known as the French Shore.

Trail maps are not to be used for navigation.

Distance: 13-kilometre linear trail (26-kilometre return).

Trailhead access: Take Route 434 toward Conche. Before the main road descends into Southwest Crouse, turn onto a short gravel road leading to a communication tower at 50.92058, -55.893638. Boat transportation can be arranged through IATNL for drop-off or pickup at the northern end. Contact IATNL for GPS references and route tracks.

Amenities: None.

Keep in mind: This is a very remote area. The best communication option is marine radio, as local mariners or the coast guard would be the first on the scene in an emergency. Map and compass skills required.

Map #: 2L13.

Permits & fees: Donations toward trail upkeep, payable to IATNL, are encouraged.

Conche

The landscape around Conche and Crouse is criss-crossed with rough hiking trails and some boardwalks, which can be hiked together or in segments, depending on your available time and fitness level.

■ **Sleepy Cove Trail**, a 2.5-kilometre linear trail, traverses Martinique Bay and affords hikers picturesque views of the village of Conche and its harbour.

■ The fully boardwalked **Captain Coublongue Trail**, an easily accessed 3-kilometre linear trail, takes hikers to Point Dos de Cheval and a lookout offering panoramic views of Southwest Crouse Harbour and the Cape Rouge Peninsula.

■ **Fox Head Trail** offers spectacular views along high cliffs with broad views of neighbouring islands and landforms. Along the 7-kilometre trail, be sure to check out Glass Hole, Cape Fox Archaeology Site, Saunders Gulch Lookout, and Conche Lookout. To return, retrace your steps on Fox Head Trail or complete a loop, passing through a World War II plane-crash site. You may also continue all the way to the Captain Coublongue Trailhead.

Return via the main road through the community or pre-arrange a shuttle.

Distance:
12.5-kilometre trail network.

Terrain/elevation: Boardwalk, gravel path, single-track path; ~80 metres elevation change.

Trailhead access:

■ In Southwest Crouse, off Route 434, park by Captain Coublongue's gravesite: 50.9015988, -55.8906291.

■ Walk back along the road into Southwest Crouse until you see Sleepy Cove Trail: 50.9044603, -55.8924412.

■ In Conche, turn left before the town wharf and park at the end of the road to access Fox Head Trail. The other trailhead begins near the World War II plane-crash site: 50.8834253, -55.8965324.

Keep in mind: Trails along the eastern side of the peninsula are on steep cliffs; stay on marked trails. It may be very windy or rainy along this shore at any time of the year; dress accordingly.

Map #: 2L13.

Permits & fees: Donations to trail upkeep are payable to the French Shore Historical Society.

Crouse Harbour

Captain Coublongue Trail

Southwest Crouse

Sleepy Cove Trail

500ft

650ft

200ft

550m

400ft

400m

150m

434

Martinique Bay

Latin Point

Conche

Silver Point

350m

500m

Chest Head

250m

Conche Harbour

Fox Head Trail

Visit the French Shore Interpretation Centre and see the French Shore Tapestry. This 216-foot-long tapestry was sewn by local women and depicts a detailed history of the area. Tours and interpretation can be provided.

Trail maps are **not** to be used for navigation.

2

Ship Cove

From the parking area, cross Route 437 to the blue sign that says "Back of the Land Trail." Treena's Trail begins here. Follow the quad track to Savage Cove, then head right as the trail climbs the 80-metre-high hills. You will see orange wooden trail markers and blue signs indicating the lookouts.

The quad trail eventually veers, and hikers should stay on the footpath heading toward Cape Onion. At Cape Onion, the trail passes by two houses—stay left of them and head toward the cemetery. A short side trail leads to a lookout; the main trail continues through the cemetery parking area and follows the road down toward the water. Walk along the road, following the shoreline, until you see the "mini village"—replicas of the first church in Ship Cove, a general store, a lighthouse, and more.

An exhibit depicting Ship Cove's heritage, by photographer Paul-Émile Miot (1827–1900), is displayed in the community. Miot was an officer in the French Navy; his photographs were the earliest photographic records of Atlantic Canada.

Continue past an old house and up into a driveway. Walk out the driveway, turn left, and continue to a blue bus-shelter-type structure. Turn right on the quad trail and follow it along the shore until it turns right onto Route 437. The parking lot will be within view.

Distance: 7-kilometre loop.

Trailhead access: Take Route 437 toward Ship Cove. About 1 kilometre before Ship Cove, park in the designated area beside a blue trailhead sign: 51.6012365, -55.6514616. The trail may also be accessed from the end of the road in Cape Onion or from the Ship Cove Cemetery.

Amenities: Lookouts, mini village.

Keep in mind: Stay back from cliff edges. Moose and coyote live in the area; dogs should be leashed.

Trail maps are **not to be used for navigation.**

Wild Bight

Whale Point Trail leads along limestone barrens, past Soup Bay, and out to Whale Point. The trail has little elevation change and is easy to follow—no trees obstruct the view.

At Whale Point, take some time to watch the water and you might be graced with a visit by a whale. Take the stairs from the point and follow the trail through the gravel pit and over to Cape Norman to the lighthouse and viewing gazebo.

The Cape Norman area is designated a "critical habitat" because of the rare species barrens willow and Fernald's braya, which are only found in this region. As you walk along the trail, look for these plants. Return to the trailhead via the Whale Point trail or walk back on the lighthouse access road.

 Whale Point was so named for the many whale-watching opportunities it offers, particularly during summer migration, when whales frequently feed in the area.

Distance: 4-kilometre linear trail (8-kilometre return).

Trailhead access: Take Route 435 through Wild Bight; after the last house, park by the trailhead sign on the right: 51.6116357, -55.9025071.

Amenities: Benches, picnic tables, information signs, gazebos.

Keep in mind: Where this trail allows access to the water, consider changes in the tides. Remember: the limestone barrens of this area are protected by federal laws. Stay on designated trails.

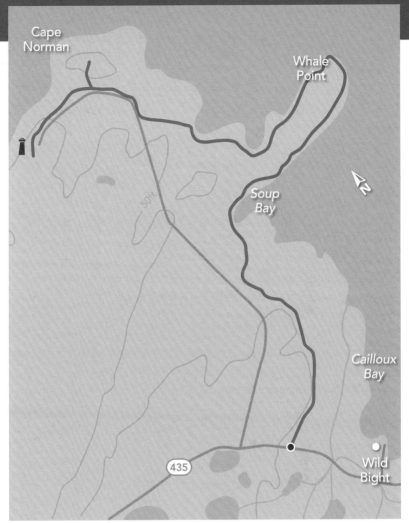

Cape
Norman

Whale
Point

Soup
Bay

Cailloux
Bay

435

Wild
Bight

Trail maps are **not to be used for navigation.**

CENTRAL NEWFOUNDLAND: BAIE VERTE & HARBOUR BRETON

This is your guide to those trails of central Newfoundland from Deer Lake eastward, including the Baie Verte Peninsula and the Connaigre Peninsula on the south coast.

Central Newfoundland boasts dozens of marked trails, 14 of which are listed below and described in this book, that take hikers along rocky coasts, into secluded beaches, and through communities where wharves, boats, and fishing gear testify to the centuries-old fishing industry and its continued importance in the 21st century. The region is visited annually by 26 species of whales and six types of icebergs.

The region has a rich Aboriginal history that dates to 5,000 years ago and includes the Dorset people and, later, the Beothuks. Most residents of the central north shore are descendants of West Country (England) fishers who worked along this coast, beginning in the 16th century. Botwood and Gander also played an important role during World War II as landing destinations for transatlantic flights.

Community trails to check out (shown on the map in red):

A. Limestone Park Trail / Smith's Harbour / <2-kilometre trail
B. Walking Trails of Botwood / Botwood / 4 short interconnected trails
C. Gorge Park Walking Trail / Grand Falls-Windsor / 1.4-kilometre trail
D. Corduroy Brook Nature Trail and Grand Falls-Windsor Hiking Trail / Grand Falls-Windsor / 16-kilometre trail network

Trails of Central Newfoundland: Baie Verte & Twillingate

55. Hummock Trail / Fleur de Lys
56. Ocean View Trail / Pacquet
57. Rattling Brook Falls Trails / Rattling Brook
58. Alexander Murray Hiking Trail / King's Point
59. Caribou Trail / Rattling Brook
60. Ocean View Trail / Jackson's Cove
61. Trail with a View / Harry's Harbour
62. Indian River Walking Trail / Springdale
63. Hazelnut Hiking & Adventure Trail / Robert's Arm
64. Beothuk Hiking Trail / Beaumont North (Long Island)
65. Maple Ridge Hiking Trail / Triton
66. Exploits Island Hiking Trail / Exploits Island
67. Oceanside Nature Trail / Leading Tickles
68. Harbour Breton Trail Network / Harbour Breton
    (on the Connaigre Peninsula, not shown)

Fleur de Lys

The Hummock Trail, well-marked by red arrows and signs, has an easy start, winding pleasantly through the forest. Some sections cross bogs, which are quite muddy and soft: stay on the boardwalks.

The next section is the toughest part of the trail. You'll gain elevation quickly—but it's worth the climb. At the top are two lookouts, each about 200 metres high, overlooking the community of Fleur de Lys and parts of White Bay. Icebergs are plentiful early in the summer. Enjoy the descent, made easier by stairs.

This trail exhibits rich boreal forest flora and fauna. The ground is covered with a variety of small boreal plants and pleasant-smelling flowers. Pitcher plants are also seen. Be wary of the high population of moose, especially on the trail's lower section; you are likely to encounter one or spot its tracks. The trail ends as it intersects with Route 410. Turn right and walk about 500 metres to the cemetery and parking area.

 Dorset Paleoeskimos lived in this area. Visit the Dorset Soapstone Quarry Interpretation Centre to find out more about their way of life.

Distance: 5-kilometre loop.

Trailhead access: On Route 410, before Fleur de Lys, watch for a large trail sign and parking area beside a cemetery on the left: 50.1183997, -56.1569853. The start of the trail is located at the end of the old baseball field on a quad trail.

Amenities: Picnic tables and lookout platforms along the trail; swimming area opposite the cemetery.

Keep in mind: Fallen trees on the trail may require short detours. The ascent has a steep section without stairs; this may be slippery and challenging in the spring and after heavy rain.

Permits & fees: Donations toward trail upkeep are payable to the Town of Fleur de Lys.

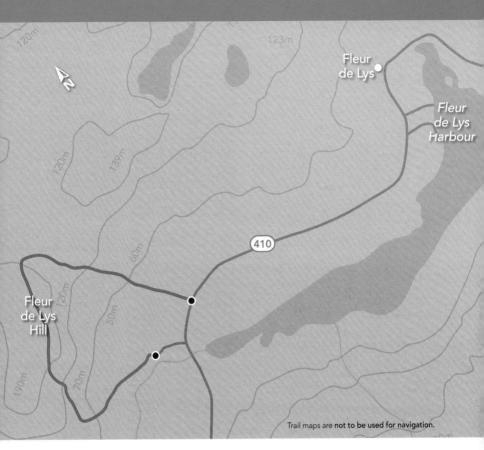

Fleur de Lys

Fleur de Lys Harbour

410

Fleur de Lys Hill

120m

123m

139m

60m

50m

120m

70m

190m

Trail maps are **not to be used for navigation.**

Pacquet

To complete a full loop of the Ocean View Trail network, start on the path without a sign (i.e., not Chelsey's Lookout). This trail starts in the forest with a gentle descent to a rocky beach before reaching the coast and views of Iceberg Alley.

Eventually the trail leads to Chelsey's Lookout, overlooking the surrounding cliffs and ocean. Continue up to Uncle Billy's Lookout, where a colony of gulls nest. You'll likely hear or smell the seabirds before you see them. With binoculars, you may glimpse the chicks, as they hang on to the cliff edges.

Most of the trail is fairly flat, except for a short climb to reach

> ★ These trails provide opportunities for viewing whales, icebergs, and a rich variety of seabirds. Some rocks in the area portray the wavy sedimentary layers formed by tectonic activity.

Uncle Billy's Lookout. Multiple trails make it easy to tailor a hike to the hiker's strength and available time. Use the interpretation panel of the trails, located at the intersection of the dirt road, to plan a route.

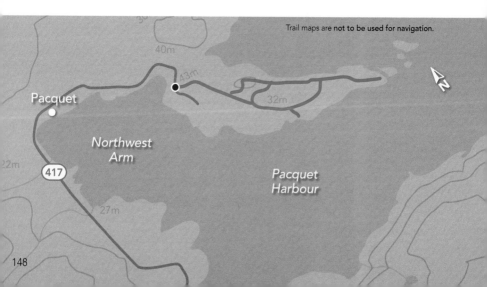

Trail maps are **not to be used for navigation.**

Pacquet

Northwest Arm

417

Pacquet Harbour

32m

40m

43m

27m

22m

Distance:
8-kilometre trail network.

Trailhead access: Take Route 417 through Pacquet until you see a wooden sign with a fleur de lys on it. Turn left and follow the signs on the dirt road to a parking area: 49.9886775, -55.8660799.

Amenities: Outhouses, picnic tables, lookout platforms, and a gazebo.

Keep in mind: Most of the coast is exposed to White Bay and the area can be windy. During storms or when the surf is high, stay away from the cliffs; waves are unpredictable and can be dangerous.

Rattling Brook

You have a choice of two trails to enjoy the majestic 800-foot Rattling Brook Falls:

Rattling Brook Falls Trail:
This path is on the west side of the road; on the east side is a small park with additional parking. From the start you will climb sets of stairs connected by well maintained trails and boardwalks. Along the way are lookouts providing great views of the face of the mountain, the falls, and Green Bay on Notre Dame Bay. The water flow over the falls depends in part on the weather. The views on the way up and from the top are worth the climb.

Top of Rattling Brook Falls:
Starting behind Windemere Cottages, take the trail as it climbs through boreal forest. Follow the signs up to the top, where you'll have views of a series of small waterfalls and of Green Bay. Return the way you came.

Rattling Brook Falls Trail

Distance: 0.5 kilometres.

Terrain/elevation: Level paths and boardwalk.

Trailhead access: Park just off Route 391 at the trailhead sign at 49.621, -56.176.

Top of Rattling Brook Falls

Distance: 1.5-kilometre (3.0-kilometre return) linear trail.

Terrain/elevation: Natural surface; steep incline, ~250-metre elevation change.

Trailhead access: Park at Windemere Cottages (49.622, -56.173) and walk behind the cottages.

Amenities: Opposite the trails is a little day-use park with picnic tables.

Keep in mind: Trails on the tundra plateaus are not always well-marked, so ensure you stay aware of your location and consider using a GPS.

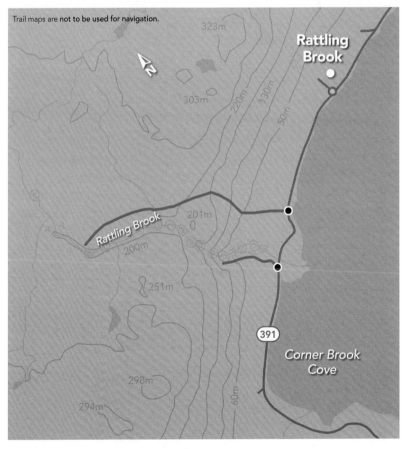

Trail maps are not to be used for navigation.

323m

Rattling Brook

303m

220m
130m
50m

201m

Rattling Brook

200m

251m

391

Corner Brook Cove

298m

294m

60m

King's Point

The first 2 kilometres of the Alexander Murray Trail meander through the forest with short stairs and boardwalks. The trail then opens up into barrens with short, stunted trees and a view of the lookout and stairs ahead. Watch for moose in the barrens on this first section of the trail.

When the trail splits, go left or right (this part of the trail is a loop) to reach the Hay Pook Lookout, the summit of the trail, at 335 metres. This challenging section climbs steeply, but a total of 2,200 stairs will help you get to the top. If you go left at the fork, the first stairs are located under the forest canopy, which offers some shade.

Take the short side trail to the bottom of the 182-metre Corner Brook Falls and gorge, particularly spectacular after a spring snow melt or heavy rains. The waterfall and pool are perfect for a swim in the heat of summer. This is a linear trail offshoot and you'll need to hike back up the stairs to continue the loop.

From the top, enjoy the landscapes of Green Bay, Gaff Topsails, and Mount Sykes. The summit also overlooks barrens and perhaps a caribou herd. Early in the summer season (May–June), icebergs float down into the bay. Return through the forest, where another waterfall awaits you. Finish the loop and return to the parking area via the linear section.

Trail maps are not to be used for navigation.

King's Point

391

302m

These trails provide opportunities for viewing whales, icebergs, and a rich variety of seabirds. Some rocks in the area portray the wavy sedimentary layers formed by tectonic activity.

Distance: 8-kilometre loop.

Trailhead access: Take Route 391 toward King's Point. Just before the community, turn left at the sign, near several red buildings: 49.5847, -56.1805.

Amenities: Washrooms and maps at the interpretation centre; viewing platforms and picnic tables along the trail.

Keep in mind: Some stairs and boardwalks need maintenance and are unstable; the stairs are slippery when wet.

Permits & fees: Donations accepted toward trail upkeep via a donation box at the trail entrance.

Rattling Brook

Starting on the ATV trail, head slightly uphill. At the fork, take the downhill (right) trail.

The Caribou Trail runs along Southwest Arm, and the views are spectacular. There are a few somewhat rough patches of terrain, and one long/steep flight of stairs, but overall most hikers should find this a lovely walk. The trail hugs the shore and you can choose to walk the shoreline or stick to the trail. It winds a bit and there are a few slopes.

Distance: 2.5-kilometre linear trail (5-kilometre return).

Trailhead access: Take Route 391 through King's Point. Drive to the end of Rattling Brook and park your vehicle at the turn-around at 49.631, -56.133. You'll see the entrance to the trail as an obvious ATV trail.

Amenities: At the end of the trail are picnic tables, fire pits, and a covered rest area.

Keep in mind: Please be sure not to block the road or the ATV trail when you park.

Rattling Brook

Trail maps are **not to be used for navigation.**

Jackson's Cove

Ocean View Trail takes hikers through a short section of forest before following the gentle coastline; it includes boardwalk sections and stairs. Three major lookout platforms along the trail provide views of Green Bay and the Baie Verte Peninsula across the bay. Whales, icebergs, and seabirds are frequently sighted.

Can you spot the sea arch? Wait until the end of the trail to look—you won't miss it, unless the day is foggy with poor visibility. From the last viewing platform, you can head down to the ocean, but be extremely wary in stormy weather and crashing waves.

Trail maps are **not to be used for navigation.**

On a bright, sunny, calm day, you may find the salt water refreshing.

Return to the parking area by the same route.

Distance: 2.5-kilometre linear trail (5-kilometre return).

Trailhead access: Follow Route 391 northward. Turn left toward Jackson's Cove and turn right at the next intersection. The trailhead and small parking area are on the left, just after the Jackson's Cove sign: 49.6913407, -55.9849749.

Amenities: Lookout platforms and picnic tables.

Keep in mind: This area, exposed to the ocean, may be very windy.

155

Harry's Harbour

Pack a picnic and spend an afternoon—even a full day—walking this trail network and swimming in the coves. The trails have little elevation gain but can become a moderate hike if you explore all 9 kilometres. The main trail is inland, with multiple shorter trails branching off toward the coast. Each short trail leads to a cove, beach, or lookout. The main trail is shared with quads, but some of the trails heading to coves are much narrower and only accessible to hikers.

From the lookout, whales are often spotted as well as an osprey pair that has a nest on top of a rock pillar. Unobstructed views of the shoreline and fascinating rock formations await at each cove. Parts of the trails are boardwalk; a few sections may be interrupted by fallen trees that you'll have to walk around.

Forest, valleys, and beach landscapes offer a diversity of scenery and make this trail a good option for hikers of all ages and interests.

 Seabirds and whales are spotted from this trail. Sea stars and sea urchins are also plentiful in many of the coves by the rocky shoreline.

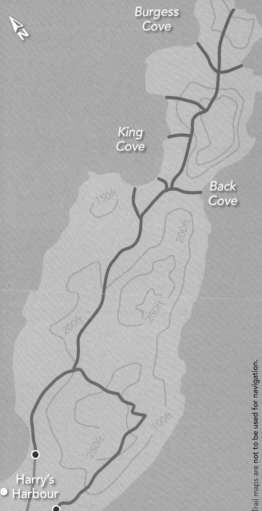

Burgess Cove

King Cove

Back Cove

150ft

200ft

200ft

250ft

250ft

100ft

250ft

Harry's Harbour

Trail maps are not to be used for navigation.

Distance:
9-kilometre trail network.

Trailhead access: Take Route 391 to Harry's Harbour. Drive to the end of the main road and turn left across from the church onto the street to Salmon Cove: 49.702841, -55.9228888.

Park by the trail sign; the trailhead is on the right.

Amenities: Outhouses, picnic tables, and lookout platforms along the trail; a shelter at the trailhead.

Keep in mind: The trail that heads to the lookout has many fallen trees. Faded or washed-out signs may be difficult to read.

2 Springdale

The wetlands and river along the Indian River Walking Trail are the natural habitat of many animals, including birds which come to nest and feed. Be sure to bring binoculars.

From the Main Street trailhead, the trail is fairly flat as it follows a marsh, then the Indian River, and meanders through the forest. The last section,

> The sand at the mouth of the Indian River and around Springdale was pushed and left there 18,000 years ago during the last ice age.
>
> The Indian River flows into Notre Dame Bay and salmon migrate upstream every year. Be sure to visit the salmon ladder by the park.

toward George Huxter Memorial Park, has more elevation change, made easy with a few short sets of stairs.

The trail, which traverses a landscape of waterfalls flowing over mafic volcanic rocks, was once farther inland; it has been remade, so stay on the new route, closest to the water. New housing and roads force the hiker onto the road at a few locations. When this happens, keep walking down the road in the direction you were heading and you'll find another entrance with garbage bins and/or signs.

Return the way you came, arrange a shuttle, or leave a vehicle at each end.

Trail maps are **not to be used for navigation.**

Distance: 6-kilometre linear trail (12-kilometre return).

Trailhead access: Take Route 390 to Springdale.

■ The first trailhead is located off Route 390 at George Huxter Memorial Park: 49.5113551, -56.1091237.

■ For the Main Street trailhead, drive through Springdale, turn right onto Main Street, drive almost to the end of the street, and park beside the trail sign: 49.4900631, -56.0744184.

Amenities: Washrooms and campsites at the park; benches, gazebos, lookouts, picnic tables, and storyboards and interpretation signs along the trail.

Keep in mind: Some sections of trail are not well-marked.

Permits & fees: Donations toward trail upkeep are payable to the Town of Springdale.

Robert's Arm

This trail has a feature unlike any other in this province: a chance to see Cressie, the monster of Crescent Lake, similar to the Loch Ness Monster. Aboriginal legends tell stories about a "pond devil" or "swimming monster." In 2008, the History Channel's "Monster Quest" aired an episode about Cressie; sightings have placed the eel-like creature between 2 and 5 metres long. Crescent Lake is 100 metres deep and connects to Robert's Arm Harbour on the southeast side, which would allow such a creature to enter the lake and offer it plenty of depth in which to hide.

Distance:
10-kilometre trail network.

Trailhead access: Take Route 380 toward Robert's Arm. The trailhead is on the right-hand side by Crescent Lake, just before the town: 49.4888783, -55.8312226.

Amenities: Gazebos, picnic tables, benches, outhouses, interpretation panels, and lookout platforms along the trail.

Keep in mind: Watch for Cressie the lake monster.

Permits & fees: Donations toward trail upkeep are payable to the Town of Robert's Arm.

Most of the Hazelnut Trail is flat and follows the shores of Crescent Lake. An optional climb of 130 metres to Hazelnut Hill offers a view of Robert's Arm, Crescent Lake, and Long Pond. Sections of the trail follow beaches, perfect for a summer swim (for those not afraid of Cressie); other sections lead through the forest. The trail is well-maintained, with boardwalks and bridges.

The trail circumnavigates the lake and ends at a dirt road. Stay left until you reach the main road (Route 380), and head left, toward the parking lot. Make this trail shorter by heading straight up Hazelnut Hill and returning to the parking lot, or longer by completing the entire trail and walking back along the road.

Sign the visitors' book on your way out and share your stories, sightings, or feedback.

Logging was the main industry in this area in the early 1930s. Pulp and paper mills were abundant and, until the 1980s, Newfoundland supplied Bowater-Lloyd (Europe's largest newsprint manufacturer) in London, England, with most of its raw material.

Robert's
Arm Pond

300ft

N

250ft

380

100ft

Robert's Arm

350ft

250ft

150ft

350ft

250ft

150ft

250ft

150ft

Crescent
Lake

200ft

150ft

Long
Lake

Trail maps are **not to be used for navigation.**

1 Beaumont North (Long Island)

A stroll along a boardwalk through forests and bogs brings you to a set of stairs, and then up and out to Western Head. These bogs are home to the carnivorous pitcher plant, which turns bright red by the end of summer. Look for the beaver dam along the trail.

From the gazebo at Western Head, take in the panoramic view of Beaumont North and surrounding islands. In season, this is an ideal location for whale and iceberg sightings.

Follow the shoreline toward Caplin Cove Head. The stairs up to Caplin Cove Head are the last of the hike, and the 360-degree view of Long Island is worth the climb. The vast horizon gives opportunities for photographs, particularly at sunrise and sunset. From Caplin Cove Head you can see China Head, where hundreds of Beothuk Indian artifacts were found.

Return to the parking lot along the same trail.

> ★ This coastal area was an ideal summer destination for Beothuks to fish and hunt—until the Europeans arrived and eventually pushed the Beothuks inland, contributing to their eventual extinction. Read the interpretation panels along the trail to learn more about the Beothuks and the artifacts that were found here.

Trail maps are **not to be used for navigation.**

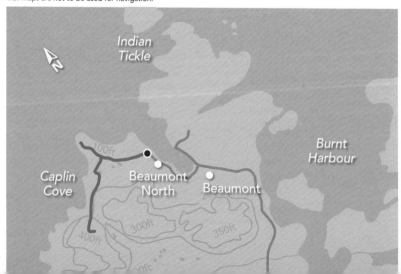

Distance: 2.5-kilometre linear trail (5-kilometre return).

Trailhead access: Follow Route 380 toward the Long Island ferry (turn left in the community of Pilley's Island). After a five-minute ferry crossing, drive to the end of the road at Beaumont North Harbour, and turn left along the bay, following the trail signs. Park at the end of the road: 49.6230138, -55.6895646.

Amenities: Gazebos and picnic tables along the trail.

Keep in mind: This trail is exposed to the ocean—beware of high winds and cliff edges.

Triton

Get ready for stairs! Most of this trail is stairs—all the way up and all the way back down. But first, the trail passes a rocky beach where summer heat may tempt hikers for a swim.

 Coloured barrels in the bay belong to a mussel farm, a form of aquaculture that uses barrels from which ropes or "socks" of mussels are suspended vertically.

After the beach comes a quick elevation gain through a forest of deciduous trees, with many maple trees, which are scarce on the island. At the lookout, a panoramic view of islands, mountains, Triton Harbour, and Notre Dame Bay awaits. Icebergs coming from Greenland and the Arctic may be seen from this vantage point during the spring and early summer. The 130-metre summit is perfect for a picnic and a well-deserved rest.

Walk back to the parking lot via the same trail. Most of the trail has either boardwalk or stairs; only a few sections are gravel-filled.

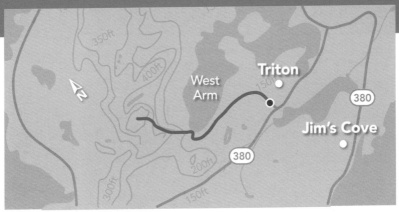

Trail maps are **not to be used for navigation.**

Distance: 2.5-kilometre linear trail (5-kilometre return).

Trailhead access: Follow Route 380 past Triton and turn left at the sign for Brighton. Shortly after the turn is a large trail sign on the right, beside a swimming pool. The trail starts by the gazebo: 49.5207422, -55.6268156.

Amenities: Gazebo, benches, and picnic tables along the trail.

Keep in mind: Stay hydrated and make several stops along the stairs.

Permits & fees: Donations toward trail upkeep are payable to the Town of Triton.

Exploits Island

Departing from Burnt Cove, the trail will lead you through fields where houses stood, decades ago. You will then pass through a boreal forest and out to the rugged coastal area where the light station is located.

Boreal forest plants flourish along the trail and many hikers spend hours photographing them. The trail is a little challenging as a result of the topography but well worth the effort if you are in reasonable shape.

Distance: 4.2-kilometre (8.4-kilometre return) linear trail.

Terrain/elevation: Rugged single track trail; 120-metre elevation change.

Trailhead access: Take a boat shuttle to Exploits harbour. Walk south to hit the trail.

Amenities: At the end of the trail are picnic tables, fire pits, and a covered rest area.

Map #: 002E11.

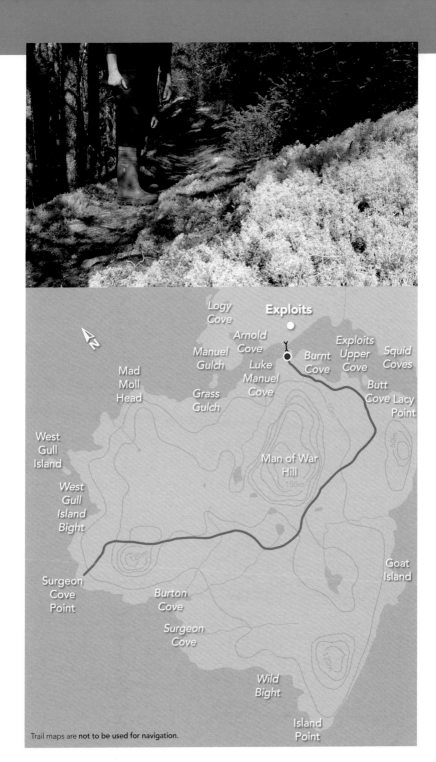

Logy Cove

Exploits

Arnold Cove

Manuel Gulch

Luke Manuel Cove

Mad Moll Head

Grass Gulch

Burnt Cove

Exploits Upper Cove

Squid Coves

Butt Cove Lacy Point

West Gull Island

Man of War Hill

150m

50m

60m

West Gull Island Bight

120m

Surgeon Cove Point

Burton Cove

Surgeon Cove

Goat Island

120m

Wild Bight

Island Point

Trail maps are **not to be used for navigation.**

1 Leading Tickles

Oceanside Nature Trail is well-marked with flagging tape. Starting from the main trailhead, the first section of the trail has boardwalks and stairs. This trail only has slight elevation changes as it wanders through the forest. Two lookouts, located close to the tip of the peninsula, offer views of Burnt Island, Thomas Rowsell Island, Seal Bay, and Notre Dame Bay.

As the trail approaches the Park Road trailhead, it veers inland, offering fewer viewpoints. Two beautiful rocky beaches, named Sprune Beach and Hannam's Cove Beach, are perfect for hikers looking to take a summertime swim.

 This small town is still quite active in the fishing industry. In season, it is also an excellent place to watch for whales and icebergs.

Distance:
3-kilometre trail network.

Trailhead access: Follow Route 350 through Leading Tickles South and over the bridge into Leading Tickles. The main trailhead is at the end of Route 350, where there is a parking area and a trail map: 49.501303, -55.4697246.

Amenities: Two lookouts and a few picnic tables along the trail.

Permits & fees: Donations toward trail upkeep are payable to the Town of Leading Tickles.

Several species of seabirds, seals, and whales can be seen from the trail. Walk back the same way you came, or veer off from the trail and follow the road back to the parking area.

Trail maps are **not to be used for navigation**.

Butler
Cove

Burnt
Island

**Leading
Tickles**

Leading
Tickles
South

150ft

100ft

50ft

150ft

50ft

50ft

150ft

Cull
Island

350

Harbour Breton

Gun Hill is a must-visit for the best view of Harbour Breton and the Harbour Breton Bay fjords. Don't forget your camera! Gun Hill is a 1.5-kilometre trail with stairs to a summit lookout at 159 metres elevation. The climb will reward you with a 360-degree view of Harbour Breton, Fortune Bay, and in the distance, the Burin Peninsula and many islands such as Brunette and the French island of Miquelon. "Coast of Bays" is a literal description of the area: huge fjords jut inland for miles while massive granite cliffs drop into the sea. Hiking up to lookouts where you can appreciate the enormity of these fjords is worth every step.

Combining Mile Pond Boardwalk and Deadman's Cove Beach Trails results in a 7.7-kilometre walk along the coastline, where you can enjoy the bog and fen around Mile Pond, as well as the shoreline and islands of Deadman's Cove. Watch sandpipers scuttling along the shore with the backdrop of islands in the distance and large cliffs to the west. This trail is ideal for bird watching in the summer, when migratory birds flock to the coastline to nest.

Trail maps are **not to be used for navigation.**

Distance:
9.2-kilometre trail network.

Trailhead access:

■ Gun Hill Trail: Take Main Road, Harbour Breton, northward and cross the bridge to the north side. Turn left on Lydia's Lane. Park at the 90-degree turn where space allows. Walk to the end of the road and onto the four-wheeler trail heading toward the tower. You will pick up the trail at 47.484, -55.795.

■ Mile Pond Boardwalk and Deadman's Cove Beach Trail: Follow Route 360 leaving Harbour Breton. Look for the parking area on Route 360; it's on your left after passing the softball field, by the "Welcome to Harbour Breton" sign at 47.455, -55.759.

Amenities: Rest spots.

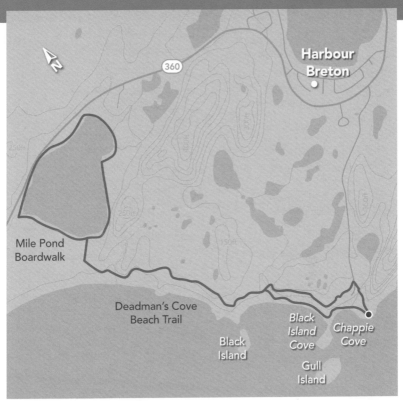

Trail maps are **not to be used for navigation.**

These hikes are located in the area referred to in the delightful Newfoundland folk song "All around the Circle" (also known as "I'se the B'y"). Tourism in this area has grown in recent years, and many accommodations and amenities are readily available for hikers. The rich local history, combined with the hospitality and services, breathtaking scenery, and hiking experiences, will make you want to return to this region again and again.

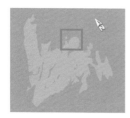

Twillingate's earliest European presence was French fishers who visited the area each summer between 1650 and 1690 and named the island Toulinquet for its likeness to a group of islands located off Brest, France. English settlers (also known as "livyers"), unfamiliar with the French language, changed the name of the island to Twillingate. Over the next centuries, Twillingate, with its rich fishing grounds and safe harbour, developed into one of Newfoundland's most prosperous ports. Merchants bought fish to sell in Spain and Portugal and provided fishers with salt and other supplies—money rarely changed hands. Today Twillingate prospers as a tourism destination.

Fogo Island sits at the extreme edge of Notre Dame Bay. It is separated from the Newfoundland mainland by Hamilton Sound and 16 kilometres of ocean. The name *Fogo* may have evolved from the Portuguese word for fire, *fuego*, perhaps referring to the forest fires that were seen regularly in the area. Portugal was one of the many European nations that fished these rich coastal waters. Fogo Island has a dramatic landscape: the northern part is an undulating plain of exposed bedrock, lichen, and treeless bogs; the southern shore is blanketed by tangled forest and boggy wetlands. Note of caution: Many of the traditional trails on the island continue beyond the descriptions we give here. Be prepared with a topographical map of the area if you wish to attempt longer hikes on unmarked trails.

Change Islands consists of three islands; the two larger islands are inhabited and connected by a causeway. Change Islands is located in Notre Dame Bay between Twillingate and Fogo. One story suggests that the name originated because ships "going down the Labrador" to fish or to hunt seals changed crews there. Another claims that the name was given because the inhabitants changed islands during the year, remaining on the north island for the summer fishing season and moving south to be closer to sources of wood for the winter months.

The Road to the Shore is a loop of highway beginning at Gambo, travelling along the northeast coast, and returning to the Trans-Canada Highway at the airport town of Gander. Gambo is famous as the birthplace of Joseph Smallwood, Newfoundland and Labrador's first premier. Farther along Route 320, near Hare Bay, is the Dover Fault, where continents collided and formed the island of Newfoundland 410 million years ago. The coastal towns of Greenspond, Badger's Quay, Wesleyville, Newtown, and Musgrave Harbour are picturesque and rich in history. The long sandy beaches of Cape Freels and Lumsden offer the opportunity to explore and wander freely along this strikingly beautiful coast.

A relatively gentle climate, sandy beaches, and scenic communities have been attracting people to the **Eastport Peninsula** for years. Now the Damnable Trail System (we'll explain that name in the pages to come!) is another reason to visit this area. Four trails ranging from easy to hard will appeal to hikers of all abilities.

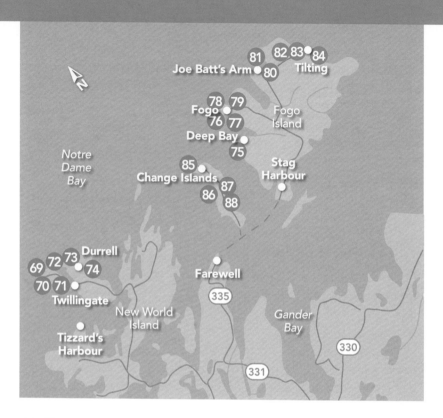

Twillingate

69. Long Point Lighthouse to Cuckhold Point Trail
70. Long Point Lighthouse to Lower Head Trail
71. Back Harbour Trails
72. French Beach to Spiller's Cove Trail
73. Spiller's Cove to Codjack's Cove Trail
74. Lower Little Harbour Trail

Fogo Island

75. Deep Bay
76. Waterman's Brook Trail
77. Brimstone Head Trail
78. Fogo Head Trail
79. Lion's Den Trail
80. Shoal Bay Trail
81. Great Auk Trail
82. Turpin's Trail West
83. Turpin's Trail East
84. Oliver's Cove Footpath

Change Islands

85. Squid Jigger Trail
86. Shoreline Path
87. Salt Water Pond Loop
88. Indian Lookout

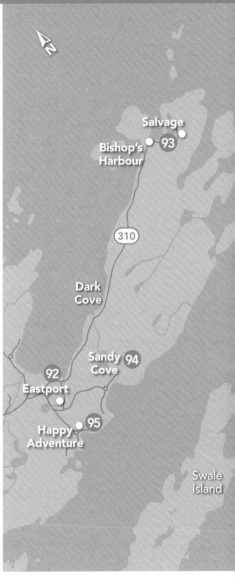

Road to the Shore

Eastport Peninsula

Crow Head (North Twillingate Island)

The Long Point Lighthouse Trail starts directly behind the light-house; a map marks the trailhead. It meanders along the rugged coastline and sharp 300-metre-high cliffs, losing and gaining elevation at various points and, if you're lucky, offering opportunities to see whales, seabirds, and bald eagles. Devils Cove provides hikers with panoramic views of nearby islands and Notre Dame Bay.

At Horney Head Cove, head down to the beach. On the right side is a sea cave to be explored. Keep hiking toward the lookout at Cuckhold Point for a view of Twillingate Harbour. The Long Point Lighthouse will be in view during most of the hike.

From Cuckhold Point, the trail leaves the shore and leads into the forest. Hikers may return the way they came, or head toward the Wild Cove / Drong Hill trailhead or the Crow Head trailhead. If you choose Crow Head, you'll reach a high point (elevation, 76 metres) with a view of the community. Stop at the Crow's Nest Café for a smoothie or coffee. The Wild Cove trail will lead you to Drong Road.

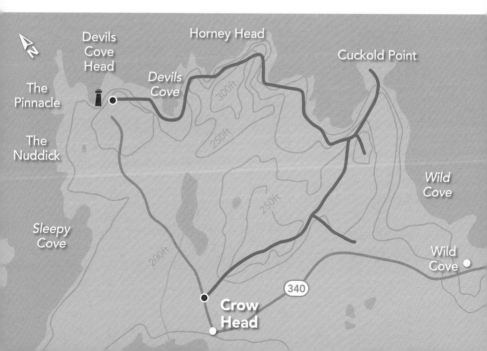

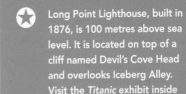

Long Point Lighthouse, built in 1876, is 100 metres above sea level. It is located on top of a cliff named Devil's Cove Head and overlooks Iceberg Alley. Visit the *Titanic* exhibit inside the lighthouse.

Distance: 5-kilometre linear trail (10-kilometre return).

Note: Combine this trail with the Long Point Lighthouse to Lower Head Trail (hike #70) to complete the loop.

Trailhead access: This trail has two trailheads:

■ Behind Long Point Lighthouse, follow Route 340 through Crow Head to Long Point Lighthouse and park: 49.6876189, -54.8009675.

■ On Main Street in Crow Head, pass Crow's Nest Café and take the first road on your right (not the one right across from the café). It is a dirt road. Park on the side of the road before you get to the first house: 49.6767782,

-54.8032394. Walk about 20 metres down a quad trail—there are no signs and the trail is a little overgrown—then turn left onto a smaller path.

Amenities: Washrooms and a gift shop which sells ice cream, drinks, and fudge at Long Point Lighthouse.

Keep in mind: If exploring the sea cave at Horney Head Cove, beware of changing tides. Stay away from cliffs, as they drop abruptly into the ocean, and gusts of wind are common. Steeper sections of the trail have loose rocks and should be hiked carefully.

Permits & fees: Donations toward trail upkeep are payable to the Town of Twillingate.

1 Crow Head (North Twillingate Island)

Long Point Lighthouse to Lower Head Trail is a coastal trail with short offshoot trails inland. Hikers may hike only the Lower Head loop, which offers views of Crow Head and Sleepy Cove and brings you back to your vehicle. This loop can be accessed from either Crow Head or Sleepy Cove.

Alternatively, hikers may walk all the way to the lighthouse. Sleepy Cove to Nanny's Hole has no elevation gain. Nanny's Hole lies directly underneath the impressive cliff on which Long Point Lighthouse is located, less than 1 kilometre away. The trail to Long Point Lighthouse is the only section requiring a short but steep climb. The trail is well-marked from Sleepy Cove to the lighthouse with maps and signs indicating distances.

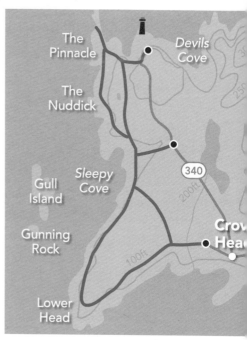

All these trails offer panoramic views of Twillingate and other islands. From the sheer cliffs along the coastline, take in the view of the ocean, and perhaps icebergs, whales, and seabirds.

Distance:
6.4-kilometre trail network.

Note: Combine this trail with the Long Point Lighthouse to Cuckhold Point Trail (hike #69) to complete the loop. This will prevent having to arrange a shuttle.

Trailhead access: Three trail access points:

■ Closest to Lower Head: In Crow Head, turn left on Broadview Street and follow it to the end (it eventually turns into a dirt road). Park by the map or cabins: 49.6767205, -54.8058554. The trail goes by cabins and then turns in to a quad trail.

■ Closest to Sleepy Cove: Before you reach Long Point Lighthouse, turn left at the hiking sign and park: 49.6831844, -54.8026623.

■ Take Route 340 to Long Point Lighthouse. Park at the lighthouse: 49.6876189, -54.8009675. The trailhead is just behind it.

Amenities: Picnic tables, and a shelter at Sleepy Cove; Long Point Lighthouse has washrooms and a gift shop.

Keep in mind: Watch out for stinging nettles—they burn the skin for a few minutes, but the sting usually diminishes quickly. Long pants are advised. Be careful when approaching cliffs, especially during high winds. If you go down to the beach at Nanny's Hole, watch for loose rocks.

Permits & fees: Donations toward trail upkeep are payable to the Town of Twillingate.

 At Sleepy Cove look for an old root cellar and remnants of the copper mine that closed in 1917. Thousands of birds such as seagulls, black guillemots, terns, and puffins live on Sleepy Cove Gull Island.

Back Harbour (North Twillingate Island)

Three relatively gentle trails start in Back Harbour. Pick one for a relaxing evening stroll, or follow all three and spend a few hours exploring North Twillingate Island.

> ★ Visit Twillingate Museum for more about the history and traditions of Twillingate Island. Just beside Twillingate museum is St. Peter's Anglican Church, one of Newfoundland's oldest wooden churches.

■ Spencer's Park Trails (3.4-kilometre trail network): From Dock Road, follow the left quad trail; it will open up onto a gravel road. The trail does not involve much elevation change. You'll reach a little cove with a rocky beach—stay and watch the sunset, if the timing is right! As you head toward Spencer's Park, you'll also have views of Batrix/Barrick's Island, Back Harbour, and Notre Dame Bay.

■ Batrix/Barrick's Island Trail (1.3-kilometre linear trail): From Back Harbour wharf, head straight toward the narrow sand beach connecting Batrix/Barrick's Island to the main island. After a short climb to the summit of Batrix/Barrick's Head, you'll have views of Back Harbour, Back Harbour Bay, Dumpling Cove, and Twillingate.

■ Back Harbour to Twillingate Museum Trail (1.3-kilometre linear trail): As you leave from Twillingate Museum, you'll see Twillingate, Back Harbour, and the shoreline. You'll also encounter St. Peter's Church cemetery along the way.

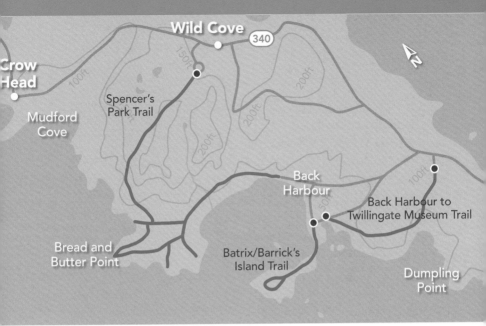

Wild Cove

340

Crow Head

Mudford Cove

Spencer's Park Trail

150ft

100ft

200ft

200ft

200ft

Back Harbour

Back Harbour to Twillingate Museum Trail

100ft

Bread and Butter Point

Batrix/Barrick's Island Trail

Dumpling Point

50ft

Trail maps are **not to be used for navigation.**

Distance:
See hike descriptions above.

Trailhead access:

■ Spencer's Park Trails: From Route 340 (Main Street) in Wild Cove turn onto Park Street and park by the "ATVs only" sign: 49.6696438, -54.7888492.

■ Batrix/Barrick's Island Trail: From Route 340 (Main Street) in Back Harbour, take Back Harbour Road, turn left on Dock Road, and drive to the wharf: 49.6576352, -54.7891308. Park out of the way of fishing operations.

■ Back Harbour to Twillingate Museum Trail: Park in the same place as you would for Batrix/ Barrick's Island Trail or park at the Twillingate Museum and St.

Peter's Church. Hike up the dirt road and turn right before the cemetery.

Amenities: None.

Keep in mind: None of these trails have signs; if you have trouble finding the trailheads, ask local residents for assistance.

Permits & fees: Donations toward trail upkeep are payable to the Town of Twillingate.

Durrell

The trailhead is located at the end of the road on the south side of Durrell's Arm near Blow Me Down Lane. The first view you'll catch along this trail is of French Beach, a stunning rocky beach of mostly pink granite pebbles. This trail has several loops to explore, depending on how much time you have to wander.

The terrain varies from sea level to 70 metres. Rugged coastal features include sea stacks, caves, and rock formations, some of which the local residents have named, including Cobra, Camel, and Indian. Vegetation varies from low shrubs on the north side of the trail to dense spruce woodland to beach and then bogland on the path from Spiller's Cove back to the start of the trail.

At Spiller's Cove, look for the enormous osprey nest, located safely on a sea stack or spiller—in early summer, you may even see chicks.

The wide beach is ideal for beachcombing or relaxing. From the beach the trail turns inland to the trailhead, or hikers may continue on to Codjack's Cove.

Offshore rocks at three different Spillars (Spillers) Coves around the province feature tall, thin, and tapered formations known as sea stacks. These place names may have derived from the term "spiller" or "spill," a small cylinder on which yarn was wound (according to the *Dictionary of Newfoundland English*), or a peg or pin for plugging a hole (*Merriam-Webster Dictionary*). Both items would have been familiar to early European sailors, who may have identified the similarities in the features and named the locations to reflect that.

Distance: 5–7-kilometre loop.

Trailhead: Blow Me Down Lane (49.400770, -54.433539).

Highlights: Rugged coastline, sea stacks.

Elev. range: 0–85 metres.

Spiller's Point

French
Head

Clam Rock
Head

0   0.5 km

N

French Beach to
Spiller's Cove Trail

French
Beach

Spiller's Cove to
Codjack's Cove Trail

Codjack's
Cove

Durrell

This trail starts in the community of Durrell near the head of the bay called Durrell's Arm. Head east at the end of Horwood Lane; trail signs in the community are clear.

This loop hike leads to Codjack's Cove and its coastal views. Sea stacks, caves, and rugged cliffs make it a photographer's paradise.

Look to the east to Main Tickle and watch for whales and grounded icebergs in the summer months. The trail continues north along the

Distance:
6.5-kilometre linear trail.

Trailhead: Horwood Lane
(49.392905, -54.435889).

Highlights: Rugged coastline, geology, beaches.

Elev. range: 0–60 metres.

coast. Hug the shoreline if the path is overgrown or unclear in places. At Spiller's Cove you can decide to take the trail leading back to Durrell or continue on to make a longer loop hike and include Spiller's Cove to French Beach.

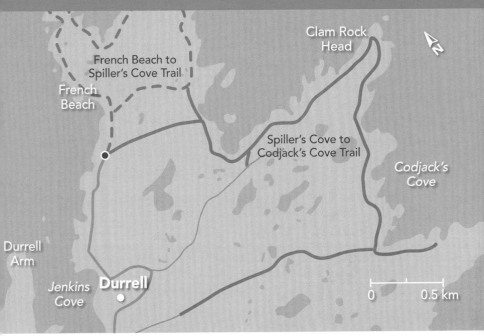

French Beach to Spiller's Cove Trail

French Beach

Clam Rock Head

Spiller's Cove to Codjack's Cove Trail

Codjack's Cove

Durrell Arm

Jenkins Cove

Durrell

0   0.5 km

Trail maps are **not to be used for navigation.**

 Codjack, according to local historians, is a codfish. The Spanish that fished off Newfoundland named it *bacalao*, after which Baccalieu Island was named. Many Newfoundlanders refer to cod as simply "fish" as it was the most common fish caught and eaten in the province.

Little Harbour

This delightful loop trail starts in Little Harbour on the east side of the island of Twillingate.

The community of Lower Cove was resettled when Newfoundland joined Canada in 1949. Part of the Confederation agreement was that all children in the new province must attend school, which forced whole families to move.

Lower Cove was also the winter residence of Thomas Sugg, who lived to be 110, one of the longest living Newfoundlanders.

The trail winds through various vegetation zones; the spongy peat-covered section of the trail is especially welcoming to weary feet. As with many headland trails in the area, there are several lookout points or smaller offshoot trails that all lead back to the main trail.

⭐ Magma dikes are formed from igneous rock. Igneous rock is formed after magma, a hot semi-liquid substance that exists below the earth's crust, cools and eventually becomes solid. Pressure and heat in the earth's core can force magmatic material through fractures in the earth's crust and make them visible in rock outcrops.

A large abandoned root cellar of the Keefe family from the 1930s is found along the way. This trail showcases fascinating geology and no examples are more prominent than the 30-metre-high sea arch and, close by it, the magma dike along the shoreline which reveals the volcanic activity that formed the region.

Distance: 5.5-kilometre loop.

Trailhead: Lower Little Harbour (49.373985, -54.423414).

Highlights: Resettled community, sea arch, magma dike.

Elev. range: 0–46 metres.

The trail winds along the coast until it reaches beautiful Jones Cove and then heads back overland to complete the loop.

Little
Harbour

Jones
Cove

**Little
Harbour**

0   0.5 km

340

Trail maps are **not to be used for navigation.**

Deep Bay

This gem of a trail is short and steep and an artist's haven. Situated within the town of Deep Bay, the trail traces a route almost due south of the starting point. In Deep Bay, park by the Shorefast House, an artist's residence on the south side of the road about halfway through town.

The hike begins with a steep climb up a wooden staircase just behind the Shorefast House. The subarctic vegetation changes noticeably as you near the top of the climb, becoming more stunted with elevation.

The trail levels out at the top, revealing a spectacular view of Brimstone Head to the north. Ground cover is sparse; harsh wind, salt spray, and thin soil deter the growth of vegetation.

The Bridge Studio is your reward for reaching the top. This is one of four artists' studios built by the Shorefast Foundation on Fogo Island. On closer inspection you will not question the positioning of the structure. One end of the building faces a small pond, providing

views of nature that would inspire anyone.

This is another one of those places where you can explore, berry pick, and relax for hours. Just remember to take a map and compass and perhaps a guide, if you want to ramble off-trail.

Distance: 0.6-kilometre linear trail (1.2-kilometre return).

Trailhead: Shorefast House (49.401786, -54.174097).

Highlights: View of Brimstone Head, orchids, berries, geology, Bridge Studio.

Elev. range: 10–250 metres.

Leveret
Islands

Hare Bay

Deep Bay

Bridge
Studio

0   0.5 km

Trail maps are **not to be used for navigation.**

Town of Fogo

This inland trail weaves through boreal forest, barrens, and pond-sides and features an abundance of wildflowers. Wild berries are plentiful in season.

The trailhead is located in a large firewood storage area on the west side of the road just before you enter the town of Fogo. The well-marked trail consists of a board-walk and steps which protect the natural vegetation.

The views of the ocean are spectacular. According to local history, men going to the lumber woods on the mainland or sealers heading to the icefields off Labrador

Distance: 4-kilometre linear trail (8-kilometre return).

Trailhead: Main road before entering the town of Fogo (49.424260, -54.162847).

Highlights: Views from Wood-peck Hill Lookout, vegetation.

Elev. range: 10–45 metres.

walked though this area to catch their ships. The trail ends at Waterman's Brook Bridge.

The view from the platform at Woodpeck Hill Lookout to the north to Brimstone Head in the town of Fogo demands a panorama lens.

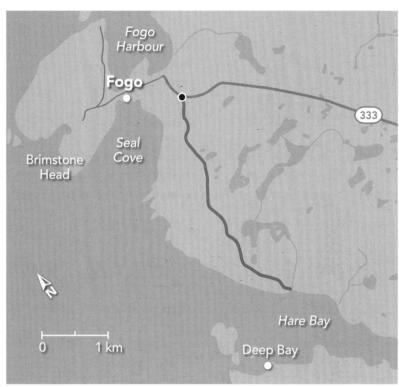

Trail maps are **not to be used for navigation.**

Town of Fogo

The town of Fogo has three trails listed which can be walked as one linear hike, but for the sake of clarity we refer to them as two trails (Brimstone Head Trail and Fogo Head Trail); the third (not described in this book) is the link between the two.

The hike to the top of Brimstone Head is not to be missed: If the steep climb on the wooden staircase doesn't take your breath away, the 360-degree view from the top certainly will. On a windy day fasten any headgear on tightly.

The geology of the area near the town of Fogo is known to be volcanic. The geologic process for the formation of Brimstone Head is more exactly described as *ignimbrite* (from the Latin *igni-* [fire] and *imbri-* [rain]).

Brimstone Head can also boast being one of the four corners of the earth, according to the Flat Earth Society.

 The Flat Earth model suggests that the earth's shape is a plane or disk. Many ancient cultures had conceptions of a flat earth, including Greece until the fifth century BC, India until 500 BC, and China until the 17th century. The Flat Earth Society has designated the four corners of the earth as Papua New Guinea, the Bermuda Triangle, Fogo, and Hydra (Greece).

Distance:
1.9-kilometre linear trail.

Trailhead: Near campground/ baseball diamond in the town of Fogo (49.425590, -54.173976).

Highlights: View from the top, one of four corners of the earth, ancient volcano.

Elev. range: 20–85 metres.

Western
Island
Middle
Rock
Garrison
Point

Fogo
Harbour

Little
Harbour

Fogo
Head
Trail

Fogo

333

Pound
Rocks

Banks
Cove

Seal
Cove

Brimstone
Head Trail

Brimstone
Head

0   0.5 km

Town of Fogo

This trail can be hiked as a stand-alone linear trail or connected to make a loop trail to include the hike to Brimstone Head and back to Garrison Point.

By the parking area at the beginning of the trail a large viewing platform displays interpretative panels explaining the history of Fogo. Six large cannons serve as reminders of military challenges in the past.

The spectacular hike includes glacial and volcanic features. Wooden staircases, built to withstand the harsh treatment by Mother Nature in this part of the globe, make it easy to walk over the rugged terrain. Several climbs along the trail are steep and seemingly endless, but viewing platforms along the way are well placed so you can catch your breath and relax. The top of Fogo Head is a magical place to take in a glorious sunset if conditions allow.

 At Garrison Point Battery, six cannons (9-pounders) were installed in 1771 as a defence against American and French privateers.

Distance:
5-kilometre linear trail.

Trailhead: The Battery above Garrison Point, town of Fogo (49.432962, -54.165431).

Highlights: View to Brimstone Head, large cannons at Garrison Point Battery, glacial features.

Elev. range: 25–103 metres.

Trail maps are **not to be used for navigation.**

Western Island

Middle Rock

Garrison Point

Fogo Harbour

Little Harbour

Fogo Head Trail

Fogo

333

Pound Rocks

Banks Cove

Seal Cove

Brimstone Head Trail

Brimstone Head

0   0.5 km

Town of Fogo

Lion's Den Trail is one of the flagship trails of Fogo Island. The trailhead is located beside the Marconi Wireless Relay Site and Interpretation Centre on the east side of the town of Fogo. This Marconi site was an important feature of this remote coast from 1912 until newer technology in 1933 made it obsolete. The building provides a view of Fogo Harbour.

The trail is well-marked. Begin by heading northeast from the parking lot. As you crest the first hill, you will catch a breathtaking view of the protected little inlet called the Lion's Den. Stories about how the inlet got its name vary, but you can imagine the name could have originated from the fiercely roaring seas as fishers and explorers navigated into what must have seemed like a lion's maw.

An interpretative panel near sea level in the Lion's Den indicates that the area was first settled in 1836 by fishers from Conception Bay looking for better fishing grounds. Wild daffodils and other once-cultivated flowers are the only reminders of the inhabitants that lived there until the late 1890s.

The hike is superb, offering views to the North Atlantic and, in season, opportunities for iceberg viewing and whale spotting.

 Seeds from cultivated plants, not native to the province, were brought over to the new world inadvertently in or stuck to packing material or ballast. Material such as sods and straw were common packing, and stone was used for ballast. Some of the plants, including daffodils along the Lion's Den Trail and mallow on parts of the East Coast Trail, flourished and adapted to their harsh new environment, and now grow wild.

Distance:
5.4-kilometre loop.

Trailhead: Marconi Site (49.431681, -54.154300).

Highlights: Resettled community, storyboards, Marconi Site.

Elev. range: 0–90 metres.

Trail maps are **not** to be used for navigation.

Lion's
Den Point

Lion's Den
Cove

Uncle
Andys
Island

Light
House
Island

Simms
Island

Barnes
Island

0   0.5 km

Fogo
Harbour

Freemans
Pond

Fogo
Head

Joe Batt's Arm

The trail to Shoal Bay begins at the side of the road about halfway between Joe Batt's Arm and the town of Fogo. It is essentially a long narrow boardwalk leading to Tower Studio, one of four architecturally designed artists' studios on Fogo Island.

Walking across a nearly treeless barren with Shoal Bay in the distance, it is impossible not to focus on the intriguingly shaped structure at the end of the boardwalk. As the name suggests, it is a tower—and yet its shape is constantly changing as your angle of view shifts. It is also important to glance down as you walk toward the studio to appreciate the variety of mosses, grasses, and bushes that cling to the rocks and peat bog.

Observe the studio from all angles: It looks solid as a rock from one side and then almost ready to topple over from another. It is a captivating design and, like all the studios, relies on solar panels and wood for electricity and heat.

Distance: 1-kilometre linear trail (2-kilometre return).

Trailhead: Between Fogo and Joe Batt's Arm (49.402936, -54.122445).

Highlights: Shoal Bay, Tower Studio.

Elev. range: Minimal.

 The artists' studios and Fogo Island Inn were designed by Todd Saunders, a Newfoundland-born architect now based in Norway. The studios and the inn, all set on sparse landscape far from any other man-made objects, appear as if they have been dropped from outer space. From a distance they look like pieces of sculpture rather than functional buildings. Closer inspection reveals, however, that they have been erected not only with an eye to aesthetics but also with concern for the environment: they have wood-burning stoves for heat, solar panels for electricity, and compost toilets. Natural materials, locally sourced where possible, have been used throughout.

Tower Studio

Shoal Bay

To Joe Batt's Arm

334

0   0.5 km

Trail maps are **not to be used for navigation.**

2 Joe Batt's Arm

This trail, which starts at Etheridges Point Community Park on the east side in the bay of the community of Joe Batt's Arm, runs almost directly true north along the coast.

Fogo Island Inn can be seen on the west side of the bay. This modern edifice has been designed to conjure the idea of a traditional fishing store perched on stilts extending toward the water.

Farther along the trail is Long Studio, another of the Shorefast Foundation's artists' studios. This geometric structure seems as if it was simply dropped into place without disturbing the surrounding natural backdrop. You can arrange ahead of time to visit the resident artist or simply walk around the building and admire its architecture on your way by.

Along this well-defined trail are terrific ocean views, community gardens, picnic spots, and rest places; wildflowers are abundant. Because of its location in the North Atlantic, this area is also a haven to migrating birds, including whimbrels.

At the end of this trail, the hiker is rewarded with the sight of a 2-metre-tall bronze sculpture of a great auk by Todd McGrain, perched upright and anchored in concrete on a massive sloping rock outcrop.

The great auk was found widely in northern habitats, including Newfoundland, Iceland, Greenland, the Faroe Islands, United Kingdom, and Norway. The species became extinct in the 1850s because of over-hunting by sailors and fishers; great auks, which did not fly, made easy prey. A great auk was approximately 70 centimetres in length and weighed 5 kilograms.

Distance: 2.7-kilometre linear trail (5.4-kilometre return).

Trailhead: Etheridges Point (49.435667, -54.092831).

Highlights: Long Studio, Great Auk sculpture, migratory bird sightings.

Elev. range: 0–10 metres.

Trail maps are **not to be used for navigation.**

Joe Batt's Point

Bronze Statue of Great Auk

Long Studio

0   0.5 km

334

Fogo Island Inn

Joe Batt's Arm

Joe Batt's Arm

Tilting

Turpin's Trail has been divided, in this book, into two experiences—Turpin's Trail West and Turpin's Trail East—as they are very different and each can be a day hike. Ample parking for Turpin's Trail West can be found on Farm Road. Unlike many of the other trails on Fogo Island, this one begins in a densely wooded area and transitions through several distinct vegetation zones. Informative storyboards along the trail present information about the vegetation and habitats you'll see along the route.

The boreal forest is the first zone encountered; this part of the island is in the North Shore Forest Ecoregion. Its climate has the warmest summers of any coastal region of the province, and the forest is dominated by black spruce and balsam fir. The trail progresses through a fen landscape, then opens into a coastal landscape.

Stones mark this low coastal part of the trail. An upturned dory and a few lobster pots have rotted and bleached in the salty spray and constant winds off the North Atlantic. At Seal Cove, an interpre-

> ★ **Fens versus Bogs**
> Because fens, wetlands that form in hollows in the landscape, are neutral in acidity, they provide an area of high productivity and greater variety of plants and animals. Bogs are dominated by sphagnum moss, which is acidic and not hospitable to a wide variety of vegetation.

tative panel describes the features of rocky shores. Explore the lovely little beach and then cool your feet in the crystal-clear water.

The trail continues in a loop back to the parking area and includes a stunning sandy beach at Sandy Cove. The history of the area is full of stories of confrontation between the local Aboriginal inhabitants, the Beothuks, and the early European settlers. The namesake of this trail, Michael Turpin, fought a battle in 1809 which cost him his head.

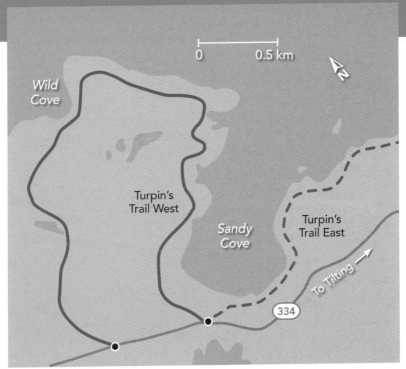

Wild Cove

Turpin's Trail West

Sandy Cove

Turpin's Trail East

To Tilting

334

0   0.5 km

Trail maps are not to be used for navigation.

SEAL COVE

Distance: 3.1-kilometre loop.

Trailhead: Farm Road parking area west of Sandy Cove Beach (49.423220, -54.032646).

Highlights: Transition of vegetation and landscapes.

Elev. range: 0–35 metres.

Tilting

The scenic town of Tilting is a photographer's paradise; be sure to allow time to stroll through the town. The homes, outbuildings, and fishing premises are generally well-preserved, teeming with history of a seafaring folk.

Turpin's Trail East starts at the award-winning Lane House Museum, the only house in Tilting with a spiral staircase. The original owner, Augie Mac, a barrel maker by trade, knew the space-saving function of a spiral design.

The trail heads in a northeast direction, over gently undulating terrain, and is clearly marked. Perched on the shoreline close to the start of the trail you will see Squish Studio, a white box-shaped structure hugging the rugged rocks. This is the fourth of the four artists' studios created by the Shorefast Foundation on the island (see hikes #46, 51, and 52 for the others).

The trail meanders past fenced vegetable gardens, sheep, abandoned lobster pots, and spectacular sea views. Seabirds are plentiful; yellowlegs are a common sight on the beach at Sandy Cove. Whales and icebergs are familiar sights from June to late August.

As you round the last headland, the view opens up to Sandy Cove Beach, a beautiful white sandy expanse that slopes gently into the ocean.

 Greater Yellowlegs, *Tringa melanoleuca*, is a medium-sized shorebird, approximately 35 centimetres in height, seen in Atlantic Canada. Its habitat includes bogs, alluvial wetlands, fens, and beaver ponds. The bird can be identified by its call, a quick whistled series of three times *tew-tew-tew.*

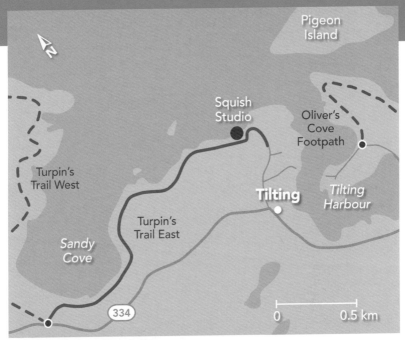

Trail maps are **not to be used for navigation.**

Distance:
4.6-kilometre linear trail.

Trailhead:
Lane House Museum
(49.422828, -54.035097).

Highlights: Historic town
of Tilting, coastal features,
seabirds, vegetable gardens,
Squish Studio, sandy beach.

Elev. range: 0–30 metres.

 Tilting

The painted fishing sheds perched on islands of granite slabs in the harbour of Tilting are memorable images. It is believed that the name of the community stems from the term "tilt," a flimsy cabin built by migratory fishers. The architecture of 21st-century Tilting no longer includes "tilts," but it has been studied and profiled in a book of the same name by the architect Robert Mellin.

This loop trail starts on the east side of Tilting Harbour. At the end of Harbour Road, head east and follow a path around to Oliver's Cove, which can include scrambling over and between huge beach rocks. The Devil's Chair is one such massive block of granite in which erosion has created a perfect perch to sit on. For gentler footing, remain on the trail in the grassy meadow.

Ocean views, and whale and iceberg viewing in season, are fabulous on this shore. Along the trail an array of wildflowers and plants, including oyster grass, add colour to your journey. At the south end of the trail, large community gardens slope to the sea. Root cellars, in particular cabbage cellars, are detailed on the storyboards.

 Root cellars were often built into the earth and covered with layers of sod. Cabbage cellars, however, were constructed a little differently, as cabbages need a drier storage. Cabbage cellars were often made from an overturned punt (a small open boat) buried in a well-drained area, with the entrance at the rear of the punt. Cabbages, with their roots still intact, were often hung from the roof (the floor of the punt) rather than on the ground, where wet rot could set in.

Distance:
4.5-kilometre loop.

Trailhead:
East side of the harbour in Tilting (49.422871, -50.033062).

Highlights: Geology, coastal features, wildflowers, gardens, root cellars.

Elev. range: 0–10 metres.

Pigeon
Island

Oliver's
Cove Footpath

Turpin's
Trail East

Tilting

Tilting
Harbour

334

Oliver's
Cove

0   0.5 km

Trail maps are **not to be used for navigation.**

1 Change Islands

This 3-kilometre linear trail takes you along the northernmost shoreline of Change Islands. Signs are plentiful along the length of the hike, which can easily be made into a loop by adding the delightful walk along the main road of this tiny community back to the beginning.

★ The waters near this trail are said to be the location that inspired the famous Newfoundland folk song "Squid Jiggin' Ground," written by native son A.R. Scammell at the age of 15. Released in 1943, this lively song with irreverent lyrics is still heard at folk-music events around the province.

The terrain varies from dry rocky lookouts to spongy bog to meadowscapes with an abundance of wildflowers in summer, including a sea of blue when blue flag irises are in bloom. Headstones in the graveyard beside the path reveal surnames common to the island.

The trail is gently undulating for the most part, with sections of boardwalk, but be careful on the stairs on steeper sections. The shoreline is pocked with small coves of crystal-clear shallow water ideal for wading or exploring by kayak.

Distance: 3-kilometre linear trail (6.5 kilometres if you make it a loop hike by walking back on the road).

Trailheads:
East side of the North Island (49.404588, -54.235691); west side of the North Island (49.404726, -54.252478).

Highlights:
Wildflowers, ocean views.

Elev. range: 0–21 metres.

The trail is perfect for iceberg viewing if you are there when these icy behemoths float by, usually between May and August. The other giants which can be viewed on this hike are whales. On a clear day you can also see one of the four corners of the earth, according to the Flat Earth Society, at Brimstone Head (see hike #77) on neighbouring Fogo Island.

Trail maps are **not to be used for navigation.**

Change Islands

This delightfully diverse path takes you through so many landscapes that it makes the name of the trail rather deceiving. The Shoreline Path is actually a series of traditional trails linked along the west side of the island approximately parallel to the main highway.

There are several entrances and exits to this 5-kilometre linear trail. Like all of the trails on the island, the joy of walking is not immediately obvious from the trailheads, but

the magic begins once you have left the view of the road behind.

At the Birch Cove entrance you will walk into thick birch woodland along a well-trodden path. You would never guess you are on a shoreline path. Signs of beaver activity are obvious: large logs strewn around bear the characteristic chatter marks from *Castor canadensis*'s long front teeth. About 10 minutes in, you'll see meadows through the trees, and then the beach at Birch Cove. You may see up to a dozen Newfoundland Ponies grazing in a large fenced paddock. Change Islands boasts a state-of-the-art pony refuge (www.nlponysanctuary.com), completed in 2015. After hiking the trails, drop in to see the animals in their new digs. Tell Netta we sent you!

Remarkable geological structures, like the almost vertical sedimentary

 The Newfoundland Pony is native to Newfoundland with ancestors, like many of the human inhabitants of Newfoundland, from the British Isles. These ponies traditionally ploughed gardens, carried kelp from the beaches, and hauled wood for the long Newfoundland winters. Their numbers in 2016 are not high. To protect against their extinction, the Newfoundland government has given them a designation of Heritage Animal; despite that effort, they are still considered an endangered species. Their average lifespan is 25 to 30 years.

South
Island

**Change
Islands**

Heritage Park
trailhead

Salt Water
Pond Loop

NL Pony
Sanctuary

Shoreline
Path

Indian
Lookout

14

Birch Cove
trailhead

0   1 km

Trail maps are **not to be used for navigation.**

layers which were initially deposited horizontally, can be seen along the trail. The beach, strewn with treasures the sea heaved upon it, is a beachcomber's paradise. Picnic spots abound.

The path weaves in and out along the shoreline, sometimes connecting with the road, and ends at Heritage Park. Climb the Bird Gaze Lookout for a full view of the coast.

Distance:
6.3-kilometre linear trail.

Trailheads:
Birch Cove (49.375603, -54.235550); Heritage Park (49.392432, -54.235313).

Highlights: Beaver, Newfoundland Ponies, geology, beachcombing, Bird Gaze Lookout.

Elev. range: 10–30 metres.

Change Islands

An easy walk around this little pond is a treat for any nature lover. The trail runs close to a main highway, which may cause some to avoid it—however, the highway or main road running north-south on Change Islands is not busy by any stretch of the imagination and will not cloud your enjoyment of the walk.

There is only one parking area, which is easy to find, by the only body of water on the east (right) side of the main road heading north from the ferry. It is about 2 kilometres south of the causeway-bridge that links the north and south islands.

This is an exceptional area for nature viewing, particularly birds, from one of the many natural "blinds" or shel-

 This salt water inlet is a birder's haven.

Distance:
1.5-kilometre loop.

Trailhead: Parking lot at Salt Water Pond (49.390269, -54.235321).

Highlights:
Birds, ducks, wildflowers.

Elev. range: Minimal change.

tered viewing spots along the trail. The boardwalk and gently undulating terrain are easy on the hiker's feet and legs.

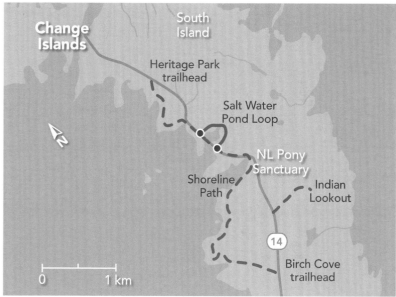

Change Islands

South Island

Heritage Park trailhead

Salt Water Pond Loop

NL Pony Sanctuary

Shoreline Path

Indian Lookout

14

Birch Cove trailhead

0   1 km

Trail maps are **not to be used for navigation.**

Change Islands

Along this coast, with its hundreds of small islands, lookout trails are common. But reaching the top of any one of them never fails to give the hiker a thrill of achievement. This trail starts at a most unlikely spot along the main road running north-south along the spine of Change Islands.

The sign is hidden slightly; it is located in a large parking lot for firewood storage. On the right side of the lot, a sign points to the Indian Lookout trail.

This is a linear trail with considerable elevation change; it is a lookout trail, after all! The trail is a pleasant hike through mixed woodland, with sets of stairs that take hikers to the highest point on the island.

The view of the coastline far below is breathtaking. Fogo Island is directly to the east.

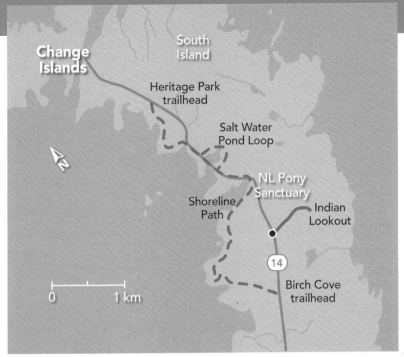

Trail maps are **not to be used for navigation.**

The origins of the trail's name are unclear. Was it named for Indians looking out for European settlers, or settlers looking out for Indians?

Distance: 1-kilometre linear trail (2-kilometre return).

Trailhead: Wood storage depot on east side of main highway (49.380618, -54.234335).

Highlights: Woodland, views from lookout, highest point of Change Islands.

Elev. range: 0–78 metres.

Gambo

The Middle Brook River Trail in the David Smallwood Park on the northern outskirts of Gambo at Middle Cove is a loop path and can be started on either side of the river.

This is a well-maintained path with many interesting storyboards about the natural history and early habitation of the area.

It is not unusual to encounter anglers along the banks of this beautiful salmon river with its many rattles and waterfalls. At the farthest point upstream, you'll find a side trail leading to a fish ladder which enables salmon to circumvent the falls. If you look down through the metal grate, it is sometimes possible to see salmon as they swim upstream—some seem to prefer to leap up the falls without the help of a ladder! Benches offer perfect viewing sites.

Another side trail, on the north side of the river, is called Madeline's Path. Madeline was a member of a Mik'maq band that lived in the area, and the path leads to a 200-year-old cemetery.

The entire trail offers a stroll more than a hike, but it is enjoyable and suitable for all ages. As the trail hugs the riverbanks, there is little elevation change but plenty of scenic picnic opportunities.

Distance: 3-kilometre loop trail.

Trailhead: David Smallwood Park (48.482118, -54.123148).

Highlights: River, waterfall, salmon ladder.

Elev. range: 1–6 metres.

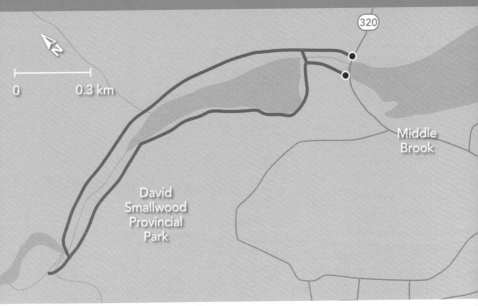

Trail maps are **not to be used for navigation.**

Greenspond

Settlers from England's West Country established a community on Greenspond Island in 1697, making it one of the oldest continuously inhabited settlements in Newfoundland. Over the centuries Greenspond has played a vital role in the cod fishery and the seal hunt. With the establishment of a customs house in 1838, it became known as the "capital of the north."

The construction of a causeway between Greenspond Island and the mainland in the 1980s has made this little gem of an island easily accessible to visitors. Signs on the main road through the community make it easy to find the trailhead for the Greenspond Island Trail, a path which hugs the coastline around most of the island.

This is an easy hike with low-lying coastal features and no steep sections. The undulating topography has been made even more pleasant to manoeuvre by long sections of substantial boardwalk and stairway. The community takes pride in the trail and a sign asks

hikers to report any areas in need of repairs.

Signs along the route identify points of interest. At Cannister Cove, hikers can turn inland to take a shortcut back to Main Road or continue along the shore to the end of the trail. The walk back through the community goes past the historic courthouse built in 1899, once the centre for justice for the entire northeast coast of Newfoundland.

Distance: 3.5-kilometre loop.

Trailhead: End of Main Road, Greenspond (49.041594, -53.335422).

Highlights: Stark, treeless topography; whale viewing; seabirds; berries in season.

Elev. range: 3–50 metres.

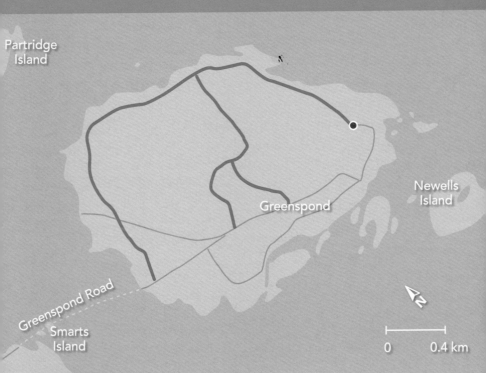

Partridge
Island

Greenspond

Newells
Island

Greenspond Road

Smarts
Island

0   0.4 km

Trail maps are **not to be used for navigation.**

Cape Freels

Anyone who has read the novel *Random Passage*, by Bernice Morgan, will know that Cape Island was the home of the Vincents and the Andrews, the principal families in the book. The Cape Island Walking Trail takes hikers out to the place where the novel is set and these families lived.

From Route 330, take the Cape Freels Road and look for the sign indicating the trailhead for the Cape Island Walking Trail. Take the

 Although the novel *Random Passage* was set on the shores of Cape Freels, the TV miniseries was filmed in New Bonaventure on the Bonavista Peninsula (see British Harbour Trail, hike #51).

Distance: 6-kilometre return.

Trailhead: Cape Freels Road (49.150748, -53.291242).

Highlights: Beach, cemetery, site of old settlement.

Elev. range: 0–5 metres.

ATV track over a small footbridge and then turn left. A path will bring you to the shoreline, where a beautiful broad sandy beach seems to stretch on forever. Turn right and walk along the beach. Look for shorebirds such as yellowlegs as you head south.

Nestled among large outcrops of smooth granite slabs at the end of the beach is a small graveyard with the headstones of members of the families who lived, toiled, and died here before the community was resettled in 1950. The location of the former settlement is nearby, but all that is left is the remains of a root cellar.

You will hardly get higher than a few metres above sea level on this hike; the shore is very low-lying—unlike most of Newfoundland's topography—but it is a starkly beautiful coastline.

Hikers have the option of taking the track or the beach back to the trailhead.

Middle Bill Cove

Cape Freels South

Cape Cove

330

0   2 km

Trail maps are **not to be used for navigation**.

1 Eastport

The white sandy beach at Eastport has long been a favourite destination for sun worshippers and swimmers. On a sunny day when the waves are rolling in on a perfect curl it is hard to imagine a prettier sight.

The beach is also the trailhead for a shoreline walk that leads to the far end of Northside Beach. A well-constructed boardwalk will lead you along the first kilometre; the trail then continues along the beach.

This is a gentle stroll and a perfect setting for a picnic and a relaxing day at the beach before taking the 1.5-kilometre walk back to the parking area.

Distance: 1.5-kilometre linear trail (3-kilometre return).

Trailhead: Eastport Beach (48.651, -53.749).

Highlights: Sandy beaches.

Elev. range: 0–5 metres.

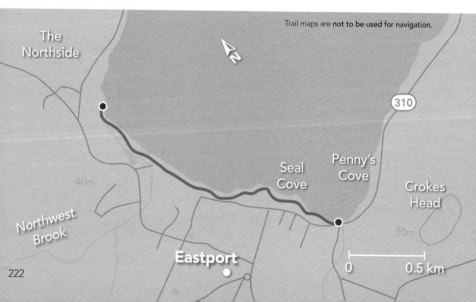

Trail maps are **not to be used for navigation.**

The Northside

310

Seal Cove

Penny's Cove

Crokes Head

40m

30m

Northwest Brook

Eastport

0   0.5 km

Salvage

Salvage is a town of remarkable scenic beauty with a network of trails that provide numerous vantage points to take it all in. The trails seem to go off in all directions at once and many hikers may choose to break it up into two separate hikes.

Distance: 7-kilometre trail network.

Trailhead: End of the main road, Salvage (48.688, -53.641).

Highlights: Great views into Newman Sound and of Salvage.

Elev. range: 5–90 metres.

The trail section at the eastern end of the town of Salvage leads to lookouts at Southern Head, Old Harry Cove, and Net Point. It is an approximately 4-kilometre loop passing Burden's Point back to the trailhead with lots of elevation change and great views.

The trail section on the westward side of town is a gentler affair and involves some road walking in the community.

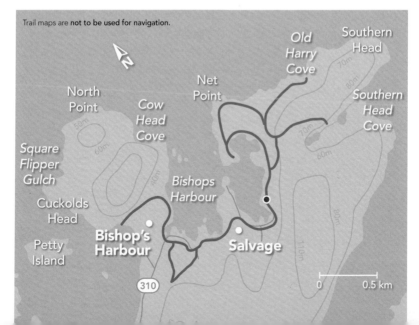

Sandy Cove to Salvage

Formerly called The Old Trails, this 13-kilometre path has been rerouted to provide more coastal views, many of which are spectacular.

Beginning the hike at Sandy Cove entails a steep climb to Sandy Cove Lookout. From here, the trail continues eastward along the ridge and eventually descends to the little beach at Smokey Hole, which is approximately the halfway point.

A little farther along, the trail comes to the resettled community at Barr Harbour, where there is a well-constructed tent deck for overnight campers.

Moving inland, the route skirts the edge of Linds Pond before beginning a steep climb up Sunrise Hill. You'll encounter one more outstanding viewpoint overlooking Broomclose Harbour before the final gentle descent into Salvage.

Most hikers should allow six hours for this hike; it features rough terrain and significant elevation changes. As of 2020, there is good signage and newly built infrastructure.

Distance: 13-kilometre linear trail.

Trailhead: Sandy Cove Beach (48.641, −53.729); Salvage (48.685, −53.646).

Highlights: High viewpoints, beaches, ponds.

Elev. range: 0 to 130 metres.

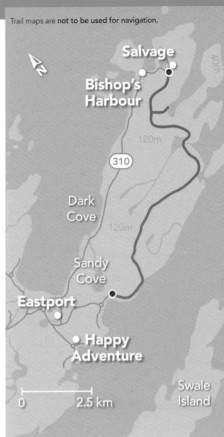

Trail maps are **not to be used for navigation.**

Salvage

Bishop's Harbour

40m

120m

310

Dark Cove

120m

Sandy Cove

Eastport

Happy Adventure

Swale Island

0   2.5 km

1 Happy Adventure

This hike is part of the Damnable trail system on the Eastport Peninsula. The trailhead is near the fish plant in scenic Happy Adventure.

Don't be put off by the uninspiring start to the hike on an uphill gravel woods road. The route soon takes a sharp turn to the right on a pathway that follows the undulating terrain. Passing beneath a sheer rocky cliff, the trail emerges into open landscape with side paths to several lookouts.

The path joins a public road and gives the option of going on to Sandy Cove or turning left and looping back to Happy Adventure.

 Damnable or *Damn the Bell* is an expression with a long history on the Eastport Peninsula. There is no certain explanation of its origins but may refer to the damnable difficulty of navigating this challenging coastline.

Distance: 3-kilometre linear trail.

Trailhead: Fishplant Road, Happy Adventure (48.638, –53.757).

Highlights: Views into Newman Sound.

Elev. range: 0–50 metres.

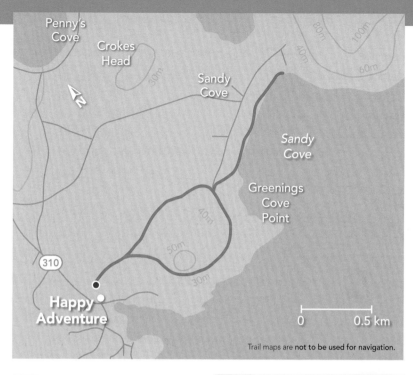

Penny's Cove

Crokes Head

Sandy Cove

30m

40m

80m

100m

60m

Sandy Cove

Greenings Cove Point

40m

50m

30m

310

Happy Adventure

0   0.5 km

Trail maps are **not to be used for navigation.**

BONAVISTA PENINSULA

Bonavista, the town that gives this peninsula its name, is where John Cabot reputedly made landfall after crossing the Atlantic from Bristol, England, in 1497. Cabot returned home with news that the waters around Newfoundland were teeming with cod, reporting that "the schools of codfish [there] were so thick you [could] walk on their backs." Fishers from Spain, Portugal, the Basque Country, France, and England were soon making regular visits.

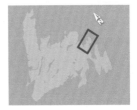

The Ryan Premises, a former fishing merchant's store and warehouse complex in the town of Bonavista, has been converted into a fascinating museum that clearly depicts the role of the cod fishery in shaping Newfoundland's history.

Another must-see is Port Union, a community created by the Fishermen's Protective Union under the leadership of William Coaker, one of Newfoundland's unique historical figures. Coaker brought modern advances to Port Union, including electrification, making it the first settlement outside of St. John's to be so served.

Trinity's many beautifully preserved houses and commercial buildings make a visit to this community seem like a step into the past. Architecture is not the only attraction: Summer in the Bight, a vibrant theatre festival held every year in Trinity, highlights the works of Newfoundland playwrights in nightly performances throughout the summer season.

The Bonavista Peninsula has numerous hiking trails of various lengths. Geology, history, coastal scenery, and wildlife ensure that these trails will not disappoint hikers of any fitness level. Moose, fox, whales, and seabirds are abundant, as are wildflowers, an attraction on any trail.

The Bonavista Peninsula has been fashioned into a tourist destination in recent years, with many B&Bs, cottages, inns, and fine restaurants, including the Bonavista Social Club in Upper Amherst Cove, Fishers' Loft and Two Whales Coffee Shop in Port Rexton, and The Twine Loft in Trinity.

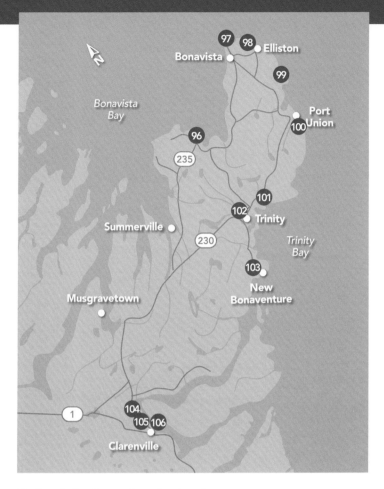

Trails of the Bonavista Peninsula

96. King's Cove Lighthouse Trail / King's Cove
97. Dungeon to Cape Bonavista / Bonavista
98. Klondike Trail / Elliston–Spillar's Cove
99. Little Catalina to Maberly Trail / Little Catalina–Maberly
100. Lodge's Pond to Murphy's Cove Trail / Melrose–Port Union
101. Fox Island Trail / Champney's West
102. Skerwink Trail / Trinity East
103. British Harbour Trail / New Bonaventure–British Harbour
104. Bare Mountain Trail / Clarenville
105. Rotary/Wellness Trails / Clarenville
106. Shoal Harbour Loop / Clarenville

King's Cove

The community of King's Cove is often overlooked in favour of some of the more heavily marketed communities on the Bonavista Peninsula, such as Bonavista and Trinity. Don't make this mistake—it is a gem. This community on the western side of the peninsula is picturesque and the trail to its lighthouse an easy and rewarding hike.

The elegant spire of Saints Peter and Paul Catholic Church is easy to spot and hikers should park near the church. The trail runs parallel to Blackhead Bay in the direction of the lighthouse about 1 kilometre away.

From the lighthouse, take the extended loop that goes by way of Fish Point Lookout and Brook Point Lookout. The sediments that are exposed on the cliff face at Brook Point are composed of 500-million-year-old Cambrian rock. The distinct colour variation is the first feature that catches your eye. The thick layers that dip sharply to the water's edge consist of red sandstones and conglomerates from the Crown Hill geological formation. The green and grey sandstone and siltstone contain copper.

The trail passes Round Pond Steady and Round Pond before traversing Pat Murphy's Meadow, made famous in "When I Mowed Pat Murphy's Meadow," the song written in the 1930s by King's Cove native J.M. Devine.

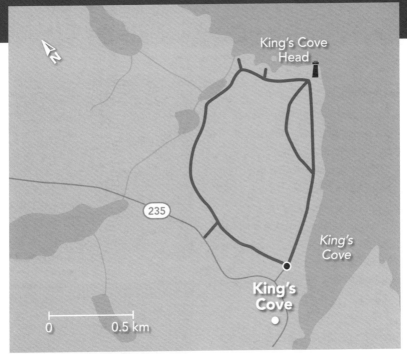

 King's Cove Lighthouse, shipped in sections from Birmingham, England, and assembled on-site in King's Cove in 1893, is an imposing structure. It was a manned lighthouse until 2000, when it was automated.

Distance: 3.5 kilometres.

Trailheads: Saints Peter and Paul Catholic Church, King's Cove (48.341052, -53.200128).

Highlights: Church, lighthouse, Brook Point.

Elev. range: 0–63 metres.

Bonavista

This gentle hike links two of the most dramatic sights on the Bonavista Peninsula: the Dungeon and Cape Bonavista. Dungeon Provincial Park features a collapsed sea cave that was once, in fact, two distinct caves. Erosion and the collapse of the cave ceiling created an enormous sinkhole, exposing two arches and allowing the ocean to flow in.

From the Dungeon, the trail travels north along the Trinity Bay side of the peninsula for approximately 2 kilometres, then crosses the Cape Shore Road on the Bonavista Bay side. It goes through a community pasture, where horses and cattle roam freely. If you would rather avoid these animals, pick up the Cape Shore Trail and walk to Cape Bonavista on the Bonavista Bay side.

During the spring and summer, the trail may offer opportunities to see icebergs and whales. Nearing Cape Bonavista, the trail comes to a large bronze statue of John Cabot. The trail officially ends at the Cape Bonavista lighthouse, but plan to spend some time bird watching and exploring the surrounding area.

 The Cape Bonavista lighthouse, completed in 1843, has a circular stone tower surrounded by a two-storey wood-frame structure. The light was traditionally fuelled by seal oil, which left a residue on the glass (frequent hand-polishing was required to clean the glass). The lighthouse has been turned into a museum which depicts the typical life of its keeper in the 1800s.

Distance:
7-kilometre linear trail.

Trailheads: Dungeon Provincial Park (48.400076, -53.050293); Cape Bonavista lighthouse (48.415265, -53.0500638).

Highlights: The Dungeon, lighthouse, Cabot statue, and whale, iceberg, and puffin sightings.

Elev. range: 2–20 metres.

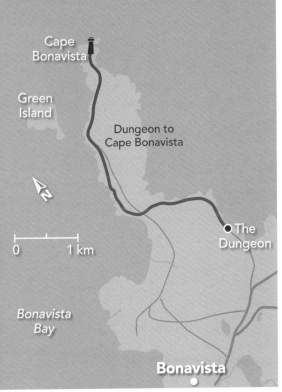

Cape
Bonavista

Green
Island

Dungeon to
Cape Bonavista

N

0   1 km

○ The
Dungeon

Bonavista
Bay

Bonavista
○

Trail maps are **not to be used for navigation**.

Elliston–Spillar's Cove

With over 100 visible root cellars, Elliston has been dubbed the "root cellar capital of the world." Wander through the town to check out the many fine examples and even take a peek inside one or two. The community also has a sealer's museum and a memorial to the sealing disasters of 1914.

After visiting these sites, explore the Klondike Trail from the north end of Elliston to Spillar's Cove.

The trail goes over L'Argent Hill and then past a cove full of sea stacks and jagged rocks. A track goes directly to the community of Spillar's Cove, but if you take this route you will miss out on a highlight of the area—an island with a colony of puffins. To see the puffin colony, follow the shoreline (instead of the dirt track); there is no developed path, and the terrain is uneven.

If you miss the puffins along the Klondike Trail, be sure to check out the puffin sanctuary on Bird Island on the main road between Elliston and Maberly. Sit for a few minutes and watch them fly off to search for food and then return to feed their young, hidden from predatory gulls, deep in their burrows.

Continue to follow the coastline into Spillar's Cove.

Distance: 5-kilometre loop around headland.

Trailhead: Elliston (north end, 48.382870, -53.033240).

Highlights: Sea stacks, puffin rock.

Elev. range: 34–60 metres.

 Puffins can dive to depths of 60 metres in search of small fish and crustaceans to feed their young. They are sometimes called sea parrots because of their large orange bills. At about seven weeks, the young puffins, now able to feed themselves, leave their burrows.

Sea stacks are pillars of rock which stand apart from the coastline. These impressive formations are formed by coastal erosion caused by wind, waves, and the freezing and thawing of water in the cracks and faultlines of the rocks.

Trail maps are **not to be used for navigation.**

Dungeon to
Cape Bonavista

Spillar's
Cove

The
Dungeon

Klondike
Trail

Elliston
Cove

Elliston

238

Bonavista

0   1 km

Little Catalina–Maberly

Allow a full day for this coastal hike which connects two Trinity Bay communities. The route is marked by black and white stakes but, as little maintenance has been done in recent years, these may not all be in place. The path hugs the coast for most of the way. There could be muddy sections if the weather has been wet.

> ⭐ The name Catalina is said to derive from *Cataluna*, the Spanish name for St. Catherine.

Maberly, just south of Elliston, also has root cellars. Now a curiosity and tourist attraction, these were once essential for preserving root crops through the fall and winter. A root cellar had to be well-constructed, dry, rodent-proof, and deep enough to keep the crops from freezing.

As you leave Maberly, look for several gazes or blinds used by seabird hunters—this area has been frequented by hunters and berry pickers for generations.

The terrain becomes more dramatic as you travel southward, with steeper cliffs and more trees. Much of this long trail goes through heathland and includes a variety of plant life, including blueberries, partridgeberries, and crowberries. Charlie's Cove is the site of a former settlement and a perfect spot to stop for refreshments.

The trail crosses bare, rocky terrain as it enters Little Catalina.

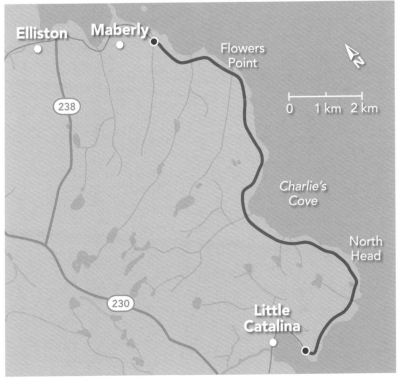

Trail maps are not to be used for navigation.

Distance: 17 kilometres.

Trailheads: Maberly
(48.370937, -53.004760);
Little Catalina (48.322945,
-53.020743).

Highlights: Cliffs and coves.

Elev. range: 2–49 metres.

Melrose–Port Union

Although this trail officially begins in Port Union next to St. Catherine's Haven (see red dotted line on map), we suggest starting at the northern end of Melrose for additional sightseeing. This well-worn scenic hike follows the shoreline of Trinity Bay and connects with the main trail at Back Cove.

From Back Cove, the trail makes its way to Burnt Point. Here you will find a viewing platform and a comfortable bench facing east to the lighthouse on Green Island directly opposite, one of the few manned lighthouses left in the province.

From Burnt Point, the trail follows the shoreline of Catalina Harbour. Look for roseroot plants along this section of the trail. About halfway back to Port Union is Murphy's Cove, once a fishing and farming settlement. The road that linked

Look for roseroot plants, also called "live-forever," in the rock crevices of this trail. Roseroot's waxy coating, a natural secretion, is a vital defence against the salt spray on the sea cliffs, where it thrives. It is an edible plant.

Distance:
8.5-kilometre linear trail.

Trailheads: Melrose
(48.290724, -53.034920); Port Union (48.294262, -53.043426).

Highlights: Shoreline, Green Island lighthouse.

Elev. range: 3–45 metres.

these communities is still visible.

The path ends in Port Union. Possibly the only union-built town in North America, Port Union was the brainchild of Sir William Coaker. Take time to visit the museum in the former Reid Railway station dating from 1917 and Coaker's bungalow.

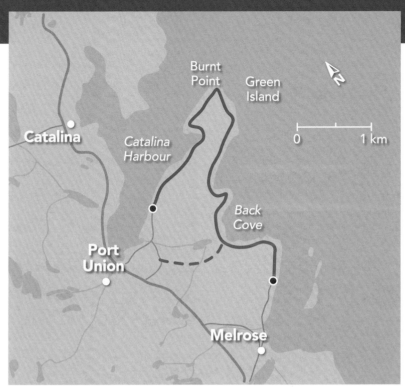

Trail maps are **not** to be used for navigation.

Champney's West

This trail starts in Champney's West at a well-marked trailhead with ample parking. The trail makes its way toward the coast, providing beautiful views of Port Rexton and Trinity Bay.

The path descends from the clifftops, arriving at a narrow beach leading to the base of Fox Island which, in fact, is not an island at all but joined to Champney's by a stretch of beach. The more adventurous will want to climb (with the aid of a rope) to the summit and enjoy the panoramic view.

Returning to the beach, follow the path along the shoreline briefly before turning inland and arriving at a road. Good signage directs you through the community passing colourfully painted fishing sheds and stages.

The path leaves the road and passes along the shore of Champney's Cove before crossing the main road and arriving back at the trailhead.

 Caplin, a major source of food for whales, seals, cod, and seabirds, are plentiful in this area. In late June and early July, large numbers of them "roll" in waves onto the beaches to spawn. People gather the little fish (about 20–25 centimetres in length) to fry, dry for later use, or fertilize their vegetable gardens.

Distance: 5-kilometre loop.

Trailhead: Main road, Champney's West (48.225975, -53.180871).

Highlights: Clifftop views, beaches.

Elev. range: 0–30 metres.

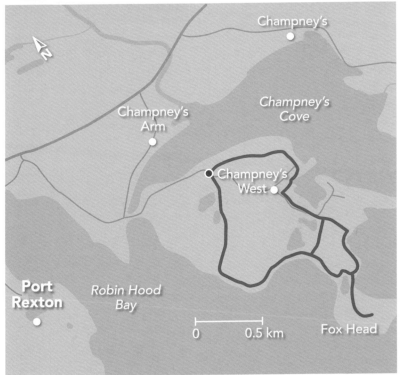

Champney's

Champney's
Arm

Champney's
Cove

Champney's
West

Port
Rexton

Robin Hood
Bay

0   0.5 km

Fox Head

Trail maps are not to be used for navigation.

Trinity East

Skerwink is another name for the shearwater, large seabirds commonly seen during the summer months off the coast of Newfoundland. The trail, which is named for these birds, is the crown jewel of hiking trails on the Bonavista Peninsula. Only 5 kilometres long, it boasts all the features hikers hope for in a coastal hike: sea stacks, cliffs, beaches, grassy headlands, and, from the summit, a panoramic view of the surrounding area.

From the well-marked parking area in Trinity East, the trail follows the old railbed to the coast and then the cliff, alternating between tree-sheltered pathways and open headlands. Kittiwakes and cormorants may be seen and, if you are lucky, a bald eagle or two.

Look for the side trail that leads to the lookout at the top of the hill. The summit affords a spectacular view of Trinity Bight and six communities; a picnic table is provided and is an ideal place to have lunch.

Returning to the main path you will soon descend to a long beach called Sam White's Cove; from there, turn right, cross a meadow, and return via a gravel path to the starting point in Trinity East.

 Travel and Leisure magazine named the Skerwink Trail one of the top 35 walks in Europe and North America. The trail has received rave reviews in national and international publications and is enjoyed by hundreds of hikers every year.

Distance:
5-kilometre linear trail.

Trailhead: Trinity East
(48.224526, -53.202473).

Highlights: Coastal views, seabirds, and icebergs and whales in season.

Elev. range: 3–60 metres.

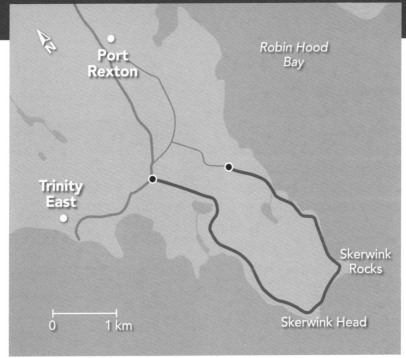

Port
Rexton

Robin Hood
Bay

Trinity
East

Skerwink
Rocks

Skerwink Head

0   1 km

Trail maps are **not to be used for navigation.**

New Bonaventure to British Harbour

This trail begins near New Bonaventure at the *Random Passage* film location. This site attracts thousands of visitors every year, and there is plenty of parking.

This linear hike is 12 kilometres return, but it is possible to avoid backtracking by taking a boat from New Bonaventure to British Harbour. Boat-tour operators provide this service during tourist season.

In 2020, only a few summer cabins remained at British Harbour, once a bustling outport of over 200 people. The trail itself begins behind the community, which was resettled in the 1970s.

The trail climbs steadily out of British Harbour as it leaves the coast, arriving at a bald rocky height of land which provides a view of British Harbour and a panorama of rugged country and ponds. Expect to encounter deadfall trees and muddy sections as this trail has had little maintenance. In a few places extra care is required as the path is steep.

Kerley's Harbour, another resettled outport, is the last point of interest

 This trail offers a chance to learn about traditional outport Newfoundland, as does the *Random Passage* site, which depicts what an isolated 18th- or 19th-century outport would have looked like.

Distance: 6-kilometre linear trail (12-kilometre return).

Trailheads: New Bonaventure (48.170817, -53.270864); British Harbour (48.154839, -53.300076).

Highlights: Resettled communities.

Elev. range: 12–156 metres.

along the trail before arriving at the film set. A road links the site to the town of New Bonaventure about 1 kilometre away.

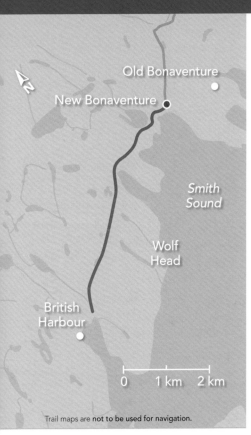

Old Bonaventure

New Bonaventure

Smith Sound

Wolf Head

British Harbour

0   1 km   2 km

Trail maps are **not** to be used for navigation.

Clarenville

Hikers may choose to begin this trail from one of two starting points: the Professional Building on Manitoba Drive in Clarenville (at the north end of the parking lot) or Hunt's Hill near the Shoal Harbour causeway. This trail can be walked as a linear trail (if you park a vehicle at each end) or as a loop.

In July 1933, in an effort to demonstrate Italy's pre-World War II air power, 20 S-55 flying boats under the command of General Italo Balbo landed on the waters of Random Sound. At the time, it was the largest fleet of aircraft to successfully complete a transatlantic flight.

Distance: 3-kilometre linear trail.

Trailhead: Parking lot, Professional Building, Manitoba Drive (48.094706, -53.582545); Hunt's Hill near Shoal Harbour causeway (48.105301, -53.583487).

Highlights: Ponds, forest, view from lookout.

Elev. range: 20–140 metres.

The highlight of the trail is, unquestionably, the spectacular view from the lookout at the top of the appropriately named Bare Mountain. On a fine day, Random Island and the town of Clarenville, separated by the sparkling waters of Random Sound, present a splendid vista. A substantial viewing platform, equipped with affixed binoculars, provides a comfortable place from which to take photographs, hydrate, and take off or add a layer of clothing. An on-site signpost gives directions and distances to various places in the province.

From the Bare Mountain Lookout the trail continues in a northerly direction over The Dam to the causeway in Shoal Harbour. If you don't have a vehicle at the Shoal Harbour trailhead, you may prefer to loop back around Stanley's Pond and return to the trailhead at Manitoba Drive.

The route winds through thick boreal forest but frequent signs make the path easy to follow. Watch for ospreys and other raptors.

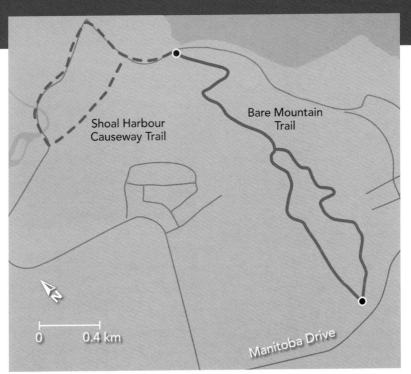

Shoal Harbour
Causeway Trail

Bare Mountain
Trail

Manitoba Drive

0   0.4 km

Trail maps are not to be used for navigation.

Clarenville

Trail builders in Clarenville have cleverly connected Rotary Trail and Wellness Trail so that they can be walked separately or linked together for a longer hike. The trails can be accessed from several trailheads; the hike can be as long or as short as you wish.

Begin where Memorial Drive meets Cormack Drive at the bridge over Lower Shoal Harbour River, which flows into Lower Shoal Harbour and then into Random Sound. The trail follows the left bank of Lower Shoal Harbour River past Elizabeth Swan Memorial Park, crosses the river near the confluence with Dark Hole Brook, and continues west.

While you are meandering through the lush boreal forest, it is easy to forget that you are still inside the Clarenville town limits. The path proceeds in a westerly direction for about 1.5 kilometres before turning north and linking up with the Newfoundland Trailway. From this point you can return to the starting point or join the Wellness Trail for a longer walk.

The Wellness Trail emerges from the woods and passes by two schools and through a busy commercial area before joining the Newfoundland Trailway. For a longer hike, cross Manitoba Drive and connect with Bare Mountain Trail (see hike #42).

There are helpful signs along the trail and trails are well-maintained. An excellent brochure on the Clarenville Trail System is available at the Tourist Information Centre.

Distance: 3–6 kilometres.

Trailhead: Memorial Drive Bridge (48.090534, -53.574422).

Highlights: Boreal forest, rivers.

Elev. range: 3–90 metres.

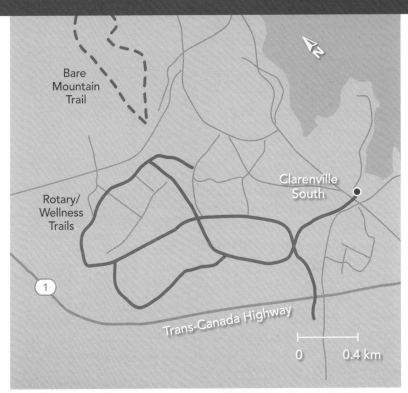

Trail maps are **not to be used for navigation.**

Clarenville

There are many places to begin this hike, but we suggest parking either just across the bridge where the Shoal Harbour River runs into the harbour, or farther along Harbour Drive near Hunt's Hill by a viewing platform. A large map of the route is posted at the base of the stairway below the viewing platform on Memorial Drive near the start of the causeway.

 The Town of Clarenville is recognized as a Canada Goose sanctuary thanks to the initiative of Clyde Tuck of Shoal Harbour, who brought two tame geese and one wild goose to the area in 1922. Large flocks can be seen in the area each spring and autumn.

Distance: 3-kilometre loop.

Trailhead: Viewing platform, Harbour Drive (48.105700, -53.584107); Shoal Harbour River bridge (48.105506, -53.591363).

Highlights: Wildlife, harbour views, lookout.

Elev. range: 3–25 metres.

This is an urban walk with a difference. It features an impressive walkway parallel to the causeway, offering a close-up view of the harbour, home to Canada geese, osprey, and eagles. Across Smith Sound is Random Island.

At the other side of the causeway, the path crosses Harbour Drive and turns left, eventually crossing Shoal Harbour River, where the river rushes into the harbour. From this point, turn onto Cedar Crescent and then quickly take a left onto the path. This will bring you to a viewing platform which has signboards detailing some of the history of the area, including the landing of an Italian seaplane fleet under the command of Captain Balbo in 1933.

Should you wish an extended hike, the northern trailhead of the Bare Mountain Trail is 50 metres farther along the Newfoundland Trailway.

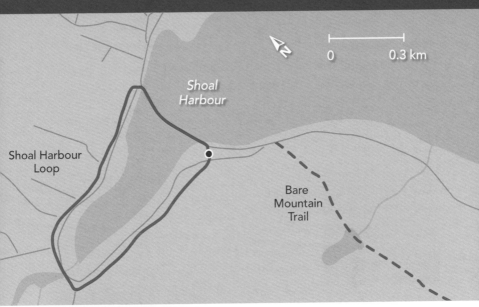

Shoal
Harbour

Shoal Harbour
Loop

Bare
Mountain
Trail

0   0.3 km

Trail maps are not to be used for navigation.

BURIN PENINSULA

The Burin Peninsula is a large appendage jutting southward into the North Atlantic from the island of Newfoundland. It is a magical place steeped in history, tragedy, and natural beauty. The towns and communities are sparsely inhabited and much of the coastline is not accessible by car.

By road, the peninsula is accessed from the Trans-Canada Highway by turning onto Highway 210 at Goobies. Swift Current is the first community strung along the highway. The next major community is Marystown, 122 kilometres to the southwest. The landscape changes dramatically as you travel south: thick forest with spruce and deciduous trees turns to large open tracts of low-growing shrubs and rock. Carry an emergency kit in your vehicle as fog and potholes could leave you on a lonely highway with little traffic for a long time.

Several side roads end at tiny communities that are well worth a stop—Bay L'Argent, Petite Forte, Rushoon, and Red Harbour, among others. At Marystown, the vistas change dramatically again, from hilly barrens to the ocean and a prosperous community where the main industry is a shipyard and fabrication facility that primarily services the province's offshore industry.

We made our first stop in the historic town of Burin for a stroll around Salt Pond. Burin has several picturesque sheltered coves, once used by rum-runners, which can be clearly seen at the base of high cliffs from Captain Cook Lookout. You can imagine pirates and privateers of bygone times sailing between hidden coves with contraband rum bought from nearby St. Pierre.

St. Lawrence is a community at the "heel" of the peninsula. Cap Chapeau Rouge looms to the southeast of Great St. Lawrence Harbour. St. Lawrence has its share of history, fame, and prosperity, including the 1942 sinking of the *Pollux* and *Truxton*. On the way to Fortune, small com-

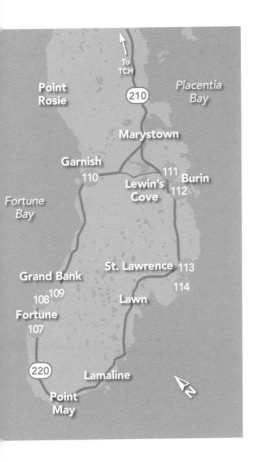

munities—Lawn, Roundabout, Calmer, and others—dot the shoreline. The French islands of St. Pierre and Miquelon can be seen on a clear day offshore from the "toe" of the peninsula.

Grand Bank wears its history well in its architecture alone. Queen-Anne-style homes topped with widow walks once owned by sea captains and wealthy merchants still stand proudly and make for great photo opportunities.

Finish the loop by heading north to Garnish. From a vantage point on the Long Ridge Trail, Garnish appears as a tidy small community surrounded by startling coastal beauty. From there the road veers east once again to take you back to Marystown.

Burin Trails

Fortune

Although Fortune is known as the jumping-off point for travellers taking the ferry to the French islands of St. Pierre and Miquelon, this historic town has much to offer in its own right. The Fortune Head Ecological Reserve is one of only three sites in the world where the transition from the pre-Cambrian to the Cambrian era is evident in the fossil record. It is also home to the Horse Brook Trail, a pleasant walking path.

Walkers can access this trail either at the Horsebrook Trailer Park just off Eldon Street or from Hornhouse Road.

Horse Brook Trail is a gentle amble along the banks of Horse Brook.

Where boardwalks were necessary, they were well built but, due to flooding, some have shifted from their footings and are a little off-kilter. Otherwise, the path is in good shape.

Horse Brook is a quiet, pretty little river for most of the year, but it is evident from erosion along its banks that it can present a different picture when water levels are high. An abundance of wildflowers grows along the riverbank in season and in late August expect a rich harvest from the many chokecherry trees.

You could leave a vehicle at either end of the trail, but as the trail is so short, it makes sense to walk both ways.

Chokecherry is a member of the Rose family. The fruit is sweet, easily recognizable by its long stems (similar to those of cherries), and easy to pick. The berries are dark purple or red when ripe and have a large pit that becomes soft and edible when cooked. Chokecherries are ripe in late August to early September and are known by a variety of names: chuckley pears, shadberries, chuck, serviceberries, wild pears, juneberries, chockly plums, Indian pears, and Saskatoon berries.

Distance:
2-kilometre linear trail.

Trailhead: Hornhouse Road (47.031630, -55.503550); Horsebrook Trailer Park 47.034982, -55.495855).

Highlights: River, wildflowers, chokecherry trees.

Elev. range: 7–16 metres.

Fortune

0   1 km

220

Trail maps are **not to be used for navigation**.

Grand Bank

Marine Trail begins at the end of College Street in the town of Grand Bank. Walk across the beach that separates Admiral Cove Pond from the ocean and then climb to the top of the cape. From this vantage point, the town is spread out like a giant map.

To the east is Fortune. To the north, in the middle of Fortune Bay, is Brunette Island, where an attempt to develop a bison herd in 1964 proved unsuccessful.

 Several large homes in Grand Bank have a widow's walk, also called a widow's watch—a railed roof walkway on a platform, often enclosed in a small cupola, at the top of a house. Some say the widow's walks were designed for women who were mourning for husbands who did not return from their sea journeys.

The path is easy to follow as it continues across the open headland and then traces the coastline toward Fortune. On a clear day, it is possible to see the French islands of St. Pierre and Miquelon. You can imagine that the headland was also a spot where people walked and waited anxiously, looking for signs of local mariners reportedly lost at sea.

Distance:
7-kilometre linear trail.

Trailhead: College Street, Grand Bank (47.060817, -55.454829); Eternity Rock, Grand Bank-Fortune highway (47.052829, -55.472842).

Highlights: Views of Grand Bank, coastline.

Elev. range: 0–47 metres.

Eventually the trail leads to L'Anse au Paul Beach. Partway down the beach, take the road that turns east and leads out to the Grand Bank-Fortune highway. Turn left at the highway and proceed along the road to the trail's end at Eternity Rock. If you don't have a vehicle waiting, walk back along the road to Grand Bank, or retrace your steps over the trail.

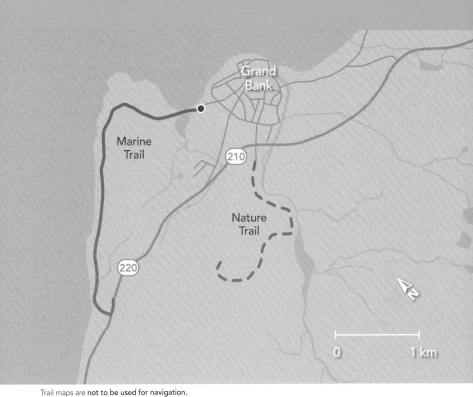

Marine Trail

Grand Bank

Nature Trail

210

220

0   1 km

Trail maps are **not to be used for navigation.**

Grand Bank

Farmer's Hill Road in Grand Bank leads to the beginning of the Nature Trail. The path follows along the bank of Grand Bank Brook and quickly arrives at a dam and fish ladder. Beyond the brook, you will enter thick woods and eventually arrive at a gazebo on Simms Ridge for an impressive view of the town and ocean. Scotch pines planted on this hillside by the local Boy Scout troop in the 1950s are an interesting

alternative to the usual fare in a Newfoundland forest.

From the gazebo, you will head toward a high communication tower. The path proceeds to Bennett's Hill Lookout and another outstanding view of the town below. From this lookout you can descend the hill to the main road or return the way you came to Farmer's Hill Road.

New trail infrastructure includes a picnic area and two lookouts. The path is generally in good condition but there is an absence of signs and, because of intersecting roads and trails, the trail can be confusing. A good signboard with a map of the trail would be helpful.

 Because of its proximity to the rich fishing banks offshore, Grand Bank was a prosperous harbour as early as the 1880s. Schooners built here to ply the waters were called Grand Bankers.

Distance:
6-kilometre linear trail.

Trailhead: Farmer's Hill Road (47.053558, -55.454392); Grandview Boulevard, (47.052688, -55.472661).

Highlights: Views of Grand Bank and coast, forest vegetation.

Elev. range: 6–79 metres.

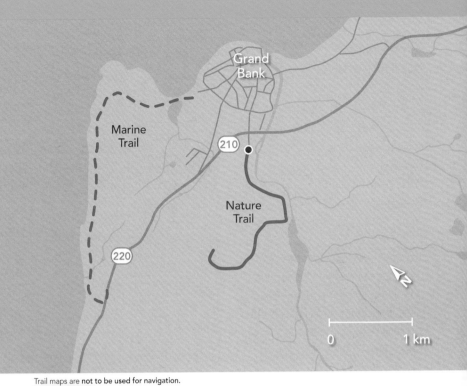

Trail maps are **not to be used for navigation**.

St. Lawrence

As you follow Pollux Crescent on the west side of St. Lawrence out of the town, the pavement soon gives way to gravel. A short way along the road is the clearly marked start to the Cape Trail that goes to the summit of Cap Chapeau Rouge.

This trail has two distinct elements: the flat section and the steep section. For the first few kilometres, the path winds through woods and then across an open bog before a steep ascent to the top of the cape.

There is some plank infrastructure but take care on old boardwalk that is not in the best of condition. The path is often wet and muddy in places.

The climb to the top can be challenging as the trail is rocky and steep. This is one of the highest points on the Burin Peninsula and the views are impressive—worth the ascent. From here, you can look down the bay to the town of St. Lawrence; in the other direction Chambers Cove and Lawn Head are easily visible.

It is always windy on top of the cape and can be foggy, so be prepared. Return via the same trail.

Distance:
4-kilometre linear trail.

Trailhead: Pollux Crescent, St. Lawrence (46.542527, -55.233923).

Highlights: Bog vegetation, views from summit.

Elev. range: 30–211 metres.

220

St. Lawrence

0   1 km

Trail maps are not to be used for navigation.

St. Lawrence

Chambers Cove near St. Lawrence would be just one of many scenic coves and bays around Newfoundland were it not for the events of November 18, 1942. On that night, three US Navy vessels ran aground in Chambers Cove and on nearby Lawn Head. Although 203 American sailors died that night, 186 were rescued by the heroic efforts of local residents.

This trail begins at the end of Iron Spring Road, an extension of Pollux Crescent in St. Lawrence. This multi-

use trail is used by ATVs as well as walkers, at least as far as Salt Cove. There, by the small hay shed where several of the first men up the cliff took shelter in 1942, a long stairway leads to the top of the cliff looking down on Chambers Cove.

The USS *Truxton* ran aground in this cove, the USS *Pollux* and USS *Wilkes* farther west on Lawn Head. Signboards explain the events of that historic night.

Hikers may wander freely on the open headland and admire the beauty of this stretch of coast, which is characterized by both dangerous rocky cliffs and sandy beaches. When you are ready to return, take the Bergeron Path by way of Salt Cove, the route taken by Seaman Ed Bergeron, the first survivor to make it ashore and who alerted men at the Iron Spring Mine of the disaster. This path brings you back to the car park at the trailhead.

> ⭐ *Standing into Danger*, by Cassie Brown, recounts the true story of the *Truxton* and *Pollux* sinkings, one of the worst disasters in Newfoundland's naval history.

> **Distance:**
> 4-kilometre loop trail.
>
> **Trailhead:** Iron Spring Road, St. Lawrence (46.530277, -55.251273).
>
> **Highlights:** Coastal scenery, historical significance.
>
> **Elev. range:** 7–60 metres.

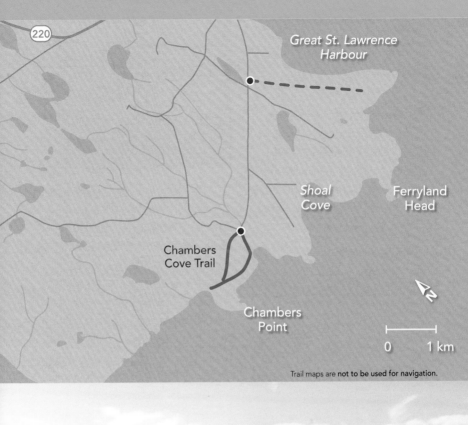

220

Great St. Lawrence Harbour

Shoal Cove

Ferryland Head

Chambers Cove Trail

Chambers Point

N

0   1 km

Trail maps are **not to be used for navigation.**

Garnish

The trailhead for the Long Ridge Trail is on the right side of Sunset Drive as you enter Garnish from Frenchman's Cove. Watch for the sign by the trail entrance; parking is located a few metres farther down the road, on the ocean side.

Distance: 1.8-kilometre linear trail (4 kilometres, including town walk).

Trailhead: Sunset Drive, Garnish (47.134290, -55.223065); Salvation Army Cemetery (47.134201, -55.214725).

Highlights: Views from the ridge, harbour walk.

Elev. range: 1–72 metres.

An interesting fact from a storyboard in Garnish: Philip and Charles Grandy, born on Jersey in the British Channel Islands, were the first to settle here, having been forced out of the French island of St. Pierre, just off the Burin Peninsula, in 1763. "Garnish" is believed to have derived from the word "Cornish," the original ancestral home of these early settlers.

It doesn't take long for this path to offer hikers beautiful rewards. As you make your way toward the ridge, the thick forest begins to thin and, at the first viewpoint, the path reveals a panoramic view of the coast. At Frenchman's Cove to the southwest you can see the long crescent beach creating a barachois behind it, and the man-made rolling greens of a nine-hole golf course. In the opposite direction is the town of Garnish with its secure little harbour and marina.

From the 70-metre peak, the trail descends back into thick forest, eventually emerging at the Salvation Army Cemetery at the northeast end of town. You could have a second car waiting there, but a better idea is to walk back through town, taking Barrisway Street to Waterfront Road by the harbour. Seaview Drive will lead you back to Sunset Drive and the trailhead.

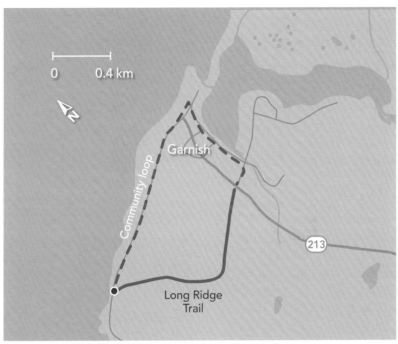

Garnish

Community loop

213

Long Ridge
Trail

Trail maps are **not to be used for navigation.**

Burin

Salt Pond is located beside Main Street as you approach Burin from Marystown. The pond empties southwest into Burin Bay Arm via a narrow channel under a bridge on Eagle Road. Salt Pond Walking Trail is a gentle 2.5-kilometre walk circling the pond and is suitable for all ages. It can easily be completed in 30 to 40 minutes.

The boardwalk and crushed-stone walkway passes at times through lush forest and, at other times, weaves its way between houses and the pond edge. Look for a wide array of wildflowers and wildlife, including ospreys hovering above the water trying to catch a fish for dinner. Walkers are almost certain to encounter a large covey of ducks near the footbridge.

The infrastructure on this walk is well built and appears to undergo regular maintenance. Viewing benches and picnic tables are provided and the dock on the west side of the pond is an especially good place to stop and picnic or just to enjoy the peace and tranquility of this area.

Distance: 2.5-kilometre loop.

Trailhead: Salt Pond, Main Street (47.055703, -55.115257).

Highlights: Birds, wildflowers, pond.

Elev. range: 1–20 metres.

Salt Pond

To Burin

0   0.3 km

Trail maps are not to be used for navigation.

Burin

This trail begins at the end of Penney's Pond Road just off Main Street on the approach to Burin. A boardwalk and stairways added in recent years have greatly improved this trail.

After passing by Penney's Pond, the trail takes hikers through thick co-niferous woods and then descends to near sea level before climbing to

James Cook, the famous Royal Navy explorer and cartographer for whom this trail is named, mapped the coastline around Newfoundland in the mid-18th century. He subsequently mapped Australia and New Zealand and circumnavigated the globe three times before being killed in an alter-cation with Hawaiian natives in 1779.

the 75-metre-high lookout. The trail is more rugged on the climb, so be careful, especially in wet conditions.

In the 18th century, this lookout provided an ideal vantage point from which to spot smugglers or the approaching pirates or privateers who periodically raided coastal settlements. You can peer down from the lookout onto fishing boats docked in Epworth, and across the bay you will see Burin and its waterfront boardwalk. Burin Inlet is picturesque and dotted with islands of all shapes and sizes.

Distance: 3-kilometre linear trail (6-kilometre return).

Trailhead: Penney's Pond Road, Burin (47.022165, -55.103678).

Highlights: Magnificent views from the lookout.

Elev. range: 6–75 metres.

Return to the trailhead by the same path.

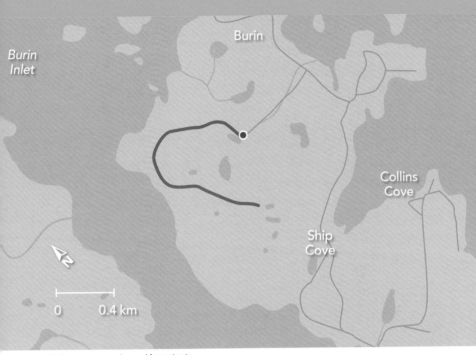

Burin

Burin
Inlet

Collins
Cove

Ship
Cove

0   0.4 km

Trail maps are **not to be used for navigation.**

AVALON PENINSULA

The Avalon Peninsula is the most densely populated area of Newfoundland and Labrador. The first permanent settlements in the region were established in the early 1600s; the area's rich cod fishery led to the steady growth of the region over the centuries.

Since the late 1990s, the offshore oil industry has spurred the rapid growth of towns and cities, particularly those in the northeast Avalon. This recent development does not mean, however, that one has to drive for hours to find the serenity and isolation of uninhabited wilderness. One of the attractions of the Avalon is the easy accessibility of walking trails that transport the hiker to places of startling natural beauty.

The terrain varies widely from one part of the Avalon to another. The treeless barrens and headlands of the southern shore or Cape St. Mary's seem a world apart from the thickly forested areas along the east coast. In some places, the land slopes gently to the sea; in others, sheer cliffs are a characteristic feature. The Labrador current brings changeable weather and encourages the subarctic vegetation of the Avalon. Hikers should be prepared for cool conditions no matter how congenial the weather when starting out; onshore winds can bring thick banks of fog on land and send the temperature plummeting.

The Avalon Peninsula trails display a variety of trail standards and infrastructure styles. Only the d'Iberville Trail takes a day to walk—and even that trail can be hiked in shorter sections. Butter Pot Hill is an inland trail; the others in this section are coastal trails.

Trails of the Avalon Peninsula

115. Centre Hill Trail / Sunnyside
116. Truce Sound Peace Garden Trail / Sunnyside
117. Cleary Walking Trail / Come by Chance
118. Bordeaux Trail / Arnold's Cove

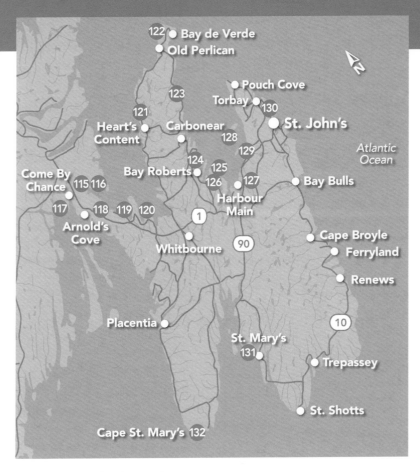

119. Coastal Trail / Chance Cove

120. Sea View Trail / Norman's Cove

121. D'Iberville Trail / Heart's Content–Winterton
and Hant's Harbour to New Chelsea

122. Grates Cove Trails / Grates Cove

123. Blackhead to Western Bay / Blackhead (Conception Bay North)

124. Bay Roberts Shoreline Heritage Walk / Bay Roberts

125. Brigus Lighthouse Trail / Brigus

126. Burnt Head Trail / Cupids

127. Butter Pot Hill Trail / Butter Pot Provincial Park

128. Gregory Normore Walking Trail / Bell Island

129. Manuels River Trail / Manuels

130. Trails of Signal Hill / St. John's

131. St. Mary's to Gaskiers Trail / St. Mary's

132. Bird Rock / Cape St. Mary's

Sunnyside

Volcanoes aren't generally associated with Newfoundland, but the large hill behind the town of Sunnyside was formed by an ancient volcano. With an elevation of 384 metres, it is the highest point in eastern Newfoundland, and a great hike. The Sunnyside town council has named this a "wilderness trail" as it can no longer maintain the boardwalk across such a long stretch of bog. Hikers should be prepared for wet and muddy sections.

Near the end of the main road through the town, you will arrive at the well-marked trailhead and parking area. Curiously, the hill that is visible from the Trans-Canada Highway is completely out of sight and remains so for much of the early part of the hike.

The trail climbs gradually, crosses a river, wends through forest, passes an old log cabin, and crosses large barrens. A freshwater spring and tent platforms are located beside a pond at the base of the hill.

From this point, the summit is only 400 metres, but it is a steep climb and the toughest part of the hike. The 360-degree panorama from the top, however, makes the effort worthwhile—all the more reason to do this trail on a sunny day with high visibility.

Walk back the way you came, enjoying the view of Placentia Bay to the south.

★ In the 1930s, a fire tower was built at the summit because of the constant threat of forest fires from steam locomotives. It has been replaced by a small gazebo, well anchored against strong and unrelenting winds.

Distance: 5-kilometre linear trail (10-kilometre return).

Trailhead: End of main road in Sunnyside (47.511925, -53.525884).

Highlights: Outstanding views from summit.

Elev. range: 1–384 metres.

Trail maps are **not to be used for navigation.**

Sunnyside

Hikers familiar with the Centre Hill Trail in Sunnyside may be tempted to overlook a shorter and less challenging trail in this community. The Truce Sound Peace Garden Trail, at 1.5 kilometres in length, could be dismissed as just a "dawdle"—but this would be a mistake.

Short it may be, but this path follows the shoreline of Truce Sound and is a pleasant walk through boreal forest, with a unique destination. From a lookout, a teepee constructed of bleached white "longers" can be seen approximately 0.5 kilometres away. At first glance, it seems that the teepee is on an island, and you might wonder if (and how) you're going to get to your destination without becoming wet. Fortunately, a narrow spit of sand or tombolo provides a safe and dry passage to tiny Frenchman's Island. Once across, go left along the shoreline to the Peace Garden memorial.

Frenchman's Island was the site of a November 6, 1612, meeting between members of John Guy's colony at Cupids and a group of Beothuk. It was a peaceful event that involved the sharing of gifts and food and was intended to mark the beginning of a mutually beneficial relationship. Unfortunately, it was not to be, and the ultimate fate of the Beothuk people lends a solemn poignancy to the site.

Tombolo is an Italian word for one or more sandbars formed by wave action that connect an island to the mainland. A lagoon can be formed by two tombolos that eventually fill with sediment. A tombolo can be a form of peninsula.

A *longer* is a long tapering pole, usually a conifer, with bark left on, used in constructing roofs, floors, or surfaces of stages and flakes. (Source: *Dictionary of Newfoundland English*)

Distance: 5-kilometre linear trail (10-kilometre return).

Trailhead: End of main road in Sunnyside (47.511925, -53.525884).

Highlights: Outstanding views from summit.

Elev. range: 1–384 metres.

Trail maps are **not to be used for navigation.**

1 Come by Chance

This trail is named for Dr. Peter Cleary and his wife, Joan Cleary, a public health nurse, who served this community for many years.

The trail parallels the banks of the Come by Chance River for about 1 kilometre, until it reaches the river estuary. There is a campsite and picnic tables here. After another kilometre of even walking, the trail crosses a gravel road. It is well worth taking a 100-metre side trip down the road to visit the site of the resettled community of Coopers Cove.

The final 1.3 kilometres of trail involves a gentle but steady climb that eventually emerges on the road near a boat marina. Beyond that the oil refinery dock is visible. From here, you return via the trail, or walk back on the gravel road until it rejoins the trail at Coopers Cove.

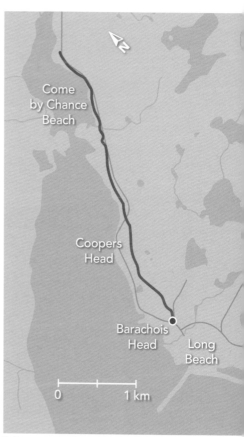

Trail maps are **not to be used for navigation**.

Distance: 3.5-kilometre linear trail (7 kilometres return).

Trailhead: End of paved main road, Come by Chance (47.839, -53.9934).

Highlights: River estuary, Coopers Cove.

Elev. range: 0–10 metres.

Arnold's Cove

Early French settlers called this area Bordeaux after their homeland in France. In the 1800s, James Adams and his family farmed the land here for over a century. A plaque has been mounted in the vicinity of the Adams family homestead.

Signs in Arnold's Cove point to the trailhead at the end of Monkstown Road, where there is ample parking. Across the bay, Merasheen Island is visible in the distance. The largest island in Placentia Bay, Merasheen Island was resettled in the 1960s.

The first part of the trail follows the shoreline, crossing beaches and grassy headlands. The Horse Meadows, Lou Point, Labours Cove, and Wild Cove are all places of interest along the way. Some old house foundations can still be seen.

This headland has long been considered an attractive place to live. Archaeologists have uncovered evidence that shows Dorset Eskimos, Beothuk Indians, and Basque fishers all spent time there.

 On the side of the main road into Arnold's Cove is the Big Pond Bird Sanctuary. This is a popular pit stop for many migratory birds, including Canada geese, pie ducks, mallards, ruddy turnstones, and sandpipers. Ospreys and bald eagles may also be seen.

The trail eventually crosses over the headland to a meadow which provides a different view of the bay and, in the distance, the trans-shipment oil facility at Whiffen Head. This is an excellent spot to relax or stop for lunch.

Allow half a day for this hike and take time for some beachcombing and exploring.

Distance: 10-kilometre loop.

Trailhead: Monkstown Road, Arnold's Cove (47.454981, -53.592369).

Highlights: Beaches, views of the bay.

Elev. Range: 0–25 metres.

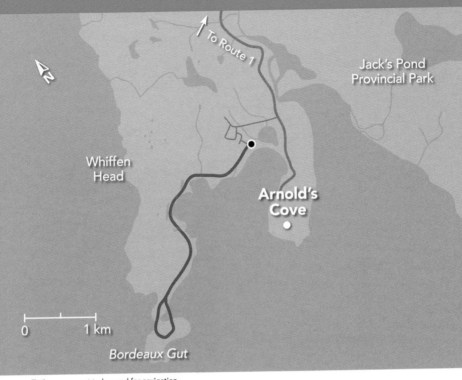

To Route 1

Jack's Pond
Provincial Park

Whiffen
Head

Arnold's
Cove

0   1 km

Bordeaux Gut

Trail maps are **not to be used for navigation.**

Wild Cove

Chance Cove

Some visitors may overlook Chance Cove in favour of its more famous neighbor, Bellevue Beach. But Chance Cove not only has a beautiful sweeping beach but also a hiking trail with features to rival any in the area.

The trail begins next to the Salvation Army cemetery on the edge of town. Approximately 1 kilometre along the path, it opens into a grassy headland. From there, it climbs through woods eventually arriving at two little hidden beaches. Knotted ropes are in place to help hikers descend to the shoreline.

The second beach has a sea cave inside a towering "island" cliff that can be entered by those willing to wade through the chilly water.

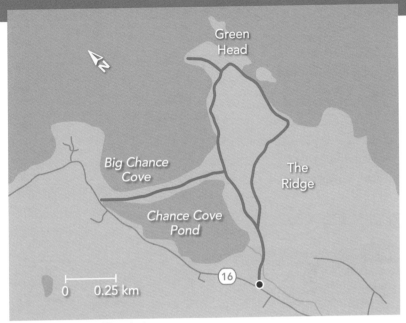

Trail maps are **not to be used for navigation**.

Distance: 5-kilometre linear trail.

Trailhead: Cemetery, Chance Cove (47.667, -53.813).

Highlights: Barrachois, hidden beaches.

Elev. range: 0–50 metres.

Norman's Cove

For a short hike with an extraordinary view, visit the Sea View Trail in Norman's Cove. Tucked into Chapel Arm at the bottom of Trinity Bay, this trail is a hidden gem.

> ⭐ **Wild roses are more than just attractive blossoms. Jams, syrup, jellies, and teas can be made from the ripened fleshy fruit or "hips" of the plant.**

A sign on Hilltop Lane near the post office in Norman's Cove points the way to the trailhead and there is plenty of parking near the cemetery. Take the track to the left. Just before you reach another cemetery, the path descends toward the cove. Turn right at the shoreline, pass a little sandy beach, and then climb a small rise to the gazebo lookout. A boardwalk crosses a pleasant meadow; the trail next takes you through thick woods and, eventually, to a clearing. Across the clearing, a 130-step staircase leads to the summit on Chapel Head 63 metres above the bay.

The picnic table at the top is an ideal place to rest and take in the

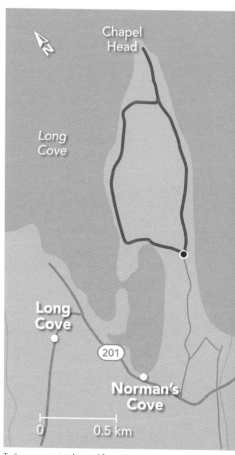

Trail maps are **not to be used for navigation.**

spectacular view of Chapel Arm, Long Cove, and the eastern shoreline of Trinity Bay. Continue along the trail as it gradually descends along the steeply angled sedimentary layers that make up the ridge of Chapel Head and brings you back to the trailhead.

Distance: 4-kilometre loop.

Trailhead: Anglican cemetery, Norman's Cove (47.340064, -53.393726).

Highlights: Views from Chapel Head, wild roses.

Elev. range: 0–63 metres.

Heart's Content–Winterton / Hant's Harbour–New Chelsea

This trail system on the east side of Trinity Bay is named for Pierre Le Moyne d'Iberville, the French commander at Placentia who led a series of destructive raids on English fishing settlements in Newfoundland in 1696.

 Pierre Le Moyne d'Iberville, sent to Placentia from New France in 1696, began raiding coastal settlements at the Colony of Avalon (Ferryland). He proceeded north to St. John's, burning and looting along the way, and then moved to Conception and Trinity bays. A total of 36 settlements were destroyed, but by the following year they had all been reclaimed by England.

Most of this trail (from Heart's Content to Winterton) can be done as a long, single-day hike. Because the trail joins the road in several places, however, it may also be tackled as a series of shorter walks.

The trail starts at the brightly painted red and white lighthouse at Heart's Content. Parts of the trail consist of an elaborate boardwalk and wooden stairs which wind in and out of wooded areas. The first section, Heart's Content to New Perlican, ends on the south side of the community of New Perlican. Follow the road through New Perlican to find a sign to show where the trail continues. The trail follows the headland to Turk's Cove. At Turk's Cove, walk along the road again before rejoining the trail to Winterton.

Although the d'Iberville Trail occasionally travels inland, it does offer some coastal views. The lookout above Winterton is the highest point and, from it on fine days, you can see across Trinity Bay. The final section of the d'Iberville Trail begins in Hant's Harbour and ends in the charming community of New Chelsea. This segment takes only an hour to walk but it climbs to 80 metres before descending into New Chelsea.

Even though the trail is segmented by Route 80, it is not difficult to locate; signs give clear directions to the trailheads and parking areas.

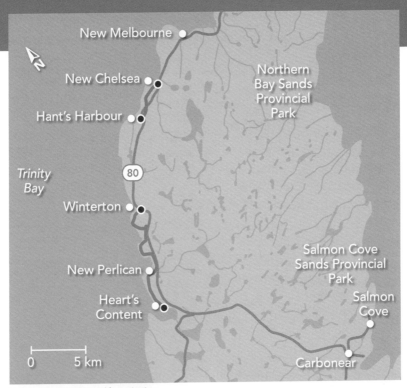

New Melbourne

New Chelsea

Hant's Harbour

Trinity
Bay

(80)

Winterton

New Perlican

Heart's
Content

Northern
Bay Sands
Provincial
Park

Salmon Cove
Sands Provincial
Park

Salmon
Cove

Carbonear

0   5 km

Trail maps are **not to be used for navigation.**

Distance: 20-kilometre linear trail.

Trailheads: Heart's Content Lighthouse (47.543175, -53.213002);
Winterton (47.571616, -53.195041);
Hant's Harbour (48.005097,
53.153002); New Chelsea
(48.013916, -53.131324).

Highlights: Ocean views.

Elev. range: 0–100 metres.

Grates Cove

Grates Cove, a community of about 200 people located at the northern tip of the Avalon Peninsula, has been inhabited by Europeans since the 17th century. Nearby Bay de Verde and Bacca-lieu Island, with its huge colony of seabirds, are two other places of interest in the area.

The Grates Cove area is devoid of trees but rich in rock, and residents put the available resources to good use. Grates Cove was designated as a National Historic Site in 1995 for its network of rock walls that enclose some 150 acres of land once used for grazing cattle, growing hay, and vegetable gardening.

Grates Cove boasts two short trails worth exploring. **Rock Walls Trail** begins on Back Road by the National Historic Site Memorial. This 2-kilometre loop trail is marked by blue arrows painted on stone, which unfortunately over time are becoming quite faded. The trail proceeds toward the coast past kilometres of stone walls and enclosures; the toil required to construct these walls

 Look for the three types of rock walls: *Thrown walls* are made of rocks cleared from fields and deposited in a row. *Piled walls* are made of some interlocking stone. *Stacked walls*, the most carefully constructed, reached heights of 1.5 metres.

Distance: See trail descriptions.

Trailheads: Rock Walls Trail: Back Road (48.095900, -52.561900); Lookout Trail: Big Hill Road (48.093786, -52.564042).

Highlights: Rock walls, panoramic views, wildflowers.

Elev. range: Rock Walls Trail: minimal change; Lookout Trail, 79–115 metres.

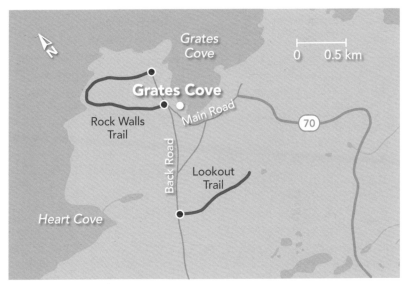

Trail maps are not to be used for navigation.

is awe-inspiring. The trail loops back to end on Main Road several hundred metres from the starting point.

Lookout Trail begins on Big Hill Road and climbs 1 kilometre to a high bluff overlooking the town. The trail consists of a boardwalk that meanders its way to the top. It is a steady climb and caution should be taken on days with high winds. The effort is rewarded by a stunning view of Conception Bay, Grates Cove, and the fields and gardens delineated by the rock walls below.

Blackhead

On the west side of Conception Bay, the small community of Black-head marks the start of a gentle hike that terminates about 7 kilometres to the north in Western Bay. Despite a lack of signs, the path is easy to follow as a well-used track parallels the coastline at least as far as Bradley's Cove.

Turn off Route 70 onto Gander Road in Blackhead. The hike begins where the cart track cuts through woods and blueberry

> Wild berries are a common sight on many of the hiking trails in Newfoundland. The colourful northern wild raisin found here is edible but not as popular or tasty as the blueberry or partridgeberry.

patches toward the shoreline. Follow the track as it passes a tiny overgrown graveyard; then the trees and bushes give way to a rugged coastline on the right and open meadows on the left.

The track brings you into the little settlement of Adam's Cove. Skirt to the left of the last house and keep heading north. Until Adam's Cove, the track is nearly level but high bare hills in the distance indicate some climbing lies ahead. At the top of the first hill enjoy the view. On clear days you can see across Conception Bay.

Below the hill is a large grassy valley. Bradley's Cove was once a thriving community but all that remains, except for a small flock of sheep, is a root cellar. The cellar, built by expert stonemasons, looks like a turf-covered igloo. The entrance to the cellar is accessible, but enter at your own risk. A small rocky beach nearby is an excellent place to stop and have lunch.

From Bradley's Cove, you have two options: stick with the cart track for the shortcut into West-

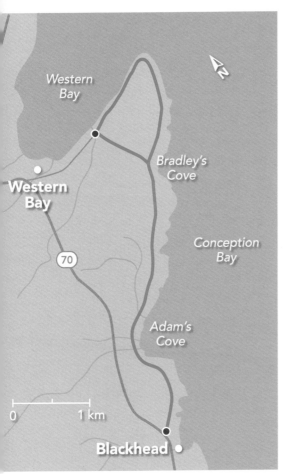

Trail maps are not to be used for navigation.

ern Bay, or keep to the right and continue out to the point, where there is an automated light in place of a lighthouse. This is a good place for whale and seabird spotting—we have seen gannets plunging from great heights into the sea. A well-used path leads to a parking area at the end of River Road in Western Bay.

Distance:
5- or 7-kilometre linear trail.

Trailheads: Gander Road, Blackhead (47.510523, -53.053527); River Road, Western Bay (47.530133, -53.041344).

Highlights: Ocean views, root cellar.

Elev. range: Minimal change.

Bay Roberts

The trailhead for this walk is situated just off Water Street in Bay Roberts East. A large sign directs hikers to a parking area at the start of the trail.

This is an 8-kilometre loop trail that combines history, culture, and scenery. A well-developed path leads hikers past signs which identify families who once dried fish and tended gardens along this shore. Several retaining walls, foundations, and root cellars have been restored by the Heritage Society; these structures prove that the local residents were also skilled stonemasons.

The path briefly joins a narrow paved road and then veers off in the direction of French's Cove. French's Cove was settled in the 17th century and destroyed twice by French raiders, in 1696 and 1705. A large photograph mounted on an interpretive panel in French's Cove shows what the community looked like before resettlement.

The landscape becomes more dramatic as the trail leads toward Juggler's Cove, with deep coves and high craggy cliffs providing views across Conception Bay. At the end of the peninsula lie Mad Rocks, which, as the name implies, can turn the shoreline into a mad fury in heavy seas.

From this point you can follow the road back to the trailhead, or, in the vicinity of Mad Rocks Café, you can loop back across the peninsula to French's Cove and return to the trailhead along the path.

Mad Rocks

French's Cove

Spaniard's Bay

Port de Grave

70

Bay Roberts

Trail maps are **not to be used for navigation.**

Distance:
8-kilometre loop.

Trailhead: Water Street,
Bay Roberts East
(47.361598, -53.135439).

Highlights: Root cellars,
stone walls, seascapes.

Elev. range:
3–45 metres.

Brigus

The lighthouse at Northern Head, the destination of this trail, seems deceptively close as you start the hike. The terrain and meandering nature of the trail makes this a bigger challenge than meets the eye.

The trailhead for this 5-kilometre hike is on Battery Road on the north side of Brigus. The hike gets under way with a fairly steep climb to the top of the ridge. Take a brief rest at the top and enjoy the view back to the historic town of Brigus. The town is renowned for its architecture, rock walls, and the annual Blueberry Festival that attracts thousands of people each August.

From the ridge, the trail descends into a valley and Brigus is lost to view. The path is not flagged, but

keep in mind that the destination is the lighthouse and, if you are in doubt, stick to the high ground and keep the ocean on your right. Finding the way is not difficult.

Allow about one and a half hours to reach the automated lighthouse. Don't be surprised if you see a small herd of goats browsing in the area. Enjoy the views from this headland before making the return journey.

⭐ Near the trailhead is Kent Cottage, a house that was occupied during the early years of World War I by American artist Rockwell Kent. He was expelled from Newfoundland on suspicion of being a German spy, although it was later recognized that the charges were bogus. Kent paid a return visit to Newfoundland at the invitation of Premier Joseph Smallwood in 1968.

Distance: 2.5-kilometre linear trail (5-kilometre return).

Trailhead: Battery Road, Brigus (47.322572, -53.122413).

Highlights: Dramatic terrain, lighthouse.

Elev. range: 12–102 metres.

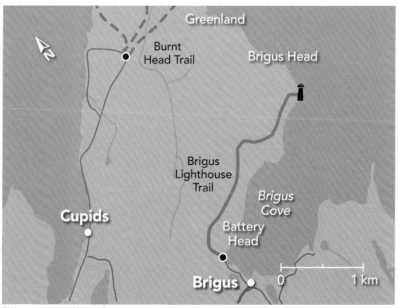

Greenland

Burnt
Head Trail

Brigus Head

Brigus
Lighthouse
Trail

Brigus
Cove

Cupids

Battery
Head

Brigus

0   1 km

Trail maps are **not to be used for navigation.**

Cupids

This trail network explores the Burnt Head-Greenland area near Cupids, Conception Bay. Cupid's Haven B&B and Tea Room at the end of Bishop's Lane is the starting point for this hike, which leads to the northeast through woods before emerging onto an open headland with meadows and beaches.

At the first fork in the trail, veer to the right in the direction of Greenland. The trail passes through a cozy sheltered picnic area and over a stream on the way to Morgan's Cove then to a viewing platform at Noder Cove. The sloping rock formations on the beach below are impressive. The trail proceeds up Windy Hill, arriving at The Arch. Take care around the edges of the cliff while taking photographs.

> Distance:
> 5-kilometre trail network.
>
> Trailhead: Cupid's Haven B&B (47.335025, -53.115546).
>
> Highlights: Sea arch (47.341905, -53.11315).
>
> Elev. range: 0–60 metres.

The trail continues up the hill to Deep Gulch and then returns to the starting point at the St. Augustine Anglican Cemetery directly across from the B&B.

 Cupids was founded by John Guy in 1610, making it the second oldest English colony in North America after Jamestown, Virginia. Originally called Cuper's Cove, the colony was abandoned in 1700. Since the 1990s, archaeologists have uncovered thousands of artifacts and several building foundations. Many of these discoveries are on display at the Cupids Legacy Centre, which opened in 2010.

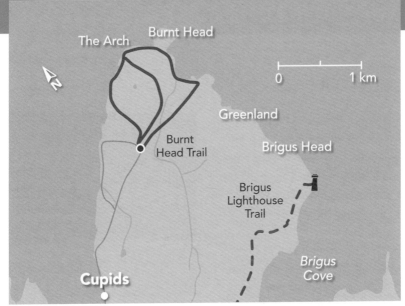

The Arch

Burnt Head

The Arch

Greenland

Burnt Head Trail

Brigus Head

Brigus Lighthouse Trail

Brigus Cove

Cupids

0   1 km

Trail maps are **not to be used for navigation.**

Butter Pot Provincial Park

Butter Pot Provincial Park, 35 kilometres southwest of St. John's along the Trans-Canada Highway, has a number of walking trails, the most notable of which is the hike to the top of Butter Pot Hill.

 A **butter pot** describes a bare rounded hilltop, sometimes referred to as a tolt. This feature also exists in Renews and Northern Bay on the Avalon Peninsula, among other locations.

From the trailhead sign at camp-site 67, follow the trail as it winds through boreal forest and past Pegwood Pond on its way to the base of the hill that gives this park its name. Watch for moose, birds, and signs of beaver activity along the way.

The summit of Butter Pot Hill is 300 metres above sea level. From it, the hiker has a bird's-eye view of the park and surrounding country-side.

The rounded pre-Cambrian rock that forms this hill is 600 million years old. Look for glacial erratics scattered over the bare hillside. This is a one-way path, so, after absorbing the view, enjoy the trail from the reverse angle on the way back.

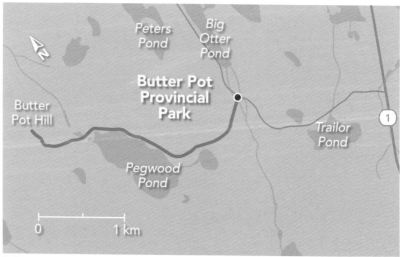

Trail maps are **not to be used for navigation.**

Distance: 3.3-kilometre linear trail (6.6-kilometre return).

Trailhead: Butter Pot Provincial Park, campsite 67 (47.233993, -53.034528).

Highlights: Mountaintop view, woodland path.

Elev. range: 155–300 metres.

Bell Island

The Gregory Normore Walking Trail, named for the first settler on Bell Island (1740), circumnavigates most of Bell Island. It is 24 kilometres in total but can be walked in shorter segments.

The obvious place to start is from Beach Hill, the first hill you meet after leaving the ferry dock. You'll find this trailhead on your right side, partway up the hill. Parking is available at the viewing platform on the left side of the road.

Follow an ATV track up the hill until you arrive at an old graveyard that contains the headstone of Gregory Normore. At this point, the ATV track veers to the left but **hikers should keep right**, closer to the coast, and follow the trail through the trees.

Once you have passed through the small forest, you'll catch a spectacular view across the tickle to Portugal Cove and Bauline. The cliffs on this side of the island are high and steep and offer the opportunity to photograph the geology of the island. As the trees thin, the path enters the open meadowland that characterizes much of this trail as it continues on north and westward around the island.

Distance: 24-kilometre linear trail (Beach Hill to lighthouse: 5-kilometre linear trail).

Trailhead: Beach Hill (47.375276, -52.552537); Belle Road (47.355798, -53.004263).

Highlights: Steep cliffs, views of Conception Bay, The Bell.

Elev. range: 23–102 metres.

The lighthouse and the Keeper's Café are approximately 5 kilometres from the trailhead and make a fitting place to stop if you are looking for a shorter hike. Beyond the lighthouse look for places named Freshwater Cove, #2 Cove, Grebe's Nest, Ochre Pit Cove, and The Bell. From Belle Road to Lance Cove there is no trail. The path resumes just to the east of Lance Cove Beach and continues on to the trailhead at Beach Hill.

This path is rated difficult, due to its length only.

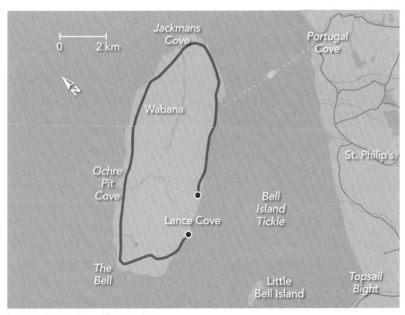

Trail maps are **not to be used for navigation.**

Manuels

A 500-million-year-old trail is something to boast about and the Interpretation Centre in Manuels does an impressive job explaining the history and geology of this very special formation.

Volcanic activity and glaciation over millions of years have created this river valley and the several trails along its banks give hikers ample opportunity to enjoy the beauty and wonder of it.

The Canyon Trail (east and west) follows the river upstream from the Interpretation Centre, and the Ocean Trail (east and west) goes downstream. The signage and infra-structure are first class.

Distance: 5-kilometre trail network.

Trailhead: Route 60 Manuels (47.520, -52.9402).

Highlights: River gorge, fossils.

Elev. range: 0–40 metres.

 Fossils are the petrified remains of extinct animals or plants. The fossils found here are called trilobites, a type of crustacean.

Trail maps are **not to be used for navigation.**

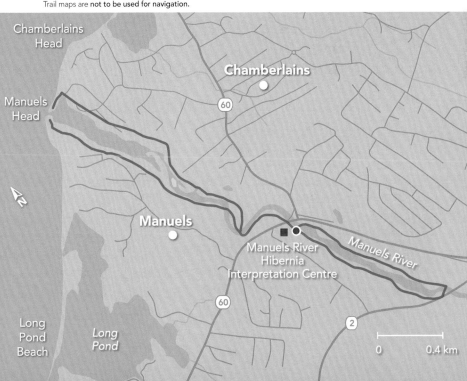

Chamberlains Head

Chamberlains

Manuels Head

60

N

Manuels

Manuels River Hibernia Interpretation Centre

Manuels River

Long Pond Beach

Long Pond

60

2

0   0.4 km

St. John's

The trails of Signal Hill are part of the Grand Concourse system of trails around the city of St. John's. Trails on and around Signal Hill can be hiked separately or linked for a more challenging 5-kilometre hike. The loop trail described here is rated "moderate," although it does include a significant climb.

 Cabot Tower was constructed atop Signal Hill in 1897 to celebrate Queen Victoria's Diamond Jubilee. That year also marked the 400th anniversary of Cabot's landfall in North America. Signal Hill is the site of the reception of the first transatlantic wireless signal by Gugliemo Marconi in 1901.

This trail is especially interesting for its geology. The Johnson Geo Centre on Signal Hill Road is a must-see either before or after the hike if you are interested in learning about the geological history of the area.

The Cuckold Cove Trail (also called the Burma Trail) begins at Georges Pond just above the Geo Centre. Park by Deadmans Pond, which is directly across the road from the Geo Centre. The trail passes by Georges Pond on the way to the Cuckold Cove Lookout just above Quidi Vidi village.

After taking in the view at Cuckold Cove Lookout, hike back up the trail for 250 metres, then turn left

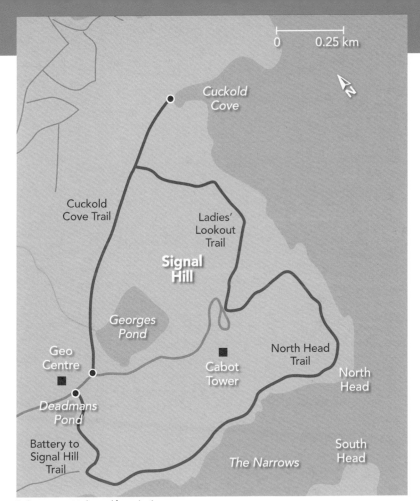

Trail maps are **not to be used for navigation.**

Distance: 5-kilometre loop.

Trailhead: Georges Pond, Signal Hill Road (47.341916, -52.411553).

Highlights: Panoramic vistas, geological features, view of St. John's Harbour.

Elev. range: 12–140 metres.

 Glacial erratics are debris transported by moving glaciers which, once the ice begins to melt, are deposited in no particular pattern in the landscape. These rocks vary in size; some on this trail are the size of a small car.

The North Head Trail, the next part of this loop, commences from the parking lot with a long stairway leading down into Ross's Valley, a glacial hanging valley created as the land rebounded (isostatic rebound) in the wake of a retreating ice cap some 10,000 years ago. Another obvious sign of glacial activity along this trail is the large glacial erratics or boulders. Less obvious to the eye but no less interesting are the stria or scratches on some of the massive flat stone surfaces on or beside the trail. These were created by

onto Ladies' Lookout Trail. A steep climb to the top on a series of wooden steps provides stunning views of St. John's to the west and the Atlantic Ocean to the east. Continue along the well-trodden trail to the Cabot Tower parking lot.

forward-moving glaciers pushing sharp debris and making gouges in the rock below the ice. The ice was up to 3 kilometres thick during the last ice age in this area of the province. The direction of ice movement can be determined by these scratches. This trail passes along the north shore of St. John's Harbour, eventually arriving at the Lower Battery.

Follow the road and turn right onto Hipditch Hill. On the left look for a staircase that goes up between two houses. Follow this trail

to Deadmans Pond and the parking lot. More information about the Signal Hill trails is available at the Parks Canada Interpretation Centre on Signal Hill.

St. Mary's

This route along the eastern shore of St. Mary's Bay, part ATV track and part traditional footpath, is used primarily by berry pickers. Although it is not a developed trail, and there are no signs, the trail is not difficult to locate or follow.

You can park near the community wharf in Gaskiers and at the trailhead in St. Mary's; or, if you prefer a shorter hike, park at the beach in Gulch.

In St. Mary's, turn off Route 90 onto Dillon's Lane and then take Battery Road a short distance to the trailhead at the Battery. Join the Back Road and follow it in a southeasterly direction until you reach a narrow footpath veering off to the right.

The footpath hugs the rugged shoreline, passing over blueberry barrens and country rich in wildflowers and grasses. It is easy walking, with little change in elevation. The depth of the peat just below the surface becomes evident as the path nears the automated light near Gulch. A picnic table near the light is a good place to stop for lunch if you have timed your arrival right.

Continue south over the meadow to the kilometre-long stony beach that separates Point La Haye Pond from the ocean. Crossing the beach is quite a slog and can be avoided by leaving a car at Gulch rather than Gaskiers. Otherwise, cross the beach, which forms a large freshwater barachois to the northeast, and follow the road through Point La Haye and Gaskiers to the community wharf.

Distance: 8-kilometre linear trail.

Trailhead: The Battery, St. Mary's (46.551855, -53.345341); community wharf in Gaskiers (46.574444, -53.364603).

Highlights: Coastline, barachois, beaches, barrens.

Elev. range: 5–35 metres.

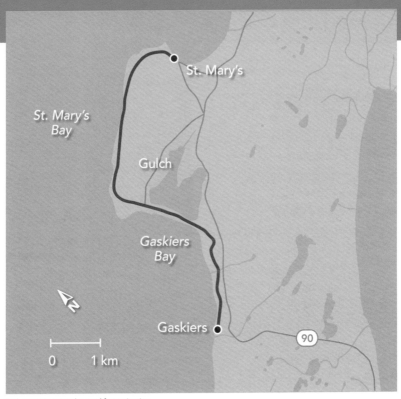

St. Mary's

St. Mary's
Bay

Gulch

Gaskiers
Bay

Gaskiers

90

0   1 km

Trail maps are not to be used for navigation.

Cape St. Mary's

The walk to Bird Rock at Cape St. Mary's is a short stroll rather than a hike, but the destination is so iconic it is impossible to ignore. Anyone who has visited this site can't help but be awed by the immense open headland at the Cape … and then there are the birds.

The Cape St. Mary's Ecological Reserve is home to common murres, black-legged kittiwakes, razorbills, and 24,000 northern gannets. The northern gannets, graceful seabirds with a wingspan of 2 metres, hatch their young on a 100-metre-high sea stack a few metres from the cliff edge. Bird Rock is the third largest, and the most accessible, nesting site for northern gannets in North America. It is endlessly fascinating to watch the birds swoop and soar as they dive for fish to feed their young.

Spring and early summer is the best time to observe the hatchlings, but foggy conditions are common at those times of the year. Late summer and early autumn usually bring warmer weather and clear skies.

Visit the interesting displays at the Interpretation Centre. The Centre also hosts a summer concert series that features traditional storytellers and musicians. Accommodations are available in nearby St. Brides.

Gannets occupy the same nest year after year. In late spring, the female lays a single egg which both parents take turns incubating until it hatches in early July. The young chick is fully feathered by September and, soon afterwards, makes its first awkward attempts at flight. Then it is on its own and must learn how to feed itself once its body fat has been used up.

Distance: 1-kilometre linear trail (2-kilometre return).

Trailhead: Cape St. Mary's Interpretation Centre (46.492310, -54.113192).

Highlights: Cliffs, headland, birds.

Elev. range: Minimal.

Trail maps are **not to be used for navigation.**

THE EAST COAST TRAIL

To many, hiking in Newfoundland means hiking the East
Coast Trail. This series of coastal paths stretching from
Topsail Beach north to Cape St. Francis and then down the
east coast of the Avalon Peninsula to St. John's and south
to Cappahayden constitute a remarkable hiking experience.

As of 2020, over 330 kilometres of trail have been developed. The trail
links many communities, providing an accessible wilderness experience
for the hiker.

Trail infrastructure has been built with an eye to interfering as little as
possible with the natural environment. Numerous bridges have been
built to facilitate stream crossings, including the impressive suspension
bridge at La Manche.

But it is the coastal scenery, not the infrastructure, that makes this trail outstanding. Path lengths vary as does the degree of difficulty, but the one constant is the trail's proximity to the ocean and the coastline, beaches, coves, and cliffs.

The ECTA was founded in 1994 with the goal of developing a coastal trail for the use of residents and visitors. It has created access to some of the most beautiful coastline anywhere in the world. To walk the East Coast Trail is to be immersed in not only the geography but also the culture and history of the east coast of this province.

New members are invited to join this volunteer-run association. More information about the trail is available at www.eastcoasttrail.ca.

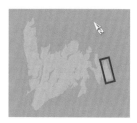

The East Coast Trail

Topsail–Portugal Cove-St. Philip's

This 17.2-kilometre path may seem daunting, but with several access points it can be walked as two or even three separate hikes.

Starting at the Topsail Beach trailhead the forested path parallels the shoreline before it turns inland and eventually joins Laurie Road. After 2 kilometres of road walking, most of it on the busy St. Thomas Line, turn left on Wards Lane and reconnect with the path which leads to Thorburn Road and St. Philip's Beach.

Distance: 17.2-kilometre linear trail.

Trailhead: Topsail Beach, Conception Bay South (47.5446, -52.9175); Thorpes Road, St. Philip's Beach; behind the Portugal Cove post office (47.6294, −52.868).

Highlights: Beaches, forest, hilltop views.

Trail maps are **not to be used for navigation.**

At the end of Thorpe's Road you rejoin the path, following the coastline for 4 kilometres to Beachy Cove. Turn left onto Beachy Cove Road and then right onto Long-marsh Road. The path soon begins the climb to the 200-metre summit of Beachy Cove Hill high above Conception Bay.

The path drops down to Nearys Pond Road and then follows Prince's Ridge for 3 kilometres before descending to the Portugal Cove trailhead and a designated parking area.

Portugal Cove–Bauline

This path has been used for many years, but changes in 2015 have made it a much-improved trail. New trailheads have been established at both ends, and the northern half of the route has been redirected so that it continues along the top of Picco's Ridge.

In Portugal Cove, take Loop Drive opposite the United Church, and turn down Harding's Hill to North Point Road, which leads to the new trailhead. In Bauline, use the parking lot at the end of Brook Path, where signs direct you to the trailhead.

Starting on the Portugal Cove side, the path leaves the ferry terminal behind as it climbs fairly steeply up newly built stairs to the top of the ridge and soon passes the Blast Hole Ponds. A farther 3 kilometres to the north is Brocks Head Pond, which empties dramatically over the cliff into Conception Bay far below. To the west, rising out of the waters of the bay, is Bell Island.

At Ocean Pond, the path turns briefly westward and then continues to the north along the top of the ridge all the way to Bauline (those familiar with the previous route will remember the trail travelled inland after Ocean Pond).

This is rugged country and as of 2020 the path had not been "hardened." Although there is little infrastructure along the trail, it is well-marked and hikers should have no problem keeping on the correct route. Expect a wilderness experience with outstanding views both inland and seaward.

Distance: 14.5-kilometre linear trail.

Trailhead: North Point Road, Portugal Cove (47.374663, -52.512882); Brook Path, Bauline (47.431696, -52.495649).

Highlights: Ponds, rivers, views of the ocean and Bell Island.

Elev. range: 14–242 metres.

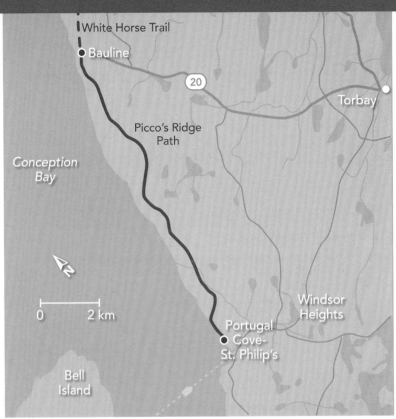

White Horse Trail

O Bauline

20

Torbay

Picco's Ridge
Path

Conception
Bay

N

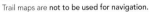

0   2 km

Windsor
Heights

Portugal
O Cove-
St. Philip's

Bell
Island

Trail maps are **not to be used for navigation.**

Bauline–Cape St. Francis

This trail incorporates the old Cripple Cove Path from Cape St. Francis and extends all the way to the town of Bauline on the eastern shore of Conception Bay. Nconditions, as well as a challenge: this trail features considerable elevation changes. A five-platform campsite (Patch Brook Campsite) is available.

Distance: 17.5-kilometre linear trail.

Trailhead: Cape St. Francis (47.48275, -52.47120); Bauline, Seaview Lane (47.43169, -52.49564).

Highlights: Rugged wilderness, ocean views, berries.

Elev. Range: 14–240 metres.

The trailhead in Bauline is at the end of Seaview Lane. Parking is available at Brook Path. On the northern end, the trailhead is near the automated light at Cape St. Francis—watch for the familiar East Coast Trail signs.

The trail from Cape St. Francis into Cripple Cove features steep climbs but the most challenging is yet to come. After Cripple Cove the path ascends to the top of the ridge 200 metres above sea level. Views along this rugged path are nothing short of spectacular.

At Little Herring Cove Pond (47.44274, -52.49153), an access path leads to Marine Park on Pouch Cove Line. This access path is in very rough condition. The main path continues south toward Bauline.

Before the path descends to the southern trailhead, a popular side trail goes to the peak of Big Hill, which towers 260 metres above the town and bay.

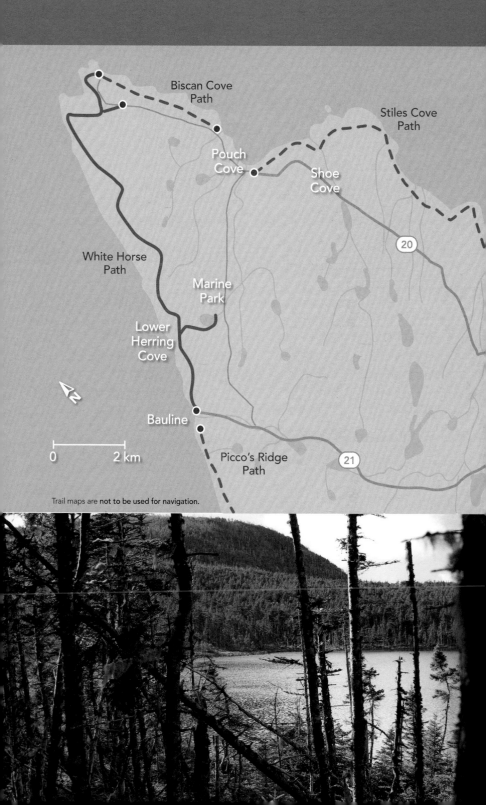

Biscan Cove
Path

Stiles Cove
Path

Pouch
Cove

Shoe
Cove

White Horse
Path

20

Marine
Park

Lower
Herring
Cove

N

0   2 km

Bauline

Picco's Ridge
Path

21

Trail maps are **not** to be used for navigation.

Cape St. Francis–Pouch Cove

Most sections of the East Coast Trail are linear trails, but loop hikes can sometimes be made by following a road back to the starting point. This is such a trail. The return road is a rough gravel road; if you choose to have a vehicle waiting at the northern end of the trail, make sure it has good clearance.

The southern trailhead is at the end of the pavement in Pouch Cove by the sign that commemorates the event of the sinking of the *Waterwitch*. Parking for hikers' vehicles is available at the ballpark about 250 metres south of the Waterwitch trailhead.

This is a fairly hilly hike with several small brooks and streams to cross. The first part of the trail leads hikers through the woods, emerging after five minutes near Horrid Gulch. It then winds to the top of Big Bald Head, which provides a view of Pouch Cove and the coastline to the south. Black and white wooden posts mark the trail on the exposed rocky outcrops.

A side path at Freshwater leads to the shoreline and a 3-metre waterfall, an ideal place to stop. The trail climbs once more to a high ridge before descending and coming out to the gravel road just south of Cape St. Francis lighthouse.

 In 1875 the schooner *Waterwitch* was heading to her home port in Cupids when she ran aground in Horrid Gulch at Pouch Cove. Men from the community responded and lowered Alfred Moores over the cliff with a "hempen rope." A letter written by Reverend Reginald Johnson of Pouch Cove to *The Times* explained that "there were twenty-five souls on board out of which [they] saved only thirteen." For his heroic efforts, Moores was awarded a medal by the Humane Society of Liverpool.

Distance: 7.3-kilometre linear trail (plus 4 kilometres on the road to complete the loop).

Trailheads: Pouch Cove (47.463184, -52.455216); Cape St. Francis (47.475704, -52.472425).

Highlights: View from Big Bald Head, Freshwater.

Elev. range: 20–123 metres.

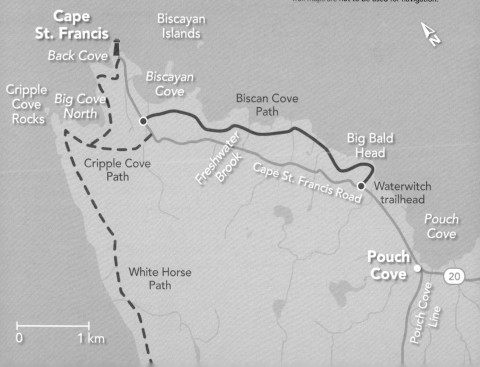

Trail maps are **not** to be used for navigation.

Cape St. Francis

Biscayan Islands

Back Cove

Biscayan Cove

Cripple Cove Rocks

Big Cove North

Biscan Cove Path

Cripple Cove Path

Freshwater Brook

Cape St. Francis Road

Big Bald Head

Waterwitch trailhead

Pouch Cove

White Horse Path

Pouch Cove

20

Pouch Cove Line

0   1 km

Pouch Cove–Flatrock

If you're looking for a 15-kilometre day hike, Stiles Cove Path from Flatrock to Pouch Cove is as good as it gets. Rivers, waterfalls, bridges, coves, and cliffs—this trail has it all.

 At Stiles Cove you will see a sobering reminder that it is dangerous to hike by the ocean. A cross and plaque memorialize a young couple who were swept off the rocks by a wave in 1993.

In Flatrock the path begins at the end of Hickey's Lane with parking at St. Michael's Church. The trail crosses over the dramatic Big River by way of a beautiful arched bridge. Steps have been cut in the stone by the trail builders for easier footholds. The trail continues through boreal forest, climbing gradually toward the top of the massive red sandstone cliff of Red Head.

From Red Head, follow the trail markers 4 kilometres north to Stiles Cove. Here Half Moon Brook tumbles over the cliff to a rocky beach below. Walk to the lookout point on the other side of the little bay and note how the water from the Half Moon Brook disappears into the beach rocks below rather than making a path to the ocean. Continuing north, the meadow at Small Point is an ideal spot to stop for lunch; it is approximately halfway to Pouch Cove.

Leaving Small Point, the trail eventually reaches its highest elevation of just over 100 metres before descending to sea level at Shoe Cove, where a bridge crosses Shoe Cove Brook. On the beach a rocky bar attempts to block the river on its unstoppable journey to the sea.

Several kilometres to the north, the trail leaves the woods, passes along the shoreline, and finally arrives at Pouch Cove post office and the northern trailhead.

This trail can be done in short segments as there are access trails to the main path at Shoe Cove, Satellite Road, and Red Head.

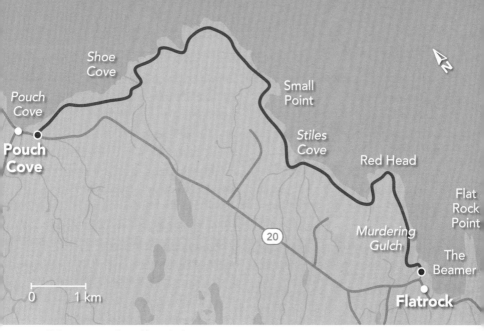

Shoe Cove

Pouch Cove

Pouch Cove

Small Point

Stiles Cove

Red Head

Flat Rock Point

Murdering Gulch

The Beamer

Flatrock

20

0   1 km

Trail maps are **not** to be used for navigation.

Distance: 15-kilometre linear trail.

Trailheads: Pouch Cove (park at St. Agnes' Church, 47.455170, -52.455377); Flatrock (park at St. Michael's Church, 47.422609, -52.422890).

Highlights: Big River, Stiles Cove, Small Point, Shoe Cove.

Elev. range: 0–103 metres.

Flatrock–Torbay

This historic trail links the towns of Torbay and Flatrock. Father Troy's Trail begins at the end of Spray Lane. After crossing the beach, you will climb to the hillside meadows on the north side of the harbour.

The trail passes through Tapper's Cove and then begins a gradual ascent and soon enters thick woods. Church Cove is one of the highlights of this path … literally. At 120 metres above sea level it provides a spectacular view of the cliff face, which is usually alive with shrieking gulls and kittiwakes.

From Church Cove, the trail follows along the top of the ridge for nearly 2 kilometres before descending to a sharp point of land that juts out into the Atlantic, known locally as the Beamer. The trail approaches the top of the Beamer, turns back, and ends at the parking area near the wharf and breakwater at Flatrock.

> **The trail is named for Father Edward Troy, who built the first Catholic church in Torbay in the early 1830s. He was banished to Merasheen Island for several years for offending church leaders and politicians, but returned to Torbay in 1848 and was the parish priest there until his death in 1872.**

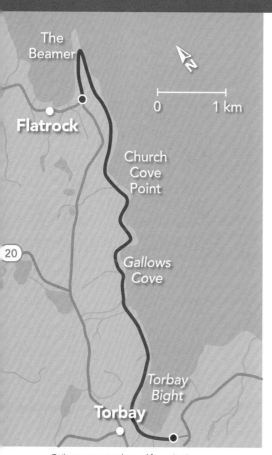

The Beamer

Flatrock

Church Cove Point

Gallows Cove

20

Torbay Bight

Torbay

Trail maps are **not to be used for navigation.**

Distance:
8.7-kilometre linear trail.

Trailhead: End of Spray Lane in Torbay (47.393309, -52.433443); breakwater in Flatrock (47.420230, -52.420818).

Highlights: Torbay, Church Cove, Beamer.

Elev. range: 2–120 metres.

Torbay–Middle Cove

This path begins on Motion Drive
in Torbay and soon leaves this
residential development behind in
favour of seashore and woodland.

A new footbridge (2020) makes for
an easy crossing of Motion River
(also called North Pond Brook).
Farther along the trail a concrete
ashram overlooks the mesmerizing
sea action of Motion.

The path crosses a meadow and
climbs into the woods eventually
arriving at the beach in Middle
Cove. This once marked the end of
the trail but proceeding up Kelly's
Hill on Marine Drive there is a footpath that skirts the edge of Stack's
Point providing wonderful views of
Middle Cove and Outer Cove.

"Motion" is commonly used in
association with Newfoundland
coastal waters. The *Dictionary of
Newfoundland English* defines it as
"a stretch of water, the turbulent
movement of which is caused by the
meeting of heavy cross-currents."

Distance: 3.8-kilometre
linear trail.

Trailheads: Motion Drive, Torbay
(47.623, −52.663); Outer Cove
(47.653, −52.6576).

Highlights: Motion, Stack's Point.

Elev. Range: 10–50 metres.

Tor Bay

Ship Cove
Point

Sculpin
Point

Middle
Cove

Marine Drive

Outer
Cove

Motion River

Marine Drive

Middle
Cove

0   0.5 km

Trail maps are **not to be used for navigation.**

Outer Cove–Logy Bay

Although it is a short trail, this hike has everything you could possibly ask for, with dramatic cliffs, majestic views, and interesting geological and architectural features.

A 10-minute walk through woods opens onto a magnificent ocean vista. The side trail down to Klondyke Gulch is worth the effort, although be prepared for a significant climb next to the top of Torbay Southern Head.

From this 130-metre-high headland, the trail descends to Cobbler Brook and then climbs again to Red Cliff

 Many of the structures on Red Cliff were built in the early 1950s when the site became part of the Pinetree Line which extended across Canada. It was established during the height of the Cold War as part of a North American radar defence system. Nearly 250 people worked there before it was abandoned in 1961.

Head, with even more spectacular views. Abandoned concrete structures, many built in the 1950s as part of a Cold War radar defence system, pepper the landscape.

The path continues through trees near the cliff top, eventually coming to a junction with Red Cliff Road and the road out to the parking area. It is possible, however, to continue on for a farther 600 metres to a viewpoint overlooking Logy Bay.

Distance:
4.7-kilometre linear trail.

Trailheads: Dorans Lane, Outer Cove (47.656, -52.673); Red Cliff Road, Logy Bay (47.638, -52.666).

Highlights: Breathtaking coastal views.

Elev. Range: 3–150 metres.

Torbay Point

Klondyke Gulch

0   0.5 km

Torbay Southern Head

Redcliff Head

Cobbler Path

Outer Cove

Doran's Lane

Outer Cove

Marine Drive

Middle Cove

Red Cliff Road

Logy Bay

Trail maps are **not to be used for navigation.**

Logy Bay–St. John's

This linear path has designated parking near the Ocean Sciences Centre in Logy Bay and near two fluid storage tanks by the northern entrance to Quidi Vidi village.

Beginning in Quidi Vidi, the path provides various views of the village and the "gut," as the little harbour

 The dummy gun bunker on this path is typical of several that can be seen along the East Coast Trail. They were constructed during the war in response to the threat from German U-boats. The fake guns are long gone but the stone constructions, though in disrepair, are still visible.

Sugar-loaf: in designation of a prominent hill resembling in its shape a cone of refined sugar (*Dictionary of Newfoundland English*).

Distance:
9-kilometre linear trail.

Trailheads: Quidi Vidi (unpaved road near end of lake, 47.345890, -52.403829); Logy Bay (next to Ocean Sciences Centre, 47.372550, -52.394749).

Highlights: Quidi Vidi, Bawdens Highlands, Sugarloaf Head.

Elev. range: 0–140 metres.

is called. During the climb to the summit of Bawdens Highlands, hikers should watch for mountain bikers—mountain bike trails criss-cross the area. Signs denote which paths are specifically designated for each activity.

Take a breather at the top and enjoy the panoramic view. Two kilometres farther along the trail, you will descend to near sea level by the pumphouse at Pump House Road; walk up a gravel road for a short distance, and then enter the woods. After passing rock formations at the Skerries, you cross the substantial John Howards footbridge, skirt Robin Hood Bay landfill, and begin the long ascent to the top of Sugarloaf Head, with its panoramic ocean views. Watch for bald eagles and fox holes along the route.

Look for the old World War II dummy gun bunker that was meant to convince enemy U-boat captains that Newfoundland defences were more robust than they actually were.

Trail maps are **not to be used for navigation.**

Logy
Bay

0   0.5 km

Robin
Hood
Bay

Skerries

Bawdens
Highlands

St. John's

Quidi Vidi
Village

Cuckold
Head

St. John's–Blackhead

This path links the Fort Amherst lighthouse on the south side of St. John's Harbour at the Narrows with the tiny community of Blackhead situated just off Cape Spear Road.

Beginning near the Fort Amherst lighthouse, the path climbs steeply to a height of land level with Cabot Tower just across the Narrows of St. John's Harbour. The terrain atop the southside hills is surprisingly varied as picturesque ponds and sunken valleys alternate with bare hilltops and offer views of the Atlantic.

Follow the black and white trail markers across the top of the south-side hills for about 3 kilometres. Next, you'll make a steep descent along Ennis River to the shores of Freshwater Bay. The trail follows the rocky barrier that separates Freshwater Pond, a lagoon, from Freshwater Bay. Storms have displaced many of the stepping stones that once facilitated this crossing; use caution here. Some wading may be necessary on the far side.

Much of the path from the rocky barrier to Blackhead is wooded but follows the cliff edge. At Small Point

the path turns sharply south, offering views of the coastline before arriving at the village of Blackhead.

 A barachois is a fresh or salt water lagoon behind a barrier of rock or sand. The barricade of large boulders that separates the freshwater lagoon from the ocean here is littered with the remains of sunken ships.

Distance:
10.6-kilometre linear trail.

Trailheads: End of Southside Road, St. John's (47.33483, -52.405709); Blackhead (47.313394, -52.392604).

Highlights: Ocean views, barachois at Freshwater Bay.

Elev. range: 4–226 metres.

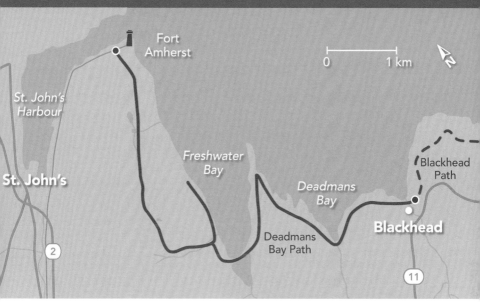

Trail maps are **not to be used for navigation.**

Blackhead–Maddox Cove

The settlement of Blackhead is the northern trailhead for this scenic 15-kilometre hike. The path traverses a 120-metre high ridge before descending into Cantwell's Cove on the way to Cape Spear lighthouse, where generations of Cantwells lived and tended the lighthouse.

When you reach Cape Spear, take some time to explore the authentic gun batteries that were built to defend the coastline. Extreme caution should be taken here, especially when high winds are blowing. Stay on the designated path.

From this easternmost point of North America, the path heads south along a high ridge toward a dramatic cove called The Basket. Here the path bends westward, and descends from a high ridge to a boardwalk that crosses a large boggy valley dotted, in season, with clusters of deep purple pitcher plants.

The terrain gradually shifts from open ground to a more thickly wooded topography before emerging in the community of Maddox Cove.

> ★ The pitcher plant is a carnivorous species. Its leaves are pitcher-shaped to hold water and enzymes which attract, and then digest, insects. The deep purple variety common to marshy areas has been adopted as Newfoundland and Labrador's provincial flower.

Cape Spear

Blackhead Path

Blackhead

(11)

Cape Spear Path

North Head

Maddox Cove

Motion Bay

Petty Harbour

|—————|—————|
0   1 km

Trail maps are **not to be used for navigation**.

Distance: 15.4-kilometre linear trail.

Trailheads: Blackhead (47.525,-52.654); Maddox Cove (47.472, -52.698).

Highlights: Cape Spear, sweeping coastal views.

Elev. range: 5–120 metres.

3

Petty Harbour–Goulds

This day-long hike begins with a 6-kilometre walk along Shoal Bay Road. The road is inland and uneven; we suggest starting the hike at the Shoal Bay trailhead and tackling it while your legs are fresh. It is also advisable to have a vehicle at both ends of the hike or at least transportation arranged before

Petty Harbour, a traditional fishing village, has also gained fame as a location site for several television series (including *Hatching, Matching, and Dispatching* and *Republic of Doyle*) and movies (including *Orca* and *Rare Birds*).

Distance:
20-kilometre linear trail
(includes Shoal Bay Road).

Trailheads: Shoal Bay Road, Goulds (47.26086, -52.45278); Petty Harbour (south side, 47.27483, -52.42166).

Highlights: Motion Head, glacial erratics, wildflowers.

Elev. range: 2–212 metres.

Campsite: Nipper's Cove.

you start. Park in Goulds at the end of Shoal Bay Road past the bus turnaround. In Petty Harbour, park at the town hall on the north side or by the Fisherman's Centre on the south side.

The Shoal Bay access road joins the East Coast Trail at Raymond Head. The path turns north and follows the coastline near sea level for about 3 kilometres before ascending to Burkes Head. A campsite, consisting of tent platforms and an open-air privy, is located nearby at Nipper's Cove.

Eventually the path descends to near sea level at Motion Head. The swirling waters offshore give the path its name. Inland is an impressive field of large glacial erratics.

The trail turns northwest and climbs some 150 metres to the top of Big Hill before descending to the picturesque village of Petty Harbour.

4

Goulds–Bay Bulls

 Spout Path, the longest segment of the East Coast Trail, requires a higher level of hiker fitness than most other sections. The hike is rated as strenuous, mainly due to its length (elevation gains are not substantial), but it is also one of the must-do hikes of the east coast of Newfoundland. It is not to be missed by anyone looking for spectacular ocean views and a challenging day on the trail.

It is best to begin this hike at Shoal Bay Road in Goulds. At Raymond Head, the path heads south and the Spout, for which this trail is named, is visible on a clear day from as far away as Long Point.

You are in for a few short climbs before the trail descends to the

 A spout may be created by a combination of wave action and freshwater streams running into gaps and holes in cliffs. They are found at several locations along the island's coastline. Heavy wave action can push water violently up these gaps or holes. The Spout along this trail can send a geyser 20 metres or more into the air in winter and summer.

Spout at about the halfway point of the hike. A nearby campsite at Little Bald Head has six tent platforms and an open-air privy.

After you pass through the campsite, there is still plenty to look forward to—sea stacks, an eagle's nest, and towering cliffs make this one of the most awe-inspiring hikes in the province. At the site of a resettled community at Freshwater, old house foundations are still visible and a waterfall follows long diagonal slabs of granite to the sea below.

The path turns west at North Head lighthouse, eventually arriving at Gunridge, where a gravel road brings you to the parking area in Bay Bulls.

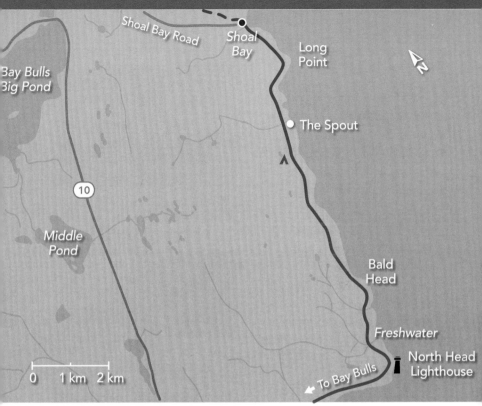

Shoal Bay Road

Shoal Bay

Long Point

Bay Bulls Big Pond

The Spout

10

Middle Pond

Bald Head

Freshwater

To Bay Bulls

North Head Lighthouse

0   1 km   2 km

Trail maps are **not** to be used for navigation.

Distance:
23-kilometre linear trail.

Trailheads: Shoal Bay Road, Goulds (47.26086, -52.45278); end of North Shore Road, Bay Bulls (47.18427, -52.46574).

Highlights: Water spout, sea stacks, lighthouse, whales.

Elev. range: 0–12 metres.

Campsite: Little Bald Head.

2 ## Bay Bulls–Witless Bay

If you are starting this hike from Bay Bulls, drive to the end of Quays Road on the south side of Bay Bulls Harbour. A narrow road leads to the path that winds through woods and meadows and along the shore.

Mickeleens Path is not a difficult hike, and it presents no great elevation changes. It is peaceful, scenic, and colourful, with a diversity of wildflowers throughout the spring and summer. Interesting place names along this path include Mutton Cove, Long Harry Cove, and Baboul Rocks.

Gull Island, which is in the Witless Bay Seabird Ecological Reserve, can be seen from Southern Head.

Whale- and bird-watching tour boats out of Bay Bulls are a frequent sight throughout the summer months. Continue along the shoreline to the trailhead at Bear Cove Road in Witless Bay.

 Icebergs are floating giants calved from glaciers in Greenland. The water contained in the ice can be thousands of years old. Companies in Newfoundland have capitalized on the purity of this water and produce popular bottled beverages such as water, beer, and vodka from it. In late spring icebergs drifting along the east coast are sometimes brought close to shore by wind and currents.

Distance:
7.3-kilometre linear trail.

Trailheads: Quays Road, Bay Bulls (47.18091, -52.48276); Bear Cove Road, Witless Bay (47.17067, -52.47537).

Highlights: Cliffs, coves, Gull Island.

Elev. range: 25–70 metres.

Spout
Path

**Bay
Bulls**

*Bay Bulls
Harbour*

Southern
Head

10

Bear Cove
Head

**Witless
Bay**

*Witless
Bay*

Gull
Island

0   1 km

Trail maps are **not to be used for navigation.**

⓵ Witless Bay–Mobile

Beginning in Witless Bay, this trail starts on Ragged Beach at the end of Gallows Cove Road. If you are walking north from Mobile, park at Mobile Central High School and cross Route 10 to the trailhead.

This path does not present any steep cliffs or demanding climbs. While pounding ocean waves can cause beach erosion—hikers should stay on the path for their own safety—this is an excellent walking trail year-round. We have been there on crisp clear winter days and the experience is exhilarating.

If you are travelling south from Ragged Beach, you can see Gull Island, a seabird ecological reserve. Farther along at Breaking Point

the path cuts through a tunnel of tuckamore, the stunted spruce trees characteristic of Newfoundland's windswept coastal headlands.

Several beaches are accessible from the path and are ideal places to stop and enjoy this beautiful coastline.

Tuckamore, also called tuckermore, tucken-more, or "tuck," are small stunted spruce and balsam fir trees frequently seen on exposed coastal areas in Newfoundland. In several places on the East Coast Trail, the path is a tunnel underneath a patch of tuckamore. In some places thick tuckamore makes the trail impenetrable to humans, but provides an ideal habitat for rabbits and birds.

Distance:
7-kilometre linear trail.

Trailheads: Ragged Beach, Witless Bay (47.154491, -52.484157); Mobile Beach, Mobile (47.145641, -52.503080).

Highlights: Seabirds, beaches.

Elev. range: Minimal change.

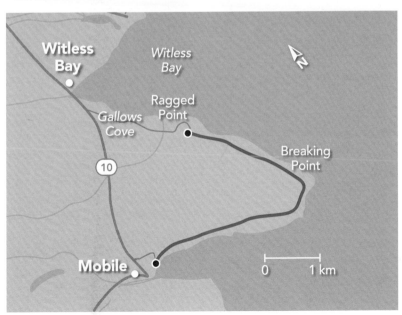

Trail maps are **not to be used for navigation.**

Mobile–Tors Cove

Only 5 kilometres long, this trail can easily be done as an out-and-back hike or combined with the Beaches Path Trail for a longer hike. Park at the end of Cod Seine Cove Road in Mobile or at Sacred Heart Church in Tors Cove.

This is a gentle low-lying path with little elevation change, which makes it ideal for children and first-time hikers. Stretches of trail pass through the woods, with occasional access to small rocky beaches. Tinkers Point, with its meadows and ocean views, is a perfect rest spot. "Tinker" is the local name for the razorbill, a seabird similar in size and colouring to the common murre.

 Although this path is named for the razorbill, hikers are more likely to see common murres or turrs, as they are often called. Large colonies exist on Baccalieu Island, Cape St. Mary's, and at the Witless Bay Seabird Reserve.

When you enter Tors Cove, you will pass an iconic image of Newfoundland, the Cribbies, a clapboarded saltbox house. Below the house lies a beautiful grassy headland and beach. Just offshore is a small island where grazing sheep can sometimes be seen.

The path leads uphill from the beach and goes directly to Sacred Heart Church and car park.

Distance:
5-kilometre linear trail.

Trailheads: Cod Seine Cove Road, Mobile (47.14249, -52.495809); Sacred Heart Church, Tors Cove (47.12525, -52.504408).

Highlights: Tinkers Point, Tors Cove Beach.

Elev. range: 0–28 metres.

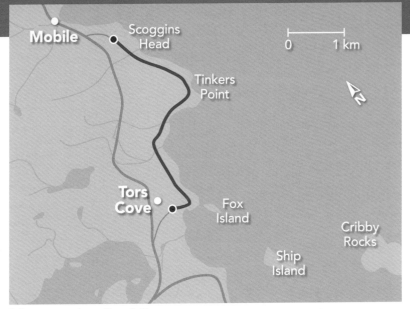

Mobile

Scoggins Head

Tinkers Point

Tors Cove

Fox Island

Cribby Rocks

Ship Island

0   1 km

Trail maps are **not to be used for navigation.**

⭐ The saltbox house is seen in many places in Newfoundland and is also popular on the eastern seaboard of the United States. It generally has a steep sloping roof, usually showing two floors from the front view then sloping sharply to show one storey at the back. It is so named because it mimics the shape of the boxes that were used to ship salt to the province. In modified saltbox-style houses, the roofline at the back half of the house has been given a more shallow pitch than the front, extending the house to provide more living space. The Cribbies displays this shallow pitch modification.

1 Bauline East–La Manche

Hikers may walk the 4-kilometre path from Bauline East into the former settlement of La Manche (French for "the sleeve"), explore the area, and return along the same path. However, from the parking area at the end of La Manche Road a 1-kilometre trail links to the old village site, so, with a vehicle parked at each end, a return trip can be avoided.

Park at the wharf in Bauline East. A gravel road brings you uphill to the start of the trail. Most of the trail is in woods but, like on many of the East Coast Trails, signposts indicate several points of interest just off the main trail. Depending on your mood, time constraints, and energy levels, you should take advantage of exploring as many of them as possible; that unusual ocean view, eagles nest, or waterfall view may just be an experience to remember. Doctors Cove on this trail is just such a place.

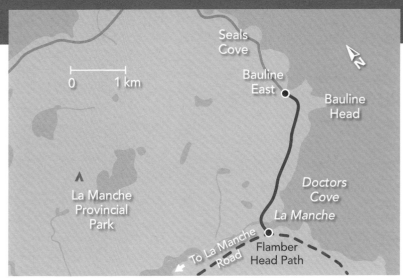

Trail maps are not to be used for navigation.

La Manche Village was nestled at the head of the narrow inlet surrounded by high hills. La Manche River flows in a torrent through a narrow gorge into the bay from Lower Pond. In 1961, the population was 25 people. A severe storm in 1966 destroyed all of the fishing stages, and the village was subsequently abandoned. Many house foundations are still visible.

Stone walls and the outlines of gardens can still be seen. Bridges over the river have been replaced at least four times. In 1999, the ECTA built an impressive 45-metre-long suspension bridge, held in place by thick steel cables bolted into solid rock.

Whales, seals, and even sea otters are occasionally seen in this peaceful cove.

Distance:
5-kilometre linear trail.

Trailheads: Bauline East wharf (47.104788, -52.503962); end of La Manche Road, off Route 10 (47.100215, -52.530564).

Highlights: Suspension bridge, old settlement, Doctors Cove.

Elev. Range: 2–64 metres.

Camping:
La Manche Provincial Park.

La Manche–Brigus South

This 12-kilometre path is more difficult than the East Coast Trail sections immediately to the north, but the extra effort is rewarded with exceptional views.

 The term *outport* comes from England and refers to a coastal settlement outside a large city like St. John's.

Cape Neddick, a high headland just off the main trail, is worth the climb. The same is true of Flamber Head, which rises to 60 metres. In between these two headlands are the rock formations at Gentleman's Head—squared chunks of rock resembling huge piles of dark chocolate, but more precisely eroded grey shale and sandstone of the St. John's Group. The nearby waterfall at the Quays is a popular place to take a lunch break or to cool your feet. This river flows eastward from Little Pond, which has several beaver lodges, so it is advisable not to drink the water before either filtering or boiling it. This is good advice to follow on any of the trails in the province.

A site to pitch tents is found at Roaring Cove, near the halfway point of the path. The nearby sea stacks and the grassy hillside leading up Flamber Head make for great photography. This was one of the major campsites for the ECTA building crews while constructing the trail to the north and south of Flamber Head.

Proceeding south from Roaring Cove the path is fairly wooded until it emerges at the picturesque outport of Brigus South.

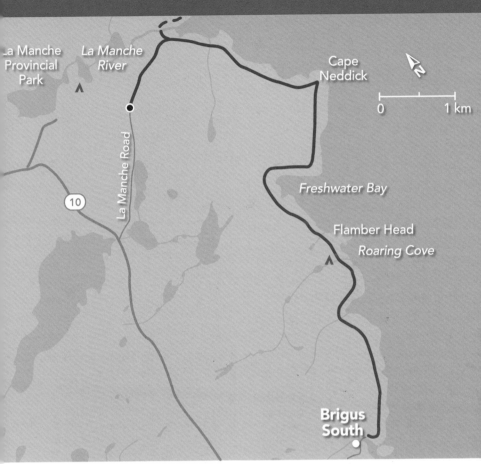

La Manche
Provincial
Park

La Manche
River

Cape
Neddick

La Manche Road

10

Freshwater Bay

Flamber Head
Roaring Cove

Brigus
South

0   1 km

Trail maps are **not to be used for navigation.**

Distance:
12-kilometre linear trail.

Trailheads: La Manche Village (park at end of La Manche Road, 47.100215, -52.530564); Brigus South (47.065207, -52.525719).

Highlights: Cape Neddick, Flamber Head, the Quays.

Elev. Range: 2–96 metres.

Camping: Roaring Cove.

Brigus South–Admiral's Cove

From Brigus South, the path climbs from near sea level to about 50 metres and more or less stays on this height of land until Tar Cove Point. Several side trails to viewpoints at Herring Cove Beach and Tar Cove Point are worth checking out.

Along with its curious name, Hares Ears Point offers an outstanding view. Cross Cove and Doctors Rock are two other viewpoints not to be missed. The path ends at Cranes Lane in Admiral's Cove.

This path can be hiked as a loop thanks to a cart track that was once part of the old Southern Shore Highway. This cart track is clearly marked on the ECTA map; it is easy to follow but not maintained and could be wet.

The parking areas are clearly marked in both communities.

Brigus South was originally called Brigus, but this name was changed in the 1920s to avoid confusing it with the town of the same name in Conception Bay.

Distance: 6.5-kilometre linear trail or 8-kilometre loop.

Trailheads: Brigus South, west side of harbour (47.06434, -52.53013); Admiral's Cove, Cranes Lane (47.060512, -52.534693).

Highlights:
Whales in summer, loop hike.

Elev. Range: 3–50 metres.

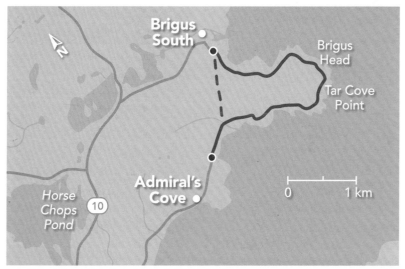

Trail maps are **not to be used for navigation.**

Cape Broyle–Calvert

This may be the most difficult section of the East Coast Trail. Even getting to the trailheads is a challenge. ECTA advises that only experienced hikers should attempt this trail and all hikers should bring survival tools and be aware that this hike could take an entire day.

At Cape Broyle, park on the un-paved portion of the Ultramar Gas Station parking lot. Walk to the end of the South Side Road to the cul de sac. Go down to the beach and walk east for several minutes. Follow black and white markers to the trail proper. This trail is mostly wooded until, at approximately 12 kilometres, at Church Cove

 The town of Calvert is named for George Calvert. The Colony of Avalon was established in his name in 1621, even though he did not visit the colony until 1627. He was subsequently granted land by Charles I of England in the Chesapeake Bay region, which became the Colony of Maryland, where he settled permanently with his family. The Colony of Avalon endured, however, and was one of the earliest permanent English settlements in North America.

Meadow it opens to an ocean view. At Cape Broyle Head the trail turns south toward Calvert.

To start at the southern trailhead, turn left off Route 10 at Power's Store in Calvert. Drive to the end of the pavement about 4 kilometres, then 1 kilometre on a dirt road to the trailhead sign. From the Calvert trailhead, the hike begins with a rigorous climb to the top of Cape Broyle Head, which provides views of the coastline and the Ferryland lighthouse. The path proceeds along the ridge to North Head and then turns west and follows the clifftops high above Cape Broyle Bay.

A side trail leads down to the sandy beach at Lance Cove. A little farther along the main trail is the Long Will campsite. It is about 7 kilometres from the campsite to the trailhead in Cape Broyle.

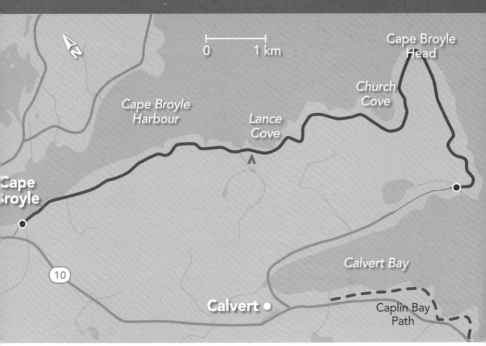

Cape Broyle Head

Church Cove

Cape Broyle Harbour

Lance Cove

Cape Broyle

10

Calvert Bay

Calvert

Caplin Bay Path

Trail maps are **not to be used for navigation.**

Distance: 18.5 kilometres.

Trailheads: South Side Road, Cape Broyle (47.051959, -52.564554); 1 kilometre past end of paved road, north side of Calvert (47.030208, -52.514872).

Highlights: View of Ferryland, Lance Cove beach.

Elev. range: 0–160 metres.

Campsite: Long Will Point.

Calvert–Ferryland

The north trailhead for Caplin Bay path is 1 kilometre south of Power's Store in Calvert. From the trailhead, the main path descends into the woods and soon comes to a side trail to a beach at Deep Cove. The main path continues past the Catholic cemetery and eventually arrives at Ferryland.

After the path crosses Route 10, it goes to the top of Fox Hill, from where there is a sweeping view of the harbour, islands, and the Ferryland lighthouse. The trail descends the hill past an old graveyard just above the Colony of Avalon Interpretation Centre.

 Archaeologists from Memorial University have been working at the Colony of Avalon dig site since the 1980s. Their discoveries reveal a complex and well-developed working colony with mansion house, forge, warehouses, dock, cobble roads, and gardens. Thousands of the recovered artifacts are beautifully displayed in the Interpretation Centre.

This short hike allows time for the hiker to visit the centre and the dig site. If you have time, walk out to the lighthouse. Gourmet picnic lunches are available at Lighthouse Picnics on Ferryland Head. It is usually necessary to book in advance.

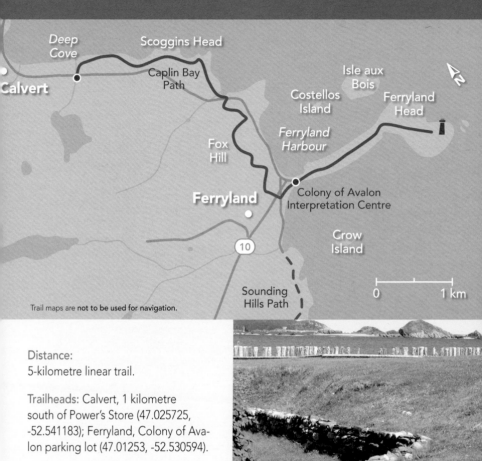

Trail maps are **not to be used for navigation.**

Distance:
5-kilometre linear trail.

Trailheads: Calvert, 1 kilometre
south of Power's Store (47.025725,
-52.541183); Ferryland, Colony of Avalon parking lot (47.01253, -52.530594).

Highlights:
Ferryland Head, Colony of Avalon,
lighthouse.

Elev. range: 15–101 metres.

Ferryland–Aquaforte

From the Colony of Avalon parking lot, head south on foot along a paved lane for about 1 kilometre. At the end of the pavement, the trail enters the woods and winds for 2 kilometres to the top of Sounding Hills. The summit offers views of Ferryland Head, Aquaforte Harbour, and Spurwink Island.

Farther along the trail is Stony River and then Spout River with its powerful current funnelling between large boulders on its way to the ocean.

Note: As of 2020, the Ferryland trailhead is closed. Hikers should check with the East Coast Trail Association (www.eastcoasttrail.com) for the latest information.

The path follows the bank of the river for about 500 metres before emerging at the Southern Shore Highway (Route 10). The designated parking area for this trailhead is just north of the bridge. If you continue to the Spurwink Island Path, you will have to walk on the road for approximately 3 kilometres. Care should be taken to face oncoming traffic until you meet the head of the next trail at the end of the pavement in the community of Aquaforte.

Distance: 6.5-kilometre linear trail (including paved lane in Ferryland).

Trailheads: Colony of Avalon parking lot, Ferryland (47.01253, -52.530594); Spout River Bridge, Route 10 (47.004433, -52.555936).

Highlights: View from Sounding Hills, Spout River.

Elev. range: 3–80 metres.

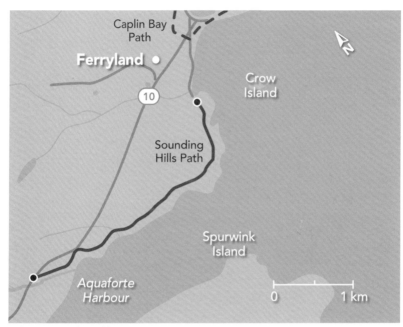

Caplin Bay
Path

Ferryland ●

10

Crow
Island

Sounding
Hills Path

Spurwink
Island

Aquaforte
Harbour

N

0   1 km

Trail maps are **not to be used for navigation.**

South West River–Port Kirwan

This is a path with three trailheads; it can be enjoyed as two separate hikes or in its entirety.

The first section, formerly the Mudder Wet Path, begins at the end of Riverhead Road in Aquaforte and welcomes hikers to spend a relaxing day walking and exploring the Little River estuary, canyon, and waterfall. A stairway leads down a steep bank to the river mouth and a side trail goes up river to the falls.

Atop the stairs the path goes up the east side of the river, offering views into the canyon below, and then loops back along the west side of the river. Approximately 2 kilometres in, the trail returns to the shoreline and an impressive view of Aquaforte Harbour. Turning right the path parallels the much larger Southwest River, arriving at Route 10 and a second parking area. The second, much longer section of this path begins here and tracks east along the south side of Aquaforte Harbour. At Big Gallows Cove, Spurwink Island comes into view. A campsite is nearby.

A little farther along is Berry Head, and the sea arch here is one of the most impressive sights on the entire East Coast Trail. A side trail will take you on top of the arch, but looking back from the main path offers the best view of this amazing formation.

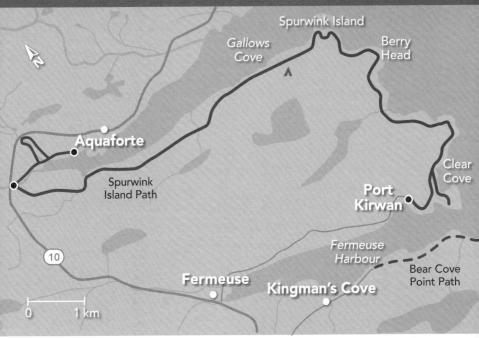

Trail maps are **not to be used for navigation**.

The path follows the coastline, passing through woods and over open headlands eventually arriving at the former settlement of Clear (Clear's) Cove. The final kilometre brings you to the third trailhead at Port Kirwin.

 A sea arch is created by erosion. Wave action, freeze-and-thaw cycles, and other forces of natural erosion can create bridges like the one at Berry Head. They are seen on many shorelines around the province and are always points of great interest.

Distance:
20.4-kilometre linear trail.

Trailheads: Riverhead Road, Aquaforte (47.0095, -52.966); Route 10, Southwest River; Port Kirwin (46.969, -52.909).

Highlights: River gorges, waterfall, sea arch.

Elev. Range: 5–75 metres.

Campsite: Gallows Cove.

Kingman's Cove–Renews

This path begins at the end of the pavement in Kingman's Cove on the south side of Fermeuse Harbour. At the beginning of the trail remains of the remains of the *Ilex*, sunk in 1948, are still visible offshore. One kilometre into the trail, a side trail leads to Trix's Cove, a blueberry picker's mecca. Remains of the former community are still visible.

Much of the path passes through woods until it reaches Bear Cove Point, where there is an automated light and foghorn. This is approximately the halfway point of this hike and a perfect spot for a boil-up. Five hundred metres farther is South Point, with a lookout where you can view the jagged sea stacks in Southern Cove.

Bear Cove Point Path stays close to the coastline as it proceeds south and finally turns west after passing Sculpin Bay and crossing a large meadow to the historic town of Renews.

> ★ Archaeologists have discovered building sites dating to the 17th century in Renews.
>
> The English and French fought over this area because of the valuable fishing grounds.

Distance: 11.5 kilometres.

Trailheads: End of the pavement, Kingman's Cove (46.575236, -52.554942); the Mount, Renews (park at church or museum, 46.551936, -52.55511).

Highlights: Bear Cove Point, South Point, Trix's Cove, town of Renews.

Elev. range: 11–56 metres.

Port Kirwan

Sleepers Point

Fermeuse Harbour

Fermeuse

Bear Cove Point

Kingman's Cove

Bear Cove Pond

South Point

10

Sculpin Point

0   1 km

Renews

Trail maps are **not to be used for navigation.**

Renews–Cappahayden

This trail, which begins at the end of the pavement on the south side of Renews Harbour, is fairly level for the first 2 kilometres, at which point it reaches Renews Head and a 50-metre climb. The path stays along this ridge for about 1 kilometre before descending to near sea level. Renews Island is about 2 kilometres south of Renews Head; a colony of cormorants nests on the island during the summer.

At Bear Cove, you will cross a bridge and then follow a dirt road for a short distance before taking a footpath back toward the beach. The path remains low and close to the coastline all the way to Cappahayden.

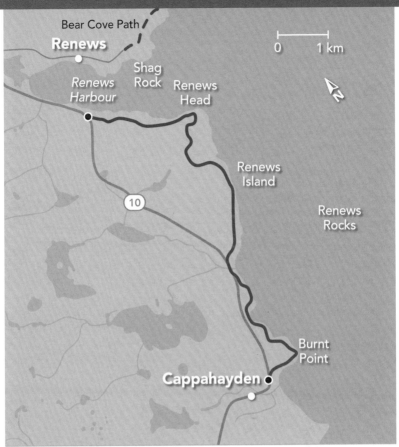

Bear Cove Path

Renews

Shag
Rock

*Renews
Harbour*

Renews
Head

Renews
Island

10

Renews
Rocks

Burnt
Point

Cappahayden

0   1 km

Trail maps are not to be used for navigation.

 Perhaps no part of the province celebrates its Irish heritage more than the area south of St. John's known as the Southern Shore. Irish immigration to Newfoundland peaked in the early 1800s, and many of the newcomers settled in the fishing communities strung along this section of the Avalon, which is part of the Irish Loop. It is still possible to meet people whose history here goes back generations yet their accents remain indistinguishable from their forebears in Waterford County.

Distance:
10-kilometre linear trail.

Trailheads: End of pavement, south side of Renews Harbour (46.545659, -52.561147); Lawlor's Road, Cappahayden (46.513846, -52.564196).

Highlights: Renews Island.

Elev. range: 3–76 metres.

Wildflowers of Newfoundland

Most of the flowers and shrubs included are found over the entire province.

Bering sea chickweed
Cerastium beeringianum
Flowers: May to September
Habitat: Gravel roadsides

Bird's-eye primrose
Primula laurentiana
Flowers: June to August
Habitat: Rocky areas, shorelines

Blue flag
Iris versicolor
Flowers: July
Habitat: Wetlands, bogs

Crackerberry (bunchberry)
Cornus canadensis
Flowers: White flower in July,
red clustered berries in September
Habitat: Forest trails

Creeping buttercup
Ranunculus repens
Flowers: May to August
Habitat: Wet areas, ditches

Fireweed
Epilobium angustifolium
Flowers: July to August
Habitat: Clearings, burned-over areas

Grass pink
Calopogon tuberosus
Flowers: July and August
Habitat: Boggy areas

Harebell
Campanula rotundifolia
Flowers: June to September
Habitat: Meadows, grassy areas

Labrador tea
Rhododendron groenlandicum
Flowers: July and August
Habitat: Bogs, fens, woodlands

Lupin
Lupines polyphyllus
Flowers: July
Habitat: Ditches, clearings, roadsides

Marsh marigold
Caltha palustris
Flowers: June
Habitat: Wet areas

Moss campion
Silene acaulis
Flowers: July
Habitat: Hilltops, coastal cliffs

Musk mallow
Malva moschata
Flowers: June to September
Habitat: Fields, roadsides

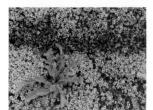

One-flowered wintergreen
Moneses uniflora
Flowers: July and August
Habitat: Forests, bogs

Orange hawkweed (devil's paintbrush)
Hieracium aurantiacum
Flowers: June to September
Habitat: Roadsides, fields

Oxeye daisy
Chrysanthemum leucanthemum
Flowers: June to August
Habitat: Roadsides, fields

Pearly everlasting
Anaphalis margaritacea
Flowers: July to September
Habitat: Gravel roadsides, pastures

Pink lady's-slipper
Cypripedium acaule
Flowers: May and June
Habitat: Wet areas, woods

Pitcher plant
Sarracenia purpurea
Flowers: May and June
Habitat: Sphagnum bogs

Roseroot
Sedum rosea
Flowers: June and July
Habitat: Rocky coastal areas

Rough-leaved aster
Aster radula
Flowers: July to September
Habitat: Wet woodlands, stream borders

Sheep laurel
Kalmia angustifolia
Flowers: Late June to July
Habitat: Various acidic habitats

Snowdrop
Galanthus nivalis
Flowers: April to May
Habitat: Wet woodlands

Starflower
Trientalis borealis
Flowers: May and June
Habitat: Woodlands, high slopes

Three-toothed cinquefoil
Potentilla tridentata
Flowers: June to August
Habitat: Acidic soil, rocky areas

Twinflower
Linnaea borealis
Flowers: June to August
Habitat: Coniferous forest, alpine barrens

Wild rose (wrinkled rose)
Rosa rugosa
Flowers: July to August
Habitat: Various habitats

Birds of Newfoundland

Newfoundland and Labrador is a magnet for birdwatchers, year-round. Here are 20 of the most common bird species seen along coastal Newfoundland—be sure to keep your eyes peeled as you hike! For additional species and detail, pick up *Birds of Newfoundland* (Boulder Books).

Herring Gull
Larus argentatus

Great Black-backed Gull
Larus marinus

Black-legged Kittiwake
Rissa tridactyla

Arctic Tern
Sterna Paradisaea

Common Tern
Sterna hirundo

Dovekie
Alle alle

Common Murre (Turr)
Uria aalge

Thick-billed Murre
Uria lomvia

Razorbill
Alca torda

Black Guillemot
Cepphus grille

Atlantic Puffin
Fratercula arctica

Double-crested Cormorant
Phalacrocorax auritus

Great Cormorant
Phalacrocorax carbo

Northern Gannet
Morus bassanus

Northern Fulmar
Fulmarus glacialis

Great Shearwater
Puffinus gravis

Sooty Shearwater
Puffinus griseus

Manx Shearwater
Puffinus puffinus

Osprey
Pandion haliaetus

Bald Eagle
Haliaeetus leucocephalus

Common Loon
Gavia immer

Land Mammals of Newfoundland

Below is a selection of land mammals you may encounter while hiking. Treat all wildlife with respect.

Arctic Hare
Lepus arcticus

Canada Lynx
Lynx canadensis

Caribou
Rangifer tarandus

Coyote
Canis latrans

Little Brown Bat
Myotis lucifugus

Moose
Alces alces

Newfoundland Pine Marten
Martes americana atrata

Newfoundland Black Bear
Ursus americanus hamiltoni

Red Fox
Vulpes vulpes

Equipment checklist for day hikes

- ❑ Small backpack/daypack
- ❑ Water (2 to 4 litres per person per day, more in hot weather)
- ❑ Sturdy shoes or hiking boots
- ❑ Appropriate clothing (warm clothes in layers and waterproof outer layers)
- ❑ Flashlight and extra batteries
- ❑ Lighter or waterproof matches
- ❑ Fire starter
- ❑ Pocket knife
- ❑ Whistle
- ❑ Cell phone
- ❑ Snacks and lunch
- ❑ Small first-aid kit
- ❑ Sunscreen and bug repellent
- ❑ Map, GPS, and compass
- ❑ Binoculars and camera

Equipment checklist for multi-day hikes

- ❏ Large backpack
- ❏ Water (2 to 4 litres per person per day, more in hot weather) and water purification system
- ❏ Waterproof hiking boots
- ❏ Appropriate clothing (warm clothes in layers and waterproof jacket and pants)
- ❏ Flashlight and extra batteries
- ❏ Lighter or waterproof matches
- ❏ Fire starter
- ❏ Pocket knife
- ❏ Whistle
- ❏ Cell phone and/or other communication device
- ❏ Food for number of days plus 1–2 days extra
- ❏ First-aid kit
- ❏ Sunscreen and bug repellent
- ❏ Map, GPS, and compass
- ❏ Binoculars and camera
- ❏ Tent, sleeping bag, sleeping pad
- ❏ Repair kit
- ❏ Stove, fuel, pots, plates, utensils, cup, etc.
- ❏ Dry bag
- ❏ Rope and carabiners
- ❏ Hiking poles
- ❏ Toilet paper
- ❏ Toiletries
- ❏ Sandals (that can go in the water; extremely useful for around camp and for crossing rivers and streams)

Further information and resources

Information is current as of publication and is subject to change.

Websites and contact information

Newfoundland Labrador Tourism:
- www.newfoundlandlabrador.com/
- For short descriptions of dozens of hikes and walks all around New-foundland & Labrador: www.newfoundlandlabrador.com/thingsto-do/hikingwalking
- contactus@newfoundlandlabrador.com
- (800) 563-6353

East Coast Trail Association, for information about the East Coast Trail, planned hikes, and official East Coast Trail map packages:
- www.eastcoasttrail.com
- information@eastcoasttrail.com
- (709) 738-HIKE (4453)

International Appalachian Trail of Newfoundland and Labrador (IATNL) is responsible for most of western Newfoundland's multi-day trails. Their website has full descriptions of trails; contact them for maps, GPS tracks, and boat shuttles to trailheads:
- www.sia-iat.com
- info@iatnl.ca
- (709) 639-3113

Newfoundland T'railway, a section of the Trans Canada Trail. For information and interactive maps:
- www.thegreattrail.ca
- www.trailway.ca

Provincial Parks of Newfoundland and Labrador. For information about locations, fees, and facilities at all provincial parks:
- www.https://www.tcii.gov.nl.ca/parks/

Provincial ferry routes, fares, and schedules (Marine Services Division, Department of Transportation and Works):

- www.tw.gov.nl.ca/ferryservices/
- (888) 638-5454

Marine Atlantic Ferry Service:

- www.marine-atlantic.ca

BonTours (providers of Western Brook Pond boat tour); reservations needed:

- www.bontours.ca
- (888) 458-2016 or (709) 458-2016
- Visit their office at the Ocean View Motel in Rocky Harbour or dockside at Western Brook Pond

Go Western Newfoundland:

- www.gowesternnewfoundland.com
- info@gowesternnewfoundland.com
- (709) 639-4787

Gros Morne National Park of Canada:

- www.pc.gc.ca/eng/pn-np/nl/grosmorne
- grosmorne.info@pc.gc.ca
- (709) 458-2417

Marble Mountain:

- www.skimarble.com/page/summer-fun
- (888) 462-7253

Lighthouse Friends for information about lighthouses in Newfoundland and across Canada:

- www.lighthousefriends.com

Photography credits

Unless otherwise indicated, numbers refer to hike numbers, not page numbers.

Hikes of Western Newfoundland (hikes 1–71)
Katie Broadhurst: 41, 45, 49, 50, 51, 52, 53, 54
Anne Alexandra Fortin: Introduction photographs, 6, 7, 12, 15, 16, 17, 18, 19, 20, 21, 25–40, 42, 43, 46, 55–71
Jenna Brake: 23
Dave Jerome: 44
Jamie Harnum and Caroline Swan: 41
Paul Wylezol: 3, 4, 47, 48, 51

Hikes of Eastern Newfoundland (hikes 72–157)
All photographs by Mary Smyth or Fred Hollingshurst, with these exceptions:
Fraser Carpenter: 83 (Yellowlegs)
Darlene Scott: 142 (barachois beach), 146 (Spout), 149 (harbour view), 156 (wildflowers)
Garry Smyth: 140 (drone photograph south to Cobbler Brook)
Rebecca Smyth and Piers Evans: bridge, 139

Wildflower photos pages 365–369 by Mary Smyth.

Birds photo credits: Saffron Blaze (Bald Eagle); Zeynel Cebeci (Great Cormorant); Richard Crossley (Dovekie, Razorbill); Dick Daniels (Great Shearwater); Bernard Dupont (Osprey); Ryan Hodnett (Double-crested Cormorant); Irish Wildlife Trust (Great Black-Backed Gull, Herring Gull); Matt MacGillivray (Northern Gannet); Sean Mack (Black Guillemot); Becky Matsubara (Black-Legged Kittiwake); Melissa McMaster (Common Murre); Kristian Pikner (Arctic Tern); Charles Sharp (Common Tern); Henrik Thorburn (Atlantic Puffin); US Fish and Wildlife Service (Thick-Billed Murre); Paul VanDerWerf (Common Loon); Matt Witt (Manx Shearwater).

Land Mammals photo credits: V.J. Anderson (Coyote), Daniel W. Carstensen (Arctic Hare); J. Jongsma (Little Brown Bat); Dan Minken (Caribou); Bailey Parsons (Pine Marten); Gérald Tapp (Moose).

Index by trail rating

The numbers that appear by hike names refer to hike numbers, not page numbers, unless otherwise noted.

 Easy

2 Moderate trails

Difficult trails

4 **Strenuous trails**
Cape Blow Me Down Trail 20
Cape Broyle Head Path 152
Gros Morne Mountain/James Callaghan Trail 40
Spout Path 145

W **Wilderness trails**
Blow Me Down Mountain Traverse 21
Devil's Bite Trail 47
French Shore Trail 51
Indian Lookout Trail 48
Lewis Hills Trail 15
Long Range Traverse 45
North Arm Traverse 23
North Rim Traverse 44
The Grand Codroy Way 4

Index by place name

The numbers that appear by hike names refer to hike numbers, not page numbers, unless otherwise noted.

About the Authors

Katie Broadhurst
Katie has been a resident and tour guide in Newfoundland since 2009. She has spent time working as trail crew with IATNL, guided tours in Gros Morne National Park and up the Northern Peninsula, and has explored western Newfoundlands trails year round. She is passionate about all things outdoors and enjoys teaching others how to explore more through her blog www.outdoorsandonthego.com.

Anne Alexandra Fortin
Alex has spent more than six years guiding and hiking all over western and central Newfoundland. After completing an Adventure Tourism Program, she became a professional outdoor guide and has worked from the southernmost tip of the Americas to Canada. Her  favorites hikes remain the ones without trails she found while exploring deep into Newfoundland's wilderness. Check out her YouTube channel Wildly Intrepid or website www.wildlyintrepid.com.

Mary Smyth and Fred Hollingshurst
Mary and Fred wrote Along the Trail, a column about hiking, in the *Telegram* from 2001 to 2010. They published their first book, *52 Great Hikes,* in 2005. Their second book, *Hikes of Eastern Newfoundland,* was published in 2014 with a new edition in 2016. They have enjoyed hiking the world-renowned East Coast Trail and many other trails throughout Newfoundland and Labrador, including in Torngat Mountains National Park. They have also explored many trails in Alberta and BC. In 2006 Fred and Mary hiked the ancient 800-kilometre Camino across Northern Spain. The Coast to Coast trail in England and the Cinque Terra in Liguria, Italy, are among their other favorite hiking experiences.

Over the years they have enjoyed outdoor adventures with their children, Amelia, Shannon, David, and Tessa, and look forward to introducing new grandson Ryan, born in September 2019, to the joys of Newfoundland's beautiful trails as soon as he can walk! Mary and Fred now live in Musgravetown, Bonavista Bay, and continue to enjoy hiking and gardening.